上海市专业学位研究生实践基地建设项目

MTI 系列教材
总主编 ◉ 冯 奇

非文学翻译教程

A Textbook of
Non-literary Translation

主 编 ◉ 唐根金　温年芳　吴锦帆

上海大学出版社

图书在版编目(CIP)数据

非文学翻译教程/唐根金,温年芳,吴锦帆主编.
—上海:上海大学出版社,2015.12
MTI系列教材/冯奇主编
ISBN 978-7-5671-1838-6

Ⅰ.①非… Ⅱ.①唐… ②温… ③吴… Ⅲ.①英语—翻译—教材 Ⅳ.①H315.9

中国版本图书馆 CIP 数据核字(2015)第 205574 号

责任编辑 刘 岚
封面设计 倪天辰
技术编辑 章 斐

非文学翻译教程
主 编 唐根金 温年芳 吴锦帆
上海大学出版社出版发行
(上海市上大路99号 邮政编码200444)
(http://www.shangdapress.com 发行热线 021-66135112)
出版人:郭纯生
*
南京展望文化发展有限公司排版
上海上大印刷有限公司印刷 各地新华书店经销
开本 787×960 1/16 印张 13 字数 213 千
2016年1月第1版 2016年1月第1次印刷
ISBN 978-7-5671-1838-6/H·316 定价:26.00元

目录 CONTENTS

导言 1
第一章　时政民生翻译 4
第二章　文化教育翻译 20
第三章　体育竞技翻译 37
第四章　旅游翻译 55
第五章　广告翻译 73
第六章　学术翻译 87
第七章　科技翻译 105
第八章　法律翻译 119
第九章　商务翻译 136
第十章　政务宣传翻译 151
参考文献 168
附录一　非文学翻译的实施步骤 171
附录二　非文学翻译的质量控制 173
附录三　英汉互译练习 175
附录四　本书附录三参考译文 190

导 言

翻译,是一个古老的话题。自从人类文明诞生以来,随着不同国家、民族之间交流和交往的出现,翻译活动便应运而生,并逐步发展繁荣起来。从最初的宗教典籍和法律条文翻译,到后来文学艺术作品的大量译介,再到后来的科技发明和商业元素的强势介入,一直到如今全方位、立体型、平民化和无所不译、无所不能译的翻译图景,可以说,翻译的发生和发展之路与人类物质文明、精神文明的进步发展始终一脉相承。

翻译,从某种意义上来说,无非是一种转换和交换。尽管有关翻译的定义往往飘忽不定,不同的人们对于翻译的理解和期待也多有不同,但是,必须承认,翻译活动的核心无不围绕转换和交换而展开。它首先是语言层面的变换和转化,这是显而易见的。此外,从更深一层的含义来看,它还应该是思想、情感和文化、文明高度的交融和传递。当然,在具体的转换和交换过程中,必然涉及使用相应的策略和方法等问题,这又另当别论。回顾历史,在千百年的中外翻译实践中,曾经产生了一大批翻译巨匠和影响深远的译作。唐朝的玄奘是中国第一个重量级的大翻译家,他不仅翻译了1 335卷佛经,还曾将老子著作的一部分译成梵文。他提出的"既须求真,又须喻俗"的翻译标准,即使在今天仍有相当重要的借鉴意义。到了清代,翻译家严复曾翻译了赫胥黎的《天演论》、亚当·斯密的《原富》、孟德斯鸠的《法意》和斯宾塞尔的《群学肆言》等作品,这些译作对于当时思想封闭的国人而言不啻是启蒙心灵的金钥匙。同时,他主张的"信、达、雅"的翻译观,也为我国翻译事业的发展作出了重要贡献。就西方而言,我们都曾听说过著名的"七十士译本"的故事。且不说因年代久远,这个故事的流传恐存有多个不同的版本,但大致的轮廓应该是,两千多年前的佩浮思岛上有那么一批翻译匠人孜孜不倦、埋头苦译，其结果就是译出了具有传奇色彩的"七十士译本"。还有罗马的圣哲杰罗姆，也曾被誉为翻译史上里程碑式的人物，他于公元382—405年翻译的《通俗拉丁文本圣经》具有重要意义，标志着《圣经》翻译取得了与世俗文学分庭抗礼的地位。就文学方面来看，经典的译家译事也是不胜枚举。乔治·查普曼在1598年至1616年翻译了《伊利亚特》和《奥德赛》，约翰·弗罗里欧于1603年译出了蒙田的《散文集》等，这些都是英语文学翻译的杰出代表。这些译家，以及其他大量甘于寂寞、隐身书斋的翻译工作者，以其刻苦和无私奉献的精神，以其智慧和令人惊叹的勇气，为世界带来了精彩，也为人类文明的融合、进步与发展贡献了力量。

翻译，也是一个全新的话题。在21世纪的今天，随着全球化进程的加快，随着互联网和其他新技术的不断推进，翻译早已突破了旧有的框架，呈现出一种全新的面貌和发展态势。

首先，翻译的内容发生了质的变化。它已从过去以文学翻译为主的模式发展成为如今以非文学翻译（即应用翻译或实用翻译）占主导的趋向，而且，这一趋势正变得越来越明朗化。从国际组织到政府机构再到民间团体的各类公文、文件和往来书信，到各国之间文化、教育、卫生、体育、旅游等层面人员和信息的密集交流，再到企业并购以及跨国公司的贸易和技术合作等，这些无不需要借助翻译的渠道才能实现信息的有效沟通。有人曾经统计过，近年来在我国的翻译图书市场上，文学翻译所占比例仅为出版翻译图书的7%到8%，其余均属于非文学翻译的范畴。

其次，译者的地位发生了根本性的变化。伴随着翻译范围的扩大和翻译内容的拓展，从事翻译的人员及其构成较之以往出现了明显的不同。在过去，翻译更像是少数人的专利。因为需求量小，那时的翻译活动基本上是兼职的，往往由某个领域的倡导者自己来完成。今天，虽然这样的翻译活动仍然存在，但绝大部分的翻译任务已经转由专业翻译人员来承担。这些人员或者在翻译公司任职，或者隶属于某个政府或非政府部门，或者从事自由职业，他们以翻译作为谋生的手段，并以此逐步开启了当今翻译职业化的一个趋势。

第三，考量翻译的标准也在悄悄发生变化。从我国翻译发展的历史来看，无论是早期的"因循本旨，不加文饰"、"五失本、三不易"和"八备说"等，还是后来的"信、达、雅"，抑或是再后来的"译意"与"译味"、"信译"、"神似"和"化境"说等，其所依托的其实都是文学翻译的大前提。也就是说，这些标准的提出都是基于文学翻译的角度,是依据文学翻译的得失来衡量的。如今,由于非文学翻译在数量上的压倒性优势,评判译文优劣的标准自然也要做出相应的调整。一般认为,对于非文学翻译,信息传递的准确和有效应该居于首要的位置。至于传统的文采辞藻和所谓的风格等,则必然退居次要的地位。

最后,关于翻译的研究也在不断发生着新的变化。翻译最初曾被认为代表一种技艺(即 craft),是一门重在实践的活计,其所讲究的无非是一些技巧、手段和方法等,仅此而已。此后,翻译也曾被看成是一种艺术(即英文所谓的 art)。但这种界定以及与此相关的研究套路似乎过于抽象,且不乏局限性。再后来,翻译成为一门科学(即 science)。至此,翻译的地位才得到了空前的提升,关于翻译的研究也步入了一个新的发展阶段。就目前的情形来看,我们不妨可以说,翻译俨然已经是一门融合了多种不同学科的综合性研究(即 interdisciplinary study)。各种理论、各种思潮和各种学科之间的嫁接和交叉融合,包括纯理论、理论和实践相结合等的研究方法层出不穷、蔚为大观。

现在就本书的编写作一个简单的说明。本书取名《非文学翻译教程》,是一本以应用文翻译实践为主,兼顾相关翻译原则和策略、方法等的专门教材,可供翻译硕士专业研究生、翻译方向的本科生和其他翻译工作者、翻译爱好者之用。本书编写的一个基本原则是不求大而全、笼而统之,但求以局部的精微和细腻,透过大量的翻译实例以及对比、分析和点评,突出实际翻译操作能力的重要性。基于这样的考虑,我们并没有纠缠于非文学翻译的概念、标准、理论和发展现状等命题,除了对书中十类文体及其基本特征展开一般性的讨论之外,我们把更多的关注点放在了译例的筛选和点评环节。本书所选的译例基本上来自编者日常教学的材料积累,其后所附的参考译文也大多出自编者之手。如果说本书有什么亮点的话,或许这可以算是其中之一。本书是上海大学外国语学院 MTI 系列教材的一种,总主编冯奇,主编唐根金、温年芳、吴锦帆。研究生李智文、武纳纳、宋飞飞、潘梅欣、吴文静和眭小雪等参与了部分译例翻译、资料整理和编写工作。最后,衷心感谢上海大学出版社刘岚编辑在本书成书过程中所提供的精心指导和帮助。

唐根金

于美国内布拉斯加林肯大学

2014 年 6 月 19 日

第一章

时政民生翻译

1.1 时政民生类文本的概念

时政和民生是一对含义比较笼统,但也相对宽泛的概念。所谓时政,应该指国际、国内和地方上的各类即时的和重大的新闻。它的内容涉及国际形势、对外交往、国内政治、各项基本国策、经济发展、文化、医疗和教育等,可以说包括了社会生活的方方面面。至于民生,它的所指相对简单清晰,但凡和民众日常生活密切相关的一切都属于民生的范围。比如,老百姓的就业、工资、物价、食品安全、交通等。一般来说,时政的内容是处于宏观层面的,而民生则是微观的和具体的。

时政民生类文本来源多以报纸、网络、杂志、电视和电台的新闻为主。特别是时政,往往出现在各类媒体的显要位置。它的形式可以是社论、述评、记者采访、现场报道等;而有关民生的文本除了上述渠道以外,还可包括各级政府机构发布的工作报告、白皮书或蓝皮书、年鉴、新闻简报、通讯和宣传材料等。

1.2 时政民生类文本的基本特征

德国功能学派的代表人物凯瑟琳娜·莱斯(Katharina Reiss)在谈到翻译活动时,曾经提出了一个著名的文本类型理论。她将文本按其功能划分为三种基本类型,即信息型(informative)、表达型(expressive)和感染型/操作型(persuasive/operative)。简单来说,信息型文本重在内容的交际,表达型文本则是按艺术手法组织文本内容的交际,而感染型/操作型文本属于一种包含说服、劝说成分的交际。莱斯还指出,一个文本可能兼具多种功能,但其中必定会有一个占主导的功能。

对照莱斯的理论,时政民生类文本一般应被归入具备信息功能的文本类型之列。虽然有关时政民生的文本涉及面很广,上至国家的政治、经济、军事、外交等领域的形势和对策,下至街道、乡镇、普通百姓的关切和诉求,甚至还有一些影响重大的突发事件(如突然爆发的流行性疾病、自然灾害等)等也包含在内,但这类文本大体上都以事实的陈述为出发点,其主要目的在于内容的交际,也即信息传递。当然,其中的一些文本,比如社论、述评等也会有相当的说服和劝诫成分。从文体学的角度来看,时政民生类文本则表现出与新闻文体基本相似的特征;有时,它也与政府公文的某些特征相重合。

首先,它在政治立场上具有明显的倾向性。时政民生类的文本,虽然性质和具体的内容各有不同,分量也有轻重之分,但是,往往事关国家的政策以及国家的整体形象,因此,确保鲜明准确的立场十分重要。特别是一些重大的时政新闻,如各大主要媒体的社论、特稿和权威述评等,因其舆论主导者的地位,更须慎之又慎。这一点,无论在我们国家,还是在世界上的其他地方(包括西方国家),莫不如此。

第二,它在内容上具有很强的时效性。时政民生类的文本,其聚焦的对象多属于此刻正在发生,或最近刚刚发生的事件。不管是国内外形势分析,还是政府政策法规的发布,抑或是国计民生的关注点,凡此种种都是特定时期或阶段的产物,都有一定的时限性。所谓"此一时,彼一时",如果某个公告或某条新闻叙述的内容早已不属于当下的语境,那么,可以想象它存在的价值必定会打折扣,人们对它的兴趣也会大大下降,因为它已经是旧闻了。

第三,它的风格简练明晰,语言平实、规范。时政民生类的文本,内容跨度极大,它所依托的发表或发布平台也不尽相同。有些可能会在国家电视台播出,或者登上权威刊物的首页,也有不少只是地方晚报上不起眼的一角。但是,无论属于哪一种情形,这一类文章的性质决定了它的首要目的是传递信息,而要迅速准确地传递信息,精确的语言和简练实用的风格是一个基本要素。比如,它的用词一般比较规范,同时又力求通俗易懂。而在句法层面,则尽量避免冗长、繁复的句式,绝不拖泥带水、纠缠不清,以利于读者迅速有效地吸收和消化信息。当然,在这一类的文本中,有时也会出现一些新生的词汇和行业专门化的用语,这是由时政民生类文本本身的性质决定的。

第四,它经常会引用大量的数据以突出所涉内容的权威性和准确性。鉴于时政民生类文本的主要目的在于传递信息,因此,其作者除了要考虑内容的正确性、时效性和语言的简明性等因素以外,还必须强调它的真实可信,以便易于为受众所接受和理解。为了达到这样的效果,文本作者往往会选择让数据说话,有时候会直接列出权威机构的统计数据;还有的时候,会采取比较和对照的办法,把两组或多组数据放在一起呈现出来,以避免空口说白话的嫌疑。此外,为了取得同样的效果,在有些情况下,文本作者也会选择引用权威人士的讲话和评论等。

1.3 时政民生类文本的翻译策略

按照翻译目的论,翻译中的最高法则应该是"目的法则"。凡涉及翻译活动,必然首先解决其所要达到的目的,而翻译的目的又与翻译文本的类型密切相关。也就是说,不同类型的文本导致出现不同的翻译目的,由此也决定了不同的翻译策略和方法。既然时政民生类文本总体上属于信息型的范畴,它不像小说、诗歌等表达型文本那样强调诉诸感官或美学意义的升华,也不像辩论、广告和宣传等感染型或操作型文本那样重在表达态度、主张和意见(当然,某些时政文本,包括社论、特稿和述评等也会包含一定的说服和劝诫的成分),那么,对此类文本的翻译应该采取怎样的策略呢?在讨论具体的策略和方法之前,让我们先来明确几条原则。

第一,正确性。所谓正确性是指译者在翻译时应充分考虑原文本的立场、态度和语气等,并确保如实地反映出原文本的意图和目的。时政类的文本(包括新闻、社论和述评等)固然包含相应的信息,但是,更重要的是,它涉及国家的政策以及对于政治事件的立场和观点等,因此,在翻译的过程中尤须谨慎处理。即使是相对琐碎的民生类别的文章,甚或是一些负面新闻的报道,比如地震、洪水等自然灾害,原作者往往也会立足于挖掘其积极的意义,突出处于困难中的人们相互关爱和互帮互助的一面,这就是舆论的引导作用。对此,译者在翻译的过程中应该始终保持清醒的认识。

第二,精确性。所谓精确性是指译者在翻译时应尽量保证信息传达的完整、准确和清晰、无误。这里的精确性,也可以被看成是忠实性,甚至是某些翻译教材里提到的译文的准确性。尽管具体的说法可能不尽相同,但它的确是翻译活动中的一条重要原则，也是译者所应该始终追求的最大目标之一。无论是何种类型的文本翻译，一旦偏离了精确性，就谈不上合格的翻译。对于时政民生类的文本，因其目的主要是向广大受众传达信息，因此，精确性显得尤为重要。译者在翻译的过程中，必须不折不扣地表达出原文本的意思，不得对原文本进行过度解读或阐释，也不能随意改动或遗漏原文本的信息。

第三，规范性。所谓规范性是指译者在翻译时应顾及原文本的文体特点并在译文中充分体现出来。时政民生类的文本具有类似于新闻文体的特征，它的语言简单明晰、通俗易懂，篇章结构往往遵循一定的格式。对此，译者必须予以高度重视。

第四，专业性。所谓专业性是指译者在翻译时应密切关注原文本中所涉及的专门化知识，并确保以职业和专业的态度在译文中呈现出来。鉴于时政民生类文本在内容上所具有的广泛性，因此，它必然涉及一些专门领域的信息。比如，在一篇关于环保的文章中，可能会出现很多化学名词，也可能同时出现一些最新的环保产品和公司的名称等。对于这种情况，就要求译者必须具备可靠的专门化知识和职业的素养。

在明确了指导时政民生类文本翻译的基本原则之后，我们现在不妨来探讨一下具体的翻译策略。说到翻译的策略，不外乎归化还是异化，形式对等还是动态对等；或者，更直白一点地说，是直译还是意译等。不过，在翻译实践中事实上并没有绝对非此即彼的策略，很多情况下，往往是几种策略兼而有之。我们已经知道，时政民生类文本的主要目的在于传递信息；同时，在不少情形之下，还涉及态度、立场和观点的表达。基于这样的出发点，我们认为，在英译汉的过程中，一般宜采用"归化"为主、"异化"为辅的策略。这既是出于照顾目的语读者或听众阅读或视听习惯的需要，避免因为语言和文化机制的差异造成阅读或视听上的困难；同时，更是为了确保译本中体现的态度和立场等不至于与国家的政策和民族意识等发生冲突。而在汉译英时，则恰好相反，我们应该追求"异化"为主、"归化"为辅的策略。这是因为，一来它有助于确保原文本的意图和目的在译文中能够得到正确的反映，二来它也有助于突出汉语语言自身独特的优势。当然，在英译汉时，适当地采用"异化"的手法，不但是可行的，有时也是必不可少的。它往往能够使译本增加新鲜感，从而更好地吸引读者的目光。同样的道理，在汉译英的实践中，恰如其分地尝试"归化"的手段，也能使译本显得更具亲和力、更易于为目的语读者和听众所接受。

现在我们来看两个例子。第一个是路透社2013年10月28日发自北京的报道，下面的这句话是该报道的一个引子：

"Five people were killed and dozens injured on Monday, the government said, when a car ploughed into pedestrians and caught fire in Beijing's Tiananmen Square, the site of the 1989 pro-democracy protests bloodily suppressed by the military."

在翻译这个句子的时候，对于最后的一个修饰部分，即the site of the 1989 pro-democracy protests bloodily suppressed by the military必须谨慎处理。其中的pro-democracy protests不宜直接翻译成"要求民主的抗议示威"，而bloodily suppressed by the military更不能直译成"遭到军方的血腥镇压"。关于发生在1989年春夏之交的"天安门广场事件"，我国政府已经形成了官方的定性和评价。这里所谓的"要求民主的抗议示威"和"遭到军方的血腥镇压"显然属于西方媒体主观的价值判断，如果原封不动地翻译出来，势必违反立场正确的原则，也不可能为中国读者所接受。因此，在翻译时必须毫不犹豫地采取"归化"的策略，要么改用具中性色彩的词语，并略去"遭到军方镇压"这样的字眼，要么干脆把整个修饰部分略而不译。实际上，鉴于这篇报道的性质是叙述一个突发事件，它的作者本该追求"短、平、快"的语言特点。他之所以不厌其烦也要加上这狗尾续貂的修饰部分，无非还是意识形态在作祟。

第二个例子引自某社区的年度工作总结，其中有这样一句话：

"……积极推进'和谐社区共同体'建设，在全市率先探索推进调整优化社区体制机制工作，按照'归口管理、明晰职责，扁平运作、高效行政'的原则，完善条块协同机制，强化社区的职能定位……"

这里的"和谐社区共同体"是一个具有时代特色的新的词汇，显然是在国家提倡建设和谐社会的背景之下提出来的，如何翻译，不能简单地采取一一对应的办法。"社区"的英文可以是living quarter, residential block或neighborhood，也可以是community等，而"共同体"一词，其对应的英文一般是community。此外，"归口管理"和"扁平运作"则是比较专门化的词汇，其中前者是我国行政和企业管理中经常提到的一种管理方法，而后者实际上是源自国外的一种企业管理理念。这两个词的翻译关键点在于要体现出专业性。"归口管理"现在一般译成 centralized management by specialized departments，而"扁平运作"有人则译为 operation in a horizontal/flat organizational structure。

1.4 翻译实例及点评

英译汉

【原文】

China's most daring adversary in Southeast Asia is, by many measurements, ill-suited for a fight (1). The Philippines has a military budget one-fortieth the size of Beijing's (2), and its navy cruises through contested waters in 1970s hand-me-downs from the South Vietnamese (3).

From that short-handed position, the Philippines has set off on a risky mission to do what no nation in the region has managed to do: thwart China in its drive to control the vast waters around it.

Analysts (4) say the Philippines' strategy, in standing up to Asia's powerhouse (5), is just as likely to backfire as succeed. But it provides a crucial test case as smaller countries debate whether to deal with China as a much-needed economic partner, a dangerous maritime aggressor, or both (6).

The Philippines doesn't view China exclusively as a threat, officials here say, noting that trade between the countries is growing. The Philippines has also used caution at times, most notably by holding off on provocative plans to drill in what could be the nation's richest oil and gas field (7). But analysts point to a series of steps taken in recent months that suggest that Manila is increasingly willing to confront Beijing. They also note that the Philippines has suspended or canceled several development deals that depended on generous Chinese aid (8).

(*Washington Post* "Philippines Pushes Back Against China", by Chico Harlan, July 23, 2013)

【译文一】

均衡来看,中国在东南亚的劲敌是足以来较量一番的(Ⅰ)。菲律宾在军事方面的预算是北京的(Ⅱ)1/40,20世纪70年代,它在有争议的海域航行的游轮多是从越南身上脱下来的旧衣服(Ⅲ)。

面对人员不足的形势,菲律宾已经开启了一场冒险的行动,而且这场行动是这个地区的任何一个国家所未曾经历的,那就是在中国试图掌控周边广袤海域的这件事上进行阻挠。

分析家(Ⅳ)称,菲律宾在力图成为亚洲强国的这一策略上可能会如逆火般获得成功(Ⅴ)。即便如此,当一些弱小国家争论是应该把中国作为一个急切需要的经济伙伴还是一个危险的海上侵略者,或者两者兼有的时候,它提供了一个关键的测试例子(Ⅵ)。

官方人员称,菲律宾并没有单单把中国视为一个威胁,指出两国之间的贸易在日渐增长。菲律宾有时也是小心谨慎的,最明显的就是推迟挖掘这个国家的石油和天然气领域的挑衅计划(Ⅶ)。但是分析人士也指出近几个月的一系列的行动表明马尼拉正在日趋地逼近北京。他们同时指出菲律宾已经搁置或者取消了若干依赖中国慷慨支援的发展交易(Ⅷ)。

(学生课堂练习)

【译文二】

多种观测结果表明,中国在东南亚地区最强劲的对手正为挑起争端而蠢蠢欲动(Ⅰ')。虽然菲律宾的军事预算只有北京的(Ⅱ')四十分之一,70年代行驶在有争议水域上的海军巡游舰(Ⅲ')还是从南越购入的。

靠着这样匮乏的海事装备,菲律宾制定了一项冒险的计划,在那个区域没有国家能成功地完成,那就是挫败中国控制其周围水域的意图。

分析者(Ⅳ')称,为了成为亚洲的强国,菲律宾的战略意图会适得其反(Ⅴ')。但此事为小国家们的辩论提供了一个重要的案例(Ⅵ'),是把中国当作一个必要的经济伙伴还是危险的海上侵略者(Ⅵ'),或者两者皆是。

这里有官员称,菲律宾没有完全把中国当成威胁,指出两国的贸易有所增长。菲律宾偶尔也谨慎行事,最明显的就是在制定开采国家丰富的石油和天然气资源的计划上有所保留。但有分析者指出近几个月来菲律宾采取的措施显示了马尼拉愿意不断的对抗北京。他们还说菲律宾已经暂停或取消了几项依赖于中国慷慨援助的发展计划。

(学生课堂练习)

【译文三】

　　从多个方面来衡量/从许多方面来看/综合各方面的因素，作为中国在东南亚地区最主要的对手，菲律宾都不具备与中国开战的资格。菲国的军费预算仅为中国的四十分之一，它的那些游弋在和中国有争议海域的舰只也是从南越淘来的 20 世纪 70 年代的老爷货。

　　不过，尽管自身实力有限，菲律宾却踏上了一段本地区其他国家未曾涉足的危险之旅，那就是试图阻挠中国对该地区广阔海域的控制。

　　分析人士认为，菲律宾选择与中国这个亚洲强国相抗衡的策略，有可能取得成功，也可能输得很惨。不过，它也为弱小国家在与中国打交道时提供了一个很有参考价值的实验样本，使这些国家明白究竟该把中国视为重要的经济合作伙伴，还是危险的海上霸主，抑或是两者兼而有之。

　　此间的官员们表示，菲律宾并不仅仅把中国看成是一个威胁，他们注意到两国之间的贸易额在增长。当然，有时候菲律宾也选择谨慎从事，特别是他们推迟了在其油气资源非常丰富的海域的开采计划，以避免刺激中国。不过，分析人士也指出，从过去数月马尼拉方面（菲律宾政府）采取的一系列步骤来看，它正变得不再畏惧与中国正面交锋。分析人士还注意到，菲律宾已经延后或取消了数个需要依赖中国慷慨援助的发展项目。

（本书作者译）

【点评】

　　本组英译汉的内容涉及国际时政的范畴，从具体的行文来看，难度并不算太大。附上的译文一和译文二均为学生的习作（译文三是本书作者提供的参考译文），在这里我们将以译文一、二为主来做一些分析和点评，特别是指出其中存在的问题和不足。这些问题和不足主要集中在两个方面，即精确性以及规范性和专业性。

　　精确性：以译文一、二的第一段为例，与原文的出入比较大，准确度和忠实度均存在诸多不足。先是原文首句中的一个短语 by many measurements，前两篇译文的处理都不理想，无论是"均衡来看"，还是"多种观测结果表明"都偏离了原文的意思。比较而言，译文三的"从多个方面来衡量/从许多方面来看/综合各方面的因素"就显得和原文更为贴近。该句翻译中的第二个问题是对 ill-suited for a fight 的理解，译文一译为"是足以来较量一番的"，译文二则译成"为挑起争端而蠢蠢欲动",显然与原文所要表达的意思恰好相反。此外,针对 China's most daring adversary in Southeast Asia,前两篇译文都没有点出菲律宾的国名,而仅仅译成"中国在东南亚的劲敌"和"中国在东南亚地区最强劲的对手"。作为开篇的首个句子,此等处理的手法读起来不免让人有方向不明的感觉。从第二个句子来看,原文中的 Beijing's 一词,两个译文都照直译为"北京的",不甚理想。原因有二:第一,以一国的首都来指代该国家的做法在英语新闻中比较常见,但在中文里却未必为一般读者所接受和认同。第二,就中文的思维习惯而言,如果文章作者以一国首都来指称该国家,有时会被认为带有一定的责难或贬低的意味。还有,对于原文中的 its navy cruises through contested waters in 1970s hand-me-downs from the South Vietnamese,译文一、二的处理也颇成问题。以第二个译文为例,前半句的"70 年代行驶在有争议水域上的海军巡游舰"就有几处缺陷。一是并没有"巡游舰"一说,此为生造出来的词语(巡洋舰倒是有的);二是"有争议水域上的"最好译为"与中国有争议水域上的";三是这些舰只并非"70 年代行驶在"那儿,因为原句中的动词 cruises 并非过去式,而且这也事关基本的常识。对原文第三段的第一句的翻译也是一个错误比较严重的地方,尤其对于 in standing up to Asia's powerhouse 的理解,两个译文的把握都不准确。不妨参考一下译文三的"与中国这个亚洲强国相抗衡",在意义上就比较精确。

规范性和专业性:这方面的问题在译文一、二中均比较突出,包括此前在讨论其精确性不足的同时,事实上也涵盖了诸多不够专业的地方。现在来看看第三和第四个段落:Analysts 被译成"分析家"和"分析者",显然不如"分析人士"更为规范和专业。在 But it provides a crucial test case as smaller countries debate whether to deal with China as a much-needed economic partner, a dangerous maritime aggressor, or both 句中,反映出来的问题则更为典型。比如,把 smaller countries 译为"小国家们",把 provides a crucial test case 译为"提供了一个关键的测试例子"以及把 maritime aggressor 译为"海上侵略者",等等。对原文第四段的第二、三和四句的翻译中,译文一出现了多处不规范和不够专业的处理。比如,"推迟挖掘这个国家的石油和天然气领域的挑衅计划"、"日趋地逼近北京"和"取消了若干依赖中国慷慨支援的发展交易",等等。

第一章 时政民生翻译

汉译英

【原文 1】

1月4日

1988年的今天,上海发生甲肝(1)。

上海市民中突然出现不明原因的发热、呕吐、厌食、乏力和黄疸等症状的病例(2)。流行期间的1月30日至2月14日,每天发病人数均超过1万例(3)。3月底疫情基本得到控制,4月以后发病率逐日下降(4)。据统计,至5月13日,共有310 746人发病,31人直接死于本病。这次上海甲肝暴发流行(5)的主要原因是市民食用了来自江苏省启东县被污染的带有甲肝病毒的不洁毛蚶和某些市民没有良好的饮食卫生习惯(6)。

(朱敏彦,2009:5)

【译文一】

January 4

Today in 1988, Shanghai in Hepatitis A (Ⅰ). Shanghai people in sudden unexplained fever, vomiting, anorexia, fatigue and jaundice and other symptoms of the disease (Ⅱ). Popular during the January 30 to February 14, daily number of cases more than 10,000 cases (Ⅲ). Basic end of March, the epidemic under control, the incidence of daily after April drop (Ⅳ). According to statistics, to May 13, a total of 310,746 human cases, 31 people died from the disease directly. The Shanghai hepatitis A outbreak (Ⅴ) is mainly due to the consumption of blood clam from Qidong County, Jiangsu Province, which was contaminated with hepatitis A virus and dirty, and some people do not have good food hygiene practices (Ⅵ).

(学生课堂练习)

【译文二】

January 4

Today in 1988, Shanghai Hepatitis A broke out (Ⅰ'). Some Shanghai citizens had fever, emesis, anorexia, languor and icterus, etc. of undetermined origins (Ⅱ'). During the epidemic period from January 30th to February 14th, the number of the ill each day reached over 10,000 (Ⅲ'). The incidence of epidemic was in control by the end of March and declined after April (Ⅳ'). According to statistics, by May 13th, 310,746 citizens were taken bad including 31 died from this epidemic. This epidemic was mainly triggered by some unclean arca subcrenata carrying HAV from Qidong County, Jiangsu Province and poor dietary health habits (Ⅵ') of some citizens.

(学生课堂练习)

【译文三】

January 4th

On this date in 1988, an epidemic outbreak of Hepatitis A hit Shanghai/a mysterious Hepatitis A epidemic swept Shanghai.

During the period around that date, many cases of unexplained/unidentified fever, vomiting, fatigue, anorexia and jaundice among local residents were reported. The situation grew worse as time progressed, and at its peak period between January 30 and February 14, the number of people inflicted with the infectious disease added up to more than 10,000 every day. It was only in late March and early April that the epidemic began to show real signs of improvement when cases of infection went down day by day. Statistics show that by May 13 as many as 310,746 individuals were affected, among whom 31 finally died of the disease. It was learned later that the direct cause for the outbreak of the epidemic was the poisoned blood clam from the neighboring Qidong County, Jiangsu Province. Some local residents, lacking a proper sense of hygiene, ate the blood clam and thus spread the virus they picked up to those around them.

(本书作者译)

【点评】

这一组汉译英的内容涉及1988年上海甲肝暴发的情形。从风格上看,有点类似新闻报道的样式,时间、地点、事情发生的经过以及原因等要素均有提及,还包括了相应的统计数字。现在我们仍然以译文一和译文二为样本,来进行一番初步的探讨,重点指出其中存在的缺陷和不足。

首先,这两个译文的总体效果均不甚理想,但译文二的质量要略好于译文一。两者的失误和缺陷有较大的相似性,主要反映在意思表达不精确和语言运用不准确、不规范。以译文一为例,在它的前三个句子中,我们始终没有看到动词的出现。比如,针对原文的"上海发生甲肝",译文一的处理是 Shanghai in Hepatitis A,缺少了必要的动词。到第四个句子,我们终于看到了动词 drop,可惜用得不是地方。还有,以 popular 对应原文中的"流行",以 good food hygiene practices 对应原文中的"良好的饮食卫生习惯"等均属于十分低级的错误。至于 Basic end of March 和 the incidence of daily after April 等也非地道的英文,令人感到难以接受。

现在来看一看译文二的情况,它的首句 Today in 1988, Shanghai Hepatitis A broke out 中的 Shanghai Hepatitis A 一说就很成问题,容易使人误以为这是一种专门的肝炎类型。其后,Some Shanghai citizens had fever, ... 等中的 some 一词则显得太随意和意思表达模糊。在随后一句中,the number of the ill 表述也很别扭,让人摸不着头脑。在接下来的这一句 The incidence of epidemic was in control by the end of March and declined after April 中,was in control 可考虑改为 was kept under control;而 declined 的前面也应该加上类似 the number of individuals affected by the disease 才比较合适。最后,dietary health habits 和译文一的 food hygiene practices 属于同样性质的问题,是译者未能跳出原文的约束、过于拘谨造成的结果。

【原文 2】

就业保障(1)

静安区把促进就业作为改善民生的首要任务,<u>全面落实"1+3"就业计划,制定实施稳定就业的"19 条措施"</u>(2)。"十一五"以来(3),静安区推行以增加就业岗位为核心(4)的促进就业政策,累计新增就业岗位 126 364 个(5);严格控制登记失业人数;<u>深化"政府购买培训成果"机制</u>(6),实现职业技能培训社会化,完成职业技能培训(农民工)57 980 人次;积极促进青年就业,<u>开设了专业化职业介绍窗口,建设了青年创业绿色通道</u>(7),实施了培训、见习、就业机制。2009年，成功扶持创业602家，帮助成功创业387人，带动就业2 714人；健全社会就业保障体系(8)，外来从业人员参加综合保险人数达到67 637人(9)，工资集体协议覆盖41 654人(10)，切实保障了劳动者的合法权益。

（www. jingan. gov. cn）

【译文一】

Employment Security（Ⅰ）

Jing'an District has taken employment promotion as the primary task to improve people's livelihood with the full implementation of "1 + 3" employment plan and establishment and implementation of "19 steps"（Ⅱ）. Since the eleventh five-year plan（Ⅲ）, Jing'an District has been accelerating its steps on the employment policy with creating more jobs as core（Ⅳ）. The number of new job opportunities has newly increased 126,364（Ⅴ）. Jing'an District has also strictly controlled the number of registered unemployed and deepened the mechanism of the government purchase training results to achieve vocational skills training socialization（Ⅵ）. Meanwhile, it has actively promoted youth employment with the creation of a specialized employment agency window and the construction of a youth entrepreneurship green channel（Ⅶ）, as well as the implementation of the training, placement, employment mechanism. In 2009, Jing'an District gave support to 602 startup companies and helped 387 people be successful in business and encouraged 2,714 people to employment. The social employment security system has been improved with the comprehensive insurance number of foreign workers amounted to 67,637（Ⅸ）and wage collective agreement 41,654（Ⅹ）to guarantee the legitimate rights and interests of workers.

（学生课堂练习）

【译文二】

Protection of Employment（Ⅰ'）

Employment promotion has become a chief task for the protection of people's livelihood in Jing'an District in Shanghai. To do so, the government has put "1+3" employment plan into practice, and at the same time, established "19 measures", aiming at stabilizing employment. <u>Since the Eleventh Five-year plan</u> (Ⅲ'), a series of measures, <u>taking job-increasing as the core</u> (Ⅳ'), has been carried out in Jing'an District, and 126,364 jobs had been added. The registered unemployed has been strictly controlled. <u>To deepen the system of "government purchases training achievements"</u>, the government has fulfilled socialization of vocational-skill training (Ⅵ'), and completed vocational-skill training for 57,980 peasant-workers. To actively <u>promote juvenile employment, the local government has established professional vocational introducing department</u> (Ⅶ'), and created new ways for juvenile startup business, and done work according to training, noticiating, employing institution. In 2009, the government has successfully supported 602 enterprises to get a start, helping to create 2,714 new jobs. <u>Social employment protection system</u> (Ⅷ') has become better, rights of labourers have been really protected, for example, <u>67,637 foreign workers have had integrity insurance</u> (Ⅸ'), and <u>41,654 workers were under the protection of Wage Collective Agreement</u> (Ⅹ).

（学生课堂练习）

【译文三】

<u>Employment Issues</u>

<u>Formulating and putting into practice "19 special measures" for employment, and implementing with full vigor the "1 plus 3" employment project</u>, the government of Jing'an District has considered employment promotion as its primary task in trying to improve the livelihood of the people living in the district. <u>Since the 11th Five-Year Plan period</u>, Jing'an District <u>has created as many as 126,364 jobs for the unemployed</u>. And its effort in this respect is also reflected in: ① working hard to bring down unemployment; ② <u>introducing the "government-sponsored career skills training programs"</u>; ③ <u>helping to push forward the marketization of</u>

vocational training programs (Over the years, the district has provided vocational training to 57,980 migrant workers); ④ laying emphasis on the employment of the young (To cater to the needs of the young, the district has opened special career centers for them, and has set up green channels for their career training and internships as well). And in 2009 alone, Jing'an District provided timely support to 602 enterprises that ran into temporary difficulty; helped 387 locals to start their own businesses; and created job opportunities for 2,714 laid-offs. In addition, it has achieved notable progress in safeguarding the best interest of all those working in the district. To date, 67,637 migrant workers in Jing'an have been covered by the Comprehensive Insurance Plan, and the number of migrant workers signing salary agreement with their employers has totaled 41,654.

(本书作者译)

【点评】

这组汉译英的内容像是政府部门的工作报告或年度总结，篇幅虽不长，但要真正译得好却也非易事。难点有二：一是原文的行文在某些环节显得不是很严谨，句式处理稍显随意（比如，第二个句子就太长了）；二是文中包含了一些专业性比较强的词汇。

译文一：第一个句子，其结构上存在一定的缺陷，后半部分的 with the full implementation of "1+3" employment plan and establishment and implementation of "19 steps"不但过于冗长，而且按照一般英文的表达习惯，也不宜放在句末。另外，其中的 establishment and implementation of "19 steps"的说法也不妥。如果说 implementation of "19 steps" 还说得过去的话，那么，establishment of "19 steps" 这样的搭配显然是不可接受的。通篇来看，这样的例子还有一些，比如，以 government purchase training results 来对应"政府购买培训成果"，以 vocational skills training socialization 来对应"职业技能培训社会化"、以 the construction of a youth entrepreneurship green channel 来对应"建设了青年创业绿色通道"等。这样的处理，具有浓重的中式英文的味道。究其原因，一是译者的语言能力有限，二是译者还放不开手脚，不敢大胆地跳出中文思维的路子。

译文二：总体而言，译文效果要略好于译文一。但是，也存在着不少类似前者的问题，即表达失当和用词不准确、不规范之处相对较多。比如，文中出现的 juvenile employment，vocational introducing department，Social employment protection system，foreign workers，integrity insurance 和 Wage Collective Agreement 等就是典型的例子。还有，"'十一五'以来"一般应译为：Since the Eleventh Five-Year Plan period。但是，译文二中 plan 没有大写，且缺少了 period 一词。（译文一更是既没有使用首字母大写，又没有加上 period。）最后，对于标题的翻译，无论是 Employment Security 还是 Protection of Employment 均不理想。

综上所述，通过对本章三组翻译（一组英译汉和两组汉译英）所进行的简单分析和讨论，可以看出每组中的译文一和译文二均存在不少问题，特别是在对原文的解读和对译文的呈现上均有较多不尽人意之处。并且，从某种意义上来说，这些缺点和不足还相当普遍。那么，如何才能避免或减少诸如此类的错误呢？换句话说，有没有什么应对之策以便改进和提高文本的翻译质量，或者说，至少使译文不至于错误迭出呢？一般认为，关键还应从译者自身入手，具体而言就是在四个方面下功夫：一是提高译者的综合素养；二是强化译者的双语能力；三是端正译者对待译文的态度；四是对译者究竟应该采取怎样具体的方法予以更多的指导和引导。对译者的这四个方面的要求具有同等重要性，切不可偏废任何一个方面，唯有真正全面重视起来才有可能使译文的质量有所改观。

第二章

文化教育翻译

2.1 文化教育类文本的概念

文化和教育是社会生活中的一个重要方面。在当今互联网时代和知识经济高度发展的背景下,各国的文化教育事业也迎来了崭新的发展机遇。就中国而言,在过去的30多年,得益于经济的腾飞和国家整体实力的提升,文化教育事业取得了空前的繁荣和发展。

文化和教育是两个既相辅相成、互为依存,但又有所区别的概念。不过,从宏观的角度来说,文化有时候被认为可以涵盖教育的范畴,这也解释了为什么在本章中我们把文化和教育归入到同一个大类。文化,实质上是一个十分抽象和模糊的概念,很难予以明确的界定;同样,对文化写作的划分也因其包罗万象的特点而似乎显得扑朔迷离。一方面,它当然可以指所有文学艺术创作的总和,也就是说,它集中了小说、戏剧、诗歌、电影、雕塑、音乐、绘画等不同的表现形式,并且,它的内容也是高雅和通俗并包,这是指它的文学性的一面。与此同时,其他人文类的写作,比如历史、地理、政治、哲学、宗教,甚至军事等方面的专门著作,就广义而言,显然也属于这一范畴。不过,还存在着另外一类与文化(包括文学艺术和历史等)和文化活动关系密切的写作。比如,文化创意园区的规划书、电影节和艺术节的宣传资料、画展的策划文字、诗人或小说家等作品推介的书面材料、影评或剧评、演出报道、人物专访或介绍,等等。这些或许可以被称为文化产品的附属产物,虽然同样以文字的形式出现,却是一种非文学性质的写作。我们在这里讨论的文化类文本基本上指后一种。关于教育类文本的范畴确认,相对简单明晰。从宏观层面来看,国家和地方的教育方针和政策、教育改革的具体措施以及历年所取得的成果等,这些是一个方面的内容。另外,各级各类学校的校园新闻、校园文化建设、学术动态、师生互动和校际交流等则构成了另一个重要的方面。

2.2 文化教育类文本的基本特征

如前所述,文化教育类文本是一种十分常见,且用途极其广泛的文本类型,它体裁多样、内容丰富,涉及文化和教育领域的几乎每一个侧面,既有宏观的政策层面的表述,也有微观的事实和细节描写,更有介于两者之间的大量信息密集的简报和快讯等。从文体风格上来看,也跨越了多种不同的类别。比如,总体规划纲要、工作总结、年度报告等,这些大致属于政府公文的范畴。又比如,策划文案、宣传手册、文化活动推介文字等,这些基本上类同于说明文的概念。再比如,演出报道、人物特写、新闻采访等,这些似可以被归入新闻文体的门类。至于书评、影评、剧评等,这些又差不多相当于文艺评论的范围。可见,文化教育类的文本,若要加以细分,其实还可以分出很多不同的小的类别。但是,总体而言,我们这里所说的文化教育类文本,其功能主要还是立足于事实表达或描述,而不是致力于唤起情感的共鸣或试图说服和劝诫对方。只不过,在某些文本条件下(比如,影评和书评等),它也会带有一定的文学色彩。

以一份文化创意园区的规划书为例,由于规模和层次上的差异,它的容量可多可少,多则或许有上百页,甚至更多,少则可能类似于一本薄薄的小册子。但是,它的核心内容不外乎描述该园区的发展前景、拟采取的一系列措施,以及希望达到的具体目标等。当然,其间还会配上一连串的数字,包括园区的总体设计框架、资金投入的额度、招商引资的数量以及预期的盈利方式和规模等。所有这些都应该被看作是从事实出发的表述,而不是诉诸情感的表达。再举一个校园文化节报道的例子。假定某高校举办了一年一度的艺术节,活动内容丰富多彩,有专题讲座、诗歌朗诵会、通俗歌曲大赛、原创话剧演出等。于是,学校广播台或电视台也及时跟进开展了采访和报道。可以想象,这一类的采访报道首先突出的是时间、地点和参与活动的人员等情况,这些是作者要传达给读者的主要信息。当然,为了增强报道的新颖性和娱乐性,作者也可能适当融入调动情感的元素。比如,以生动的语言描绘演出的场景和观众热烈的现场反应等,这是一种由信息延伸出来的恰当的补充。

通过上述分析不难看出，对照莱斯的文本类型理论，文化教育类文本应被归入信息型文本的序列，这一点是毋庸置疑的。那么，这一类文本又体现出一些怎样的特征呢？

第一，它具有信息特征强的特点。凡属文化教育类的文本，总体上以事实描述和信息传递为其根本。即便是影评和书评等，虽往往会带有一定的文学色彩，但它们的核心部分仍然是信息。以一则影评为例，构成其文本主体的内容不外乎该电影的故事梗概、导演和演职员阵容、摄影技巧、音响效果、服装、道具等。此外，还可能包括制片公司的资金投入规模、预期的票房等。当然，为了增强文章的可读性，作者也会适时加入一些拍摄花絮和幕后镜头等细节方面的描述。

第二，它具有文风简单平实、语言通俗易懂的特点。像新闻报道一样，文化教育类文本的目的是要迅速准确地传达信息，为了达到这一目的，语言的简洁和明晰是一个基本要求。也就是说，它的基本语汇、篇章结构和行文风格等必须易于为普通读者所接受。

第三，它也体现出一定的行业专门性特点。一般认为，文化教育类文本似乎不像自然科学领域的文章那样艰涩难懂，它应该和我们的日常生活比较接近，但实际上它覆盖的范围也十分广泛。除了那些基本的、常识性的东西以外，它还包括很多普通人不一定了解的专门领域的内容。比如，特殊教育、考古挖掘等，再比如，某个自然科学领域的前沿信息等。关于这些方面的文章，就势必牵涉专门的知识和特殊的语汇。如果要把它们翻译成另一种语言，则译者在翻译之前和翻译之中，必然要花费大量的心血，做好相应的知识储备和准备。

最后，它还具有辐射面广的社会宣传效应。文化教育类文本除了提供信息以外，有些涉及意识形态方面的问题。从一定意义上来说，它体现出与宣传类文本相近的某些本质特征，往往被认为充当着舆论风向标的作用，因此，文章作者在主旨和基调的把握上有时候显得比较谨慎。

2.3　文化教育类文本的翻译策略

文化教育类文本是一个十分庞大的体系，其内容既涉及政府和政策的层面，有时候也与众多教育机构和文化企业有关，同时还牵连到普通百姓的日常生活。对于这一类文本的翻译，首先要明确以信息传递为主的出发点。在此基础上,为了确保信息传递的迅速和有效,则应该进一步强调翻译过程中的三个要点:准确性、规范性和可读性。这三个要点与文化教育类文本自身所呈现的特征相互呼应,构成了此类文本翻译的基本准则。

先来谈一谈准确性,这主要是指译文在内容上应该忠实地反映出原文的风貌。也就是说,译者在翻译时必须尽最大的努力保证准确无误和恰当地传达出原文所包含的信息,不得有任何疏漏、歪曲、更改或添加的成分。文化教育类文本的基本属性是信息含量丰富,因此,在翻译过程中对于准确性的考量必然居于首要位置。此外,基于文化教育类文本有时还兼具社会宣传和舆论导向的作用,这里的准确性还包括要求译文在态度和立场上与原文保持一致。

至于规范性,它所要求的主要是译文在形式上应该保持与原文的统一。比如,它对语言、篇章结构和行文风格等的选择,包括对一些专业领域和专门术语的处理等都应该体现出严格的规范性,不得偏离原文本来的风格。由于文化教育类文本本身是一个相对笼统的概念,其中包含了多种不同的体裁,有类似于政府公文的文体,或相当于新闻报道的文体,也有基本上属于说明文范畴的文本,甚至还有书评、影评、剧评和音乐评论等文学和文艺评论类的文本,因此,译者在具体的翻译操作过程中必须时刻保持高度的清醒,针对不同风格的原作,采取与之相对应的策略,以最大限度地实现译文的规范性。

在文化教育类文本翻译中,译者需要审慎把握的第三个原则是可读性。所谓可读性,既包括译文内容的完整准确,也包括其在表现形式上的合理、通达晓畅。从某种意义上来说,它应该是译文准确性和规范性的有机结合。既然文化教育类文本总体上属于信息型文本,它的目的是要向读者、听众或观众(也就是信息的受众)迅速和有效地传递信息,那么,就存在一个判断信息传递是否准确和有效的问题。在解决这一问题的过程中,译文的可读性是一个十分重要的参考标准。

现在让我们来谈一谈具体的翻译策略和手段。从大的方面来说,对于此类文本的翻译仍应采用归化和异化相结合的策略。在英译汉时,主张以"归化"为主、"异化"为辅。这主要是出于保持民族文化和语言自主性的需要,同时,也是为了照顾目的语读者或听众阅读或视听习惯的需要,避免因为语言和文化机制的差异造成阅读或视听上的困难。当然,对于原文中某些异族文化特有的现象,有时适当地采用"异化"的手法,也是必不可少的。这样既有利于信息的传达,还能够使译本增加新鲜感,从而更好地吸引读者的目光。在汉译英的时候,则正好相反,我们应该追求"异化"为主、"归化"为辅的策略。理由也相同,一则有助于确保原文本的意图和目的在译文中能够得到正确的反映,二则也有助于突出汉语语言自身独特的优势。当然,在汉译英的实践中,适度地尝试"归化"的手段,也能使译本显得更具亲和力、更易于为目的语读者和听众所接受。

至于具体的操作方法,一般说来,适用于其他文本的翻译方法,如增补、删节、转译、换译、正反和反正、合句和分句等,也大致适用于文化教育类文本的翻译。只不过由于文化教育类文本非文学性的特点,在具体的翻译过程中,类似引申、替代、阐释、转换和重构等手段恐相对较少采用。至于究竟采用何种方法,并无成规,一切应视具体的语境而定。

下面我们来看一个例子:"Jin" named the word of the year by cross-strait netizens("进"字被海峡两岸网民选为年度汉字)。这是 CHINADAILY.com.cn 2013 年 12 月 20 日一篇报道的标题。在这个标题的翻译中,译者就用到了增词法。译者把英文 word 翻译成"汉字",而不是简单的"字"。这样的处理是合理的,也完全符合读者的期待。

再看另一个引自相同网站的例子:The power of poetry and its hold on the public imagination is still alive and well if a recent event is anything to judge by. 这个句子出现在一篇关于某个赛诗会的报道中,现把它试译为:"如果以最近的一场赛诗会来衡量的话,可以说,诗歌的魅力及其对公众的吸引力仍在。"在这段译文中,原文的两个形容词 alive 和 well 被合二为一,is still alive and well 也被简化成"仍在"。虽然看似有所省略,但信息却显得更为集中和突出。

总之,针对文化教育类文本的翻译,关键的一点是要强调信息传递的迅速、准确和通俗晓畅。从这个意义上来说,某些翻译手段,比如增补、删节、改译、强化和弱化等的使用就会显得更加频繁,也更加有效。

2.4 翻译实例及点评

英译汉

【原文】

Harvard President's Remarks on Women Draw Fire (1)

CAMBRIDGE—The president of Harvard University, Lawrence H. Summers, sparked an uproar at an academic conference Friday when he said that <u>innate differences between men and women might be one reason fewer women succeed in science and math careers</u>(2). Summers also questioned <u>how much of a role discrimination plays</u>(3) in the dearth of female professors in science and engineering at elite universities.

Nancy Hopkins, a biologist at Massachusetts Institute of Technology, walked out on Summers' talk, saying later that if she hadn't left, "<u>I would've either blacked out or thrown up.</u>"(4) <u>Five other participants reached by the Globe</u>(5), including Denice D. Denton, chancellor designate of the University of California, Santa Cruz, also <u>said they were deeply offended</u>(6), while four other attendees said they were not.

Summers said <u>he was only putting forward hypotheses based on the scholarly work assembled for the conference</u>(7), not expressing his own judgments—in fact, he said, more research needs to be done on these issues. The organizer of the conference at the National Bureau of Economic Research said Summers <u>was asked to be provocative</u>(8), and that he was invited as a top economist, not as a Harvard official.

However, the problem of women in academia is one that Summers is confronting in his role as university president. <u>The percentage of tenured job offers made to women by the university's Faculty of Arts and Sciences</u>(9) has dropped dramatically since Summers took office, prompting vigorous complaints from <u>many of Harvard's senior female professors</u>(10). Summers has called last year's results, when only four of 32 tenured job offers went to women, unacceptable and promised to work on the problem. However, some Harvard professors have questioned his <u>commitment</u>(11) to the issue.

(*The Boston Globe*, by Marcella Bombardieri, January 17, 2005)

【译文一】
萨默斯对女人的评判引起轩然大波(Ⅰ)
坎布里奇——当哈佛大学校长劳伦斯·H.萨默斯在星期五的学术会议

上指出男女之间天生的差异是只有极少数女性在科学和数学事业上成功的原因之一时,这一论断引起了一片哗然。萨默斯同时质疑在天才大学里,关于在科学和工程领域中女性教授短缺这件事上,歧视占据了多大的分量。

麻省理工大学的生物学家南希·霍普金斯反对萨默斯的言论,之后回应说如果她没有离开,"我可能已经熄火或者被扔出去了。"(Ⅳ)由环球剧院所联系到的其他五位参与者中(Ⅵ),来自加州大学圣克鲁斯分校的代理校长丹尼斯·D.丹顿也称自己被深深地中伤了,但是其他四位参与者认为没有。

萨默斯说他只是针对事先为这次会议所编排的学术工作进行了一类假设(Ⅶ),并没有表明他自身真正的评价。实际上,他说,在这个议题上还需要做更多的研究。这次会议的组织者在国家经济研究总局上说萨默斯是被要求"挑衅的"(Ⅷ),并且说他这次是作为一名顶尖的经济学家而不是哈佛行政人员的身份被邀请的。

然而,学术界的女性问题是萨默斯作为大学校长需要面对的。自萨默斯上任以来,艺术和科学学院中提供给女性工作者(Ⅸ)终身任职的比例急剧下降,这引发了哈佛大学的许多高级女教授(Ⅹ)的强烈抱怨。去年32个终身任职的名额只有4个给了女性工作者,萨默斯保证会更好地解决这个难以让人接受的问题。然而,哈佛的一些教授已经对他解决这项问题的信誉(Ⅺ)产生了怀疑。

(学生课堂练习)

【译文二】
萨默斯评论女性的言论引热议

在周五的一个学术会议上,哈佛大学校长劳伦斯·H.萨默斯说男人与女人天生的不同可能是导致自然科学和数学领域成功的女人较少的原因之一(Ⅱ'),此说法一出引起一片哗然。萨默斯还质疑,在女性教授缺乏的名牌大学的自然科学和工程学专业,性别歧视扮演了多么重要的角色(Ⅲ')。

麻省理工学院的生物学家,南希·霍普金斯,在萨默斯演讲时走开了。后来她说她要是不离开的话,"我不是晕掉了就是吐了。"其他五名在场者,包括即将上任圣克鲁兹加利福尼亚大学校长的丹尼斯·丹顿也说他们深感受到侵犯了(Ⅵ')。

萨默斯说他只是为了此会议在整合了学术研究结论的基础上提出的假

设,而不是自己的看法——他说,实际上这件事情还要进一步研究。此次会议的主办方国家经济调查局说萨默斯被要求发言的时候具有启发性一些,他是作为一流的经济学家被邀请的,而不是哈佛大学的领导。

然而,萨默斯作为大学校长,女性在学术界的生存问题是他要面对的问题之一。自他上任以来,<u>艺术和科学院就职女性教授(IX')的比率大大下降了</u>,这激起了许多资深女教授不停的抱怨。萨默斯觉得去年的结果不甚理想并承诺会解决这个问题,当时 32 个终身职位教授只有 4 名为女性。然而,一些哈佛教授质疑他对此事的努力。

(学生课堂练习)

【译文三】

哈佛校长有关女性的言论招来非议

剑桥——在上周五的一次学术会议上,哈佛大学校长劳伦斯·H.萨默斯表示<u>男女之间先天的差异可能是造成女性在科学和数学领域缺乏建树的原因之一</u>。此言一出,举座哗然。同时,针对精英大学里科学和工程方面女教授队伍人数偏少与性别歧视有关的观点,他也提出了质疑。/同时,萨默斯还质疑精英大学里科学和工程方面女教授队伍不够壮大的现象究竟<u>在多大程度上应该归咎于性别歧视</u>。

麻省理工学院的生物学家南希·霍普金斯在萨默斯发言时即愤而离席。事后,她解释说,如果当时继续留在会场,"我就算不晕过去也会想要吐"。<u>本报(《波士顿环球报》)联系到的五名与会者</u>——包括加州大学圣巴巴拉分校候任校长丹妮丝·D.丹顿——也表示他们<u>对萨默斯的讲话非常不满</u>。不过,另外四名当时在场的专家却不以为然。

萨默斯声称,他的发言并不代表自己的判断,他<u>只不过是根据会议收到的论文提出一些假设性的意见</u>。事实上,关于这些问题还需要开展进一步的研究。会议的主办方——国家经济研究局——则表示是他们<u>希望萨默斯的发言可以起到抛砖引玉的作用</u>,而且,萨默斯参会的身份是顶尖经济学家,并不是哈佛校长。

不过,女性在学术界的地位问题正是萨默斯作为大学校长所面临的一个难题。自从他就任校长以来,哈佛文理学院提供给<u>女性的终身教职比率直线下降</u>,这引起了很多<u>资深女教授</u>的强烈不满。萨默斯已经表示,去年的 32 个终身教职中仅有四席由女性获得,这是无法接受的,他承诺要加以改进。不过,一些哈佛教授则怀疑他是否能信守诺言。

(本书作者译)

【点评】

本组英译汉的原文节选自美国《波士顿环球报》的一篇报道,内容涉及前哈佛大学校长萨默斯在一次学术会议上的讲话。当时,该事件一经披露,曾引起了美国社会,甚至世界范围的广泛关注。就此处提供的译文一和译文二的总体表现来看,后者的质量要略好于前者。现在让我们来作一番具体的讨论,重点针对其中出现的问题和不足做一些分析和点评。

准确性:不管是何种类别的翻译,准确性始终是居于第一位的,否则,就谈不上翻译。在原文第二段第一句中有一句引言:"I would've either blacked out or thrown up."第一位译者的译文是:"我可能已经熄火或者被扔出去了。"这个翻译与原文所要表达的意思相距甚远,同时,它也破坏了其与上下文之间逻辑上的合理性。比较而言,第二个译文的处理就要准确、合理一些("我不是晕掉了就是吐了。")还有,第一位译者在翻译 Five other participants reached by the Globe 时,竟然把其中的 the Globe 误译成"环球剧院",这是严重的失误。常识告诉我们,世界著名的环球剧院位于伦敦,它以上演莎翁剧作而出名,而此处文中的 Globe 应该是哈佛大学所在地美国波士顿市的一份报纸——《波士顿环球报》(*Boston Globe*)的一个简称。再来看一下第三段第一句话前半部分的翻译,译文一为:"萨默斯说他只是针对事先为这次会议所编排的学术工作进行了一类假设"。在这半个句子的翻译中问题不少。且不说别的,仅以"编排"来对应原文的 assembled,以"学术工作"来对应原文的 scholarly work 就属于典型的"硬译"和"死译",没有吃透原文的意思。

规范性和可读性:译文的规范性和可读性当然首先是建立在准确性基础上的,也就是说,只有具备了准确性,才有可能进一步讨论译文的规范性和可读性。不过,从另一个方面来说,如果某个译文的规范性和可读性很成问题,那么,它的准确性自然也就大打折扣了。我们先以译文一为例,挑出其中的几个片段来加以评判。先是标题中的"对女人的评判",然后是最后一段里面的"高级女教授"、"女性工作者"和"对他解决这项问题的信誉产生了怀疑"。这些中文表达要么不规范,要么不具可读性,要么是两者兼而有之。不必去对照英文的原文,我们只要读到这样的文字表达,就基本可以对它整体的翻译质量做出判断。现在来看一看译文二的情况。它的标题"萨默斯评论女性的言论引热议"相对要好得多,特别是"女性"一词显得更为合乎规范。当然,所谓"引热议",其意思表达上还略有不足。根据原文的 draw fire,如果译成"招来非议"、"惹来麻烦"或"引火烧身"等则更为理想。不过,在正文首句的翻译中,译文二却出现了"哈佛大学校长劳伦斯·H.萨默斯说男人与女人天生的不同可能是导致……"的表述,这里的"男人与女人"属于口语化的表达,应考虑译为"男女之间"或"男性和女性之间"才较为合理。此外,针对原文第二段最后的... also said they were deeply offended,译文二给出的翻译是:"他们深感受到侵犯了"。这是很容易引起理解偏差的处理手法,因为"受到侵犯",可能使人联想到 sexual harassment,或者至少是"某种权利受到侵犯"之类的,而此处文中所指显然并非其人身或其他权利受到了侵犯(译为"冒犯"可能较为合理)。还有,对原文末尾的 the university's Faculty of Arts and Sciences 的翻译也不太理想。译文一是"艺术和科学学院",译文二是"艺术和科学院",而真正规范的翻译应该是"文理学院"。凡此种种,都与译文的规范性和可读性(或者也可以说是准确性)有关。

汉译英

【原文1】

2007年1月3日
2007年的今天《2007年上海市民阅读报告》出炉(1)

上海市民平均周读书时间达到 11.94 小时,读书成为上海市民<u>以增长知识为主导生活方式的重要体现</u>(2)。调查显示,近年来,市民的读书习惯较为稳定,阅读最多的媒介,依然是<u>报纸这类能够快速获取信息而耗时不多的读物</u>(3)。市民获取信息途径的前三位依次为:报纸,比例为47.2%;电视,比例为26.1%;网络,比例为19.1%。

(朱敏彦,2009:5)

【译文一】

On January 3rd 2007, <u>the Reading Report of Shanghai Citizens in 2007</u>

was published（Ⅰ）.

Shanghai citizens spent 11.94 hours in reading on average per week, embodying the lifestyle of Shanghai citizens in favor of economic growth（Ⅱ）. According to the survey, in recent years, the majority of citizens tend to read through paper media, like newspaper, convenient instead of time-consuming（Ⅲ）, which is still the most popular media. The top three ways of acquainting information for citizens: 47.2% from newspaper; 26.1% from TV; 19.1% from internet.

（学生课堂练习）

【译文二】

On January 3rd, 2007, Book Report of Shanghai Citizen in 2007 has been released（Ⅰ'）.

The reading time of Shanghai citizen has reached 11.94 hours per week. This has showed that reading is becoming the leading way of enhancing knowledge in Shanghai（Ⅱ'）. According to the statistics, the reading habits among citizens are relatively unchanged in recent years. Certainly, the reading material is still newspaper through which you can get information quickly without consuming much time（Ⅲ'）. The report says, the leading way of acquiring knowledge for Shanghai citizen, in turn, are Newspaper (47.2%), TV (26.1%), Internet (19.1%).

（学生课堂练习）

【译文三】

January 3, 2007

Today/On this day in 2007, "2007 Shanghai Residents Reading Fact Sheet" was released.

According to this report, Shanghai residents spend an average of 11.94 hours on reading every week, showing how much of a role reading played in their everyday life in the context of information explosion. Newspapers, with an acceptance rate of 47.2%, still remained the top choice for local residents. They were most favored by local residents because of their wide coverage of information and easy access. The other two media also popular with Shanghai locals were TV (26.1%) and internet (19.1%).

(本书作者译)

【点评】

　　这一组汉译英篇幅比较短,从内容上看,体裁类似地方报纸刊登的简讯或者政府部门编撰出版的年鉴。应该说,译文一和译文二的表现是各有优劣、各有得失。

　　首先,对于原文标题的处理,译文一、二均有所不足。把"阅读报告"译为 Reading Report 或 Book Report 就很值得商榷。Reading Report 是一个比较奇怪的表述,而对于 Book Report,大家都知道应该是"书评"的意思。事实上,原文中虽有"报告"一词,但在翻译的时候,却不应该简单地以 report 套上去。还有,对于原文标题中的"出炉"一词,译文一译作 was published,译文二译作 has been released。单就词语选择而言,release 比 publish 表义更为精确,但问题是选择现在完成时的 has been released 就不对头了,因为此前已表明该报告出炉的日期是 2007 年 1 月 3 日。

　　其次,在一些关键词语的选择和搭配上也有偏颇。比如,译文一中:Shanghai citizens spent 11.94 hours in reading on average per week, embodying the lifestyle of Shanghai citizens in favor of economic growth,撇开其他方面的问题不说,embodying 一词用得大而无益,违背了此类文本的翻译应力求 idiomatic 的原则(基于原文新闻报道的文体风格,建议译者在此处考虑使用 indicating 和 showing 等)。另外,in favor of economic growth 部分,意思表达与原文也存在出入。还有,译文一最后一个句子中的 acquainting information 则属于乱译,因为并不存在这样的搭配(或许,这个 acquainting 是 acquiring 之误)。在这两个环节的处理上,译文二显得相对成熟。

　　第三,在逻辑合理性方面处理的不足。既然原文标题已点明正文内容引自《阅读报告》,那么,尽管原文报道并没有出现"调查显示"或其他类似的字眼,在实际翻译中仍应考虑把 According to this report 或 According to the survey 等提前到正文的开头才比较合适。这样一来,整个译文读起来才会显得合理、流畅。可惜译文一、二均未能对此有所考虑和调整,而只是一味刻板地按照原文的词序来安排翻译。

另外,译文二的总体表现虽然要强于译文一,但是,个别地方的处理还是显得过于随意。比如,Certainly, the reading material is still newspaper through which you can get information quickly without consuming much time 句中的 you,就与全篇其他地方的指称不协调、不匹配,甚至发生了冲突;而 quickly 和 without consuming much time 似乎又是明显的重复表达。

【原文2】

序

30多年改革开放,中华大地沧桑巨变(1)。我国国际地位显著提高,中外交往与日俱增(2)。上海,作为中国最大的经济中心城市,是中国改革开放和社会主义现代化建设的缩影,成为国际友人来华访问的重要城市。(3)

《第一夫人在上海》(4)用镜头展现了近20年来访问上海的近200位世界各国第一夫人、国宾夫人和女政治家的风采。本书与之前出版的《国宾在上海》一样,从一个侧面反映了国际社会对上海的关注,也形象地展示了这座开放的城市与世界交流、合作不断深化的进程。

当前,上海正按照中央要求(5),朝着加快建设国际经济、金融、贸易、航运中心和社会主义现代化国际大都市的宏伟目标迈进,我们相信,随着中国2010年上海世博会的举办,一个更加开放的上海,一个与世界联系更加紧密的上海,必将吸引越来越多来自国际社会的关注目光,上海人民将一如既往地敞开胸怀(6),热忱欢迎更多来自五湖四海的国内外朋友(7)。

(许根顺,2010:"序")

【译文一】

Preface

China has experienced the tremendous changes over the past 30 years since the reform and opening-up(Ⅰ), with the significant improvement of the international status and the continuous increase in foreign exchanges(Ⅱ). And Shanghai, as China's largest economic center and the miniature of China's opening-up reform and socialist modernization, has become the most destination for foreign friends(Ⅲ).

This photography collection, <u>First Ladies in Shanghai</u> (Ⅳ), shows the elegant demeanour of nearly 200 great women, including first ladies, <u>ambassador ladies</u>, and stateswomen, who came to visit this city during the last two decades. Same as the previous <u>Ambassador in Shanghai</u>, this collection also reflects the more and more attention by the international society for this city, and vividly shows the increasing global communications and cooperations.

Now, <u>according to the central requirement</u> (Ⅴ), Shanghai is striving to become the economic, financial, trade and shipping center in the world, and <u>is on her way to build herself</u> into a modern international metropolis under the socialist system. And we believe that, as the World Expo 2010 Shanghai being held, the <u>more extrovert and globalized Shanghai</u> (Ⅵ) will attract more international attention, and we embrace friends from all of the world.

（学生课堂练习）

【译文二】

Preface

<u>Past over 30 years</u> (Ⅰ') has witnessed the historic changes of China since the Reform and Opening-up. China's international status has significantly promoted and its exchanges with the rest of the world has greatly increased. <u>Shanghai, the largest economic center in China, its development and socialist modernization are the microcosm of the whole country</u> (Ⅲ'). Therefore, it has been regarded as one of the important destinations by friends from all over the world paying their visits in China.

<u>First Ladies in Shanghai</u> (Ⅳ') is the photograph album about nearly 200 elegant and excellent ladies in the political field around the globe, including first ladies, wives of state guests and stateswomen from different countries. Like <u>State Guests in Shanghai</u> (which is the other work by Xu Shunsheng who is the photographer of both), this book not only reflects that Shanghai attracts the broad international attention, but also

demonstrates that it performs very well in further enhancement and cooperation with other countries.

Currently, Shanghai, in accordance with the Central Government's policies, is forging ahead towards building a modern socialist, metropolis which is an economic, financial, trade, and shipping center in the international arena. We believe that with the opening of the 2010 Shanghai World Expo, <u>it is more accessible and easier to invest in and cooperate with Shanghai</u>（Ⅵ'）. As always, Shanghai people <u>welcome all the friends from both China and overseas</u>（Ⅶ'）.

（学生课堂练习）

【译文三】

Preface

<u>Sea changes have taken place since China embarked on its journey of reform and opening up three decades ago. With its remarkably enhanced international status and increasing exchanges with other nations, China has received an unprecedented level of attention from the world.</u> Shanghai, the largest economic center of China, <u>epitomizes the achievements of China's reform</u>, opening up, and socialist modernization drive; as a result, Shanghai always stays in focus of the world's attention and <u>makes one of the most popular destinations in China for overseas visitors.</u>

<u>First Ladies in Shanghai</u> holds a record of the visits of about 200 first ladies, <u>wives of state guests' and female statespersons</u> to Shanghai in the past 20 years. Like *State Guests in Shanghai*, which has already come out, this book is not only a pictorial chronicle of the ever deepening international exchanges and cooperation of this open city, but also one telling demonstration of the world's interest in Shanghai.

<u>In line with the national development strategy</u>, Shanghai is striding towards the ambitious goal of turning itself into an international economic, financial, trading and shipping center and a modern international metropolis with a socialist identity. It's our firm conviction that Shanghai,

with increasing openness and closer links to the outside world, and with the approach of the 2010 Shanghai World Exposition in particular, will attract more and more attention from the international community. <u>Citizens in Shanghai will as always be ready to extend our warmest welcome to friends from all over the world.</u>

（本书作者译）

【点评】

  <u>这一组汉译英的原文为一本中英对照摄影图集的"序言"</u>。就译文一、二来看，均存在不少瑕疵和不足。在这些瑕疵和不足中，有些涉及意思表达不准确或不够精确，有些是词语搭配、句式选用和语法等方面的失当和不符合规范，还有一些则两者兼而有之。

  以译文一为例，其第一个句子就有几处明显的缺陷。先是 China has experienced the tremendous changes ... 中的 the 属于多此一举。其后的 since the reform and opening-up 又与此前的 over the past 30 years 不搭配（建议可改为 with 或 because of its reform and opening-up policy, 或者也可考虑改为 since its adoption of the reform and opening-up policy, 并将此置于句首）。另外，这个句子的后半部分，即 with the significant improvement of the international status and the continuous increase in foreign exchanges 也有问题。一是其本身的词语选择和搭配不够精准，二是其与此前的主句部分衔接失当。在第二句中，译文中的 miniature 属于死译、硬译，译者的意图是要和原文的"缩影"对应起来，可惜，在变通方面还是欠了些火候（译文二处理成 microcosom 同样不理想）。此外，诸如 become the most destination for foreign friends, ambassador ladies, according to the central requirement 和 the more extrovert and globalized Shanghai 等，也都是典型的中式英文。

  就译文二而言，情况要好一些，但也有不少需要改进的地方。比如，第一句中的 Past over 30 years 就很令人疑惑。如果要把"30多年"翻译成英文，要么是 For over 30 years, 要么是 Over the past 30 years（或者也可考虑 Over the past 30 years or so）。当然，究竟取何种翻译，还事关后面的搭配问题。再比如，它的第三句实质上是一个不完整的句子，没有出现谓语动词。此外，在倒数第二个句子的后半部分 it is more accessible and easier to invest in and cooperate with Shanghai 中，不但 it is more accessible 不可取，整个部分也与此前的部分不相匹配。还有，针对原文中的"热忱欢迎更多来自五湖四海的国内外朋友"，译文二的翻译是：welcome all the friends from both China and overseas，这个处理还是有点想当然。原文虽然的确是"欢迎……国内外朋友"，但是，其实只要译出"外国朋友"的意思就可以了。或者，至少可以模糊化处理，把它翻译成类似 welcome friends far and near。最后，在翻译《第一夫人在上海》和《国宾在上海》两个书名时，译文一、二均未能按惯例使用斜体（并且，译文一的翻译与原文有出入）。

第三章

体育竞技翻译

3.1 体育竞技类文本的概念

在人类文明发展的过程中,体育始终扮演着重要的角色。人类历史上最早的体育活动,实际上与我们祖先日常的劳作密不可分。由于自然环境的险恶和人类自身文明程度尚十分低下,因此,早期的先民为了基本的生存必须练就强悍的体魄。到了公元前776年,随着古希腊奥林匹克运动会的出现,体育竞技的概念开始逐步走进人们的头脑,体育比赛也成为和平条件下人们追逐光荣与梦想的一个途径。之后,在1896年希腊又成功举办了第一届现代奥林匹克运动会,现代体育的雏形就此逐步开始成型。

在21世纪的今天,体育已经发展成为人们生活中一个不可或缺的方面。奥运会、世界杯足球赛、田径黄金大奖赛、世界游泳锦标赛、F-1大奖赛、四大网球公开赛等,无不吸引了世界各地观众热切关注的目光。不仅如此,在相当程度上,现代体育已经超越了以锦标和金牌为唯一目标的局限,成为世界各国人民增进了解、发展友谊和共同进步的一个欢乐大舞台。

伴随着各类体育活动的蓬勃兴起,与此相关的写作自然也成为一种风尚,更多地进入了人们的视野。所谓体育竞技类文本,从广义上来说,其功能主要是记录体育界的人和事。它一般以新闻报道的形式出现,内容覆盖与体育相关的各个侧面,比如,赛事筹备进展报告、赞助商介绍、项目特点总结、比赛现场报道、运动员和官员采访,甚至还包括一些花边新闻或丑闻的追踪报道等。体育竞技类文本的发布平台以专业的体育报纸、杂志和电视台、电台以及网站为主。同时,在大部分非体育专业的纸面媒体和电视、广播以及网站上一般都辟有固定的体育板块,专供此类文章的发表。

值得一提的是,有时候人们也会把体育和竞技区分开来,把它们看成是一个整体的两个相互关联的方面。在这种情况下,前者往往指以强身健体为目的的大众体育运动或活动(比如,在我国不少地方开展得热火朝天的全民健身运动就是一例);而后者则专门指训练有素的运动员之间竞争激烈的各类专业比赛。

3.2 体育竞技类文本的基本特征

体育竞技类文本属于新闻报道的范畴,它的文体种类和样式相对固定和程式化,不外乎简讯、特稿、专访、现场播报和系列报道等。一般说来,此类文本的目的主要是向受众传达相关的信息。比如,一则简讯往往是通报某个比赛的结果;一篇特稿很可能是对于某个赛事的回顾和总结,或者,也可能是赛前的种种分析和展望。至于专访,其对象有可能是运动员,也有可能是代表团的官员,甚或是裁判员,不管是何种情形,必然包含大量有关规则、术语、训练安排、比赛、营养和康复等方面的内容。总之,体育竞技类文本的核心要素是信息,只要该信息能被受众及时、有效地接受,那么,它就达到了目的。因此,若对照莱斯的文本类型理论,它显然应该被划入信息型文本的序列。当然,必须看到,在这一类别的文本中,也存在着一定程度的情绪渲染和鼓动的成分。比如,在比赛进行过程中同步实时发出的现场直播或报道,就常常会令人产生激情澎湃、热血沸腾的感觉,这是因为负责现场播报的播音员或记者都会刻意在选词和用词方面强化情感的投入以感染听众或观众。另外,在体育竞技类文本中也或隐或现地流动着文化的影子。人们常说"文体不分家",指的也许就是文化和体育之间的相互渗透与交融。

如果要对体育竞技类文本的总体特征作一个简单梳理的话,我们认为,它至少体现出以下几个方面的特点。

第一,它的文风趋于简洁、明朗。体育竞技类文本多以事实陈述或信息传递为要旨,基于此,它的整体风格讲究简单、明晰和直截了当。这一点,无论从它的篇幅、文章的架构,还是具体的遣词造句上都能得到充分的反映。凡涉及体育竞技的文本,不管其出现在哪一类的媒体中,一般篇幅比较紧凑,较少看到洋洋洒洒的长篇大论。它的句式和篇章结构也是透明简单、单刀直入,不常见到层层叠叠的虚饰。

第二,它的语言多接近普通人的日常生活,在表达上既有明显的口语化倾向,同时又力求生动形象、不落俗套。当然,为了加强文本的可读性,作者有时也会在行文过程中特意选用一些具有煽情意味的词语。但是,这些意在营造独特效果的语汇也往往是读者或听众所喜闻乐见的,不可能云山雾罩、高深莫测。事实上,在长期的实践中,体育竞技类文本已经形成了一套属于自己的语言表达体系,那就是人们所说的体育语言。所谓体育语言,是一种有别于其他门类写作的语言,它以通俗、简明和风趣、幽默为其标志。

第三,它在态度或立场上多体现出一定的倾向性。由于体育运动本身所追求的"更快、更高、更强"的原则,特别是由于竞技类项目竞争激烈和对抗的性质,其结果往往是非胜即负、非赢即输。那些专业记者,也就是体育竞技类文本的作者,在某种程度上也是普通的观众,有自己对比赛的判断,也有自己对某个运动员和运动队的好恶和情感所属。尽管他们在撰写采访和制作现场报道等的时候,一般力求客观公正,但是,不可否认,在具体的行文过程中仍或多或少能体现出作者本人的态度和立场。这一点,从其词语的色彩以及笔触和基调上即可得到证明。比如,有这么两个句子:其一为"经过上下半场的激烈较量,顽强的主队最后以1分惜败",其二为"经过反复拉锯,强大的客队最后终于以1分的优势险胜"。这两个句子叙述的虽然是同一个事实,但是,作者在对待主客两队的态度上显示出了明显的差异:前一个句子的作者偏向主队,而后一个句子的作者则偏向客队。

第四,它的内容具有专业性强的特点。体育竞技是一个十分宽泛的概念,囊括了大众体育和竞技体育范围的所有项目。其中,有些项目是我们平时比较熟悉的,但还有相当一部分是我们接触较少,甚至完全没有听说过的。即使是那些我们了解较多的体育运动或项目,实际上也还有一些规则和专门的术语等不为一般人所熟悉,更不要说其他一些我们本来就知之甚少的项目和比赛等。因此,可以想象,有关体育竞技类的文本中必然常常会看到一些专门化的词汇和表达。这些专业性较强的词汇和表达可能与某项体育运动或比赛本身的发生和发展密切相关,也可能与体育医学、体育营养学和体育社会学等相关的新兴领域有关。

最后,基于体育竞技类文本的社会辐射效应,该类文本在一定程度上还承载着独特的文化意义。体育,和音乐一样,常常被看作是一门国际通用的语言。它既是民族的,同时又是世界的。透过体育竞技类文本,我们不仅能观照本民族的文化内涵和文化传承,有时还能体悟到依附在体育背后的异族文化特质。

3.3 体育竞技类文本的翻译策略

关于体育竞技类文本的翻译,和此前的时政民生类文本以及文化教育类文本翻译一样,也首先要考虑其文本的属性和特征。我们已经知道,体育竞技类文本具有非文学的性质,其主要目的是向受众(读者、听众和观众)传达和体育相关的信息。基于此,在讨论具体的翻译策略和手段之前,我们有必要先来确定几条指导性的原则。

第一,要突出体育的专业性。体育竞技类文本是一种特殊的写作形式,它的涉及面很广,无论在内容上,还是在表达手段上,都有一套独特的符号和系统。在当今世界,体育和竞技的概念何其宏大,从足球、篮球、网球、田径、游泳等广受欢迎和关注的运动项目,到诸如藤球、壁球、卡巴迪等不为一般人所知的小众项目,体育的触角可以说无所不在。若要追根溯源,每一项运动或比赛都有它发生、发展的历史,也有它与众不同的规则、要求、比赛氛围和裁判标准等。这就要求译者在从事此类文本的翻译时,必须具备专业的素养,以专业的态度来对待具体的翻译任务。也就是说,他必须学会用体育的方式来演绎体育界的人和事。不管文本涉及的项目是大众所喜闻乐见的,还是生僻的、冷门的,他都必须在译文中力求最大限度地反映出体育的专业性。

第二,要强调受众的接受度。体育竞技类文本面向的对象是普通读者、听众或观众,由于此类文本专业性强的特点,若要想译文取得好的效果,还需要考虑受众的反应和接受度。这就意味着译者在翻译的过程中需要把体育的专业性和大众化、普及性巧妙地结合起来,把通俗易懂、简单明晰和风趣幽默的语汇贯穿在译文之中,唯有如此,其译文才有生命力,才能得到受众的欢迎和肯定。

第三,要着意挖掘体育之外的美学、人文和道德意义。体育和竞技绝非简单的身体比拼,尤其在21世纪的今天,随着全球化进程的加快,随着各国人民生活水平和质量的普遍提高,随着体育与科技、人文之间关系的日益紧密,体育已经被赋予越来越多的外延含义。作为体育运动和竞技比赛宣传的载体,体育竞技类文本必然在这一点上也有所反映。因此，这就对译者的翻译活动提出了更高的要求。他不仅要专注于文本所包含的传统体育元素，比如力量、技巧和智慧等，还要兼顾由此衍生出的美学价值、道德寓意、文化特质，甚至娱乐效果等，并以恰当的方式表现出来。

现在让我们来谈一谈体育竞技类文本的翻译策略、手段和方法问题。从广义的角度看，可用于指导此类文本翻译的理论不少，比如目的论、译者主体性的理论、接受美学和奈达的功能对等理论等。究竟取何种理论为导向，或者，是否应该结合多个不同理论，实际上并无定规，一切取决于翻译的任务、目的、要求和文本的性质。至于具体的操作手段和方法，当然也是灵活多变，而非一成不变的，但也不外乎直译、意译、音译和综合译法等几种方法。

我们来看几个例子：bungee（蹦极），Chelsea FC（切尔西足球俱乐部），ace（网球比赛中的爱司球），bogey（高尔夫球比赛术语，译为柏忌，即高于标准杆一杆），这些属于音译。一般说来，专用的人名地名、球队名称、运动项目的某些术语等宜采用音译法。再看下面的几个例子（均选自 http://sports.yahoo.com）：Sampras returns to Aussie Open to present trophy.（桑普拉斯回到澳网将担任颁奖嘉宾。）Benson Henderson will enter the Octagon without the lightweight title around his waist for the first time in nearly two years at Saturday's UFC on Fox 10.（周六由福克斯第 10 频道直播的终极格斗比赛将是本森·亨德森近两年来首次在失去轻量级金腰带的情况下走进八角笼。）这两个句子中，前者是一篇网球比赛报道的标题，其中的 Aussie Open 是 Australian Open 的缩略形式，此处直接译成"澳网"。后者出现于一篇对现在在亚洲地区开始流行的终极格斗比赛的报道中，在这里，原文的 Octagon, the lightweight title around his waist，UFC 和 Fox 10 被以直译的方法分别译为"八角笼"、"轻量级金腰带"、"终极格斗比赛"和"福克斯第 10 频道"。再来看一个意译的例子：Sergio Ramos is very good in the air. 这个句子应该译为"塞尔吉奥·拉莫斯头球技术出众。"因为 in the air 这个短语在足球范围内可表示"争顶头球"，如果按其通常的意思译作"在空中"，则会令读者感到莫名其妙。最后请看这个例子：Arsenal 4 - 1 Coventry: Podolski hits double as Gunners cruise into FA Cup fifth round. 参考译文是："阿森纳 4 比 1 击败考文垂：波多尔斯基梅开二度，帮助枪手顺利挺进足总杯第五轮。"在这个标题的翻译中，可以说综合了多种手法。

3.4 翻译实例及点评

英译汉

【原文】

Pacers proved no pushovers

WALTHAM—The Celtics might not have drawn a red circle around the date on their calendars. But there is a heightened sense of awareness that tonight's opponent, Indiana, is <u>the only team that has defeated them convincingly this season</u>(1).

On Nov. 1, <u>the Pacers took a 95-79 victory</u>, <u>providing a discouraging end to an extraordinary week</u>(2) for the Celtics, <u>who had raised their 17th NBA championship banner and won twice in previous days</u>(3).

But <u>that defeat</u> also signaled a wake-up call for the Celtics (17-2), who <u>have gone 15-1 since</u>(4) and have a nine-game winning streak, best in the league this season.

"We do know they beat us, and I thought they played better than us," Celtics coach Doc Rivers said yesterday. "We struggled on both ends of the floor. <u>Give them credit</u>(5). <u>If you look at their losses, they've lost more games at the buzzer than any team in the league.</u>(6)

For us, we've got to play our game and we can't worry as much about what other teams are doing. We've got to keep trying to correct what we are not doing better."

The Celtics had taken a 96-80 victory over Chicago the previous night, then arrived at their Indianapolis hotel at 4 a.m.

"The tough part is having TV games when they are the first of a back-to-back(7)," Rivers said. "The 8 o'clock start — <u>a half-hour doesn't seem big, but it is, especially when you have a 2 1/2—or three-hour flight</u>(8). But everyone goes through that, not just us."

"Indiana is very good. I think they will be a playoff team. <u>They've just lost heartbreaking games,</u>(9) and <u>eventually the basketball gods will turn</u>

their way (10). And when that happens, they'll be a good team."

（*The Boston Globe*，by Frank Dell'Apa，December 3，2008）

【译文一】

步行者队绝非泛泛之辈

沃尔瑟姆—凯尔特人可能没有在日历上把这个日期用红色圆圈圈起来。但是他们越发强烈地感觉到今晚的对手印第安纳是<u>在本赛季唯一一个令人信服地击败自己的团队</u>（Ⅰ）。

11月1号这一天，<u>步行者们</u>（Ⅱ）以95∶79的成绩赢得这场比赛，<u>为凯尔特人这一周来非凡的成绩画上了一个苍凉的结局</u>（Ⅲ），要知道凯尔特人已经举起了17届NBA总冠军的旗帜，并且<u>在过去的两天里赢了两次</u>（Ⅲ）。

但是这次击败为曾经有着17∶2的业绩的凯尔特人敲响了一个警钟，<u>他们曾经获过15∶1的成绩，在本赛季的联赛中荣获九连胜，表现最好</u>（Ⅳ）。

"我们都知道他们打败了我们，我认为他们比我们打得好。"凯尔特人的教练里费斯昨天说道。"我们在攻防两端挣扎，<u>给他们得分</u>（Ⅴ）。如果你观看一下他们的失分状况，就可以发现<u>从蜂鸣器响起的那一刻开始，他们就失去了比联盟的任何一个团队都多的赛事</u>（Ⅵ）。

对于我们来说，我们只会打好自己的球，对于别的球队在做什么，我们不会关心太多。我们正在努力地去纠正现在做的不是太好的东西。"

凯尔特人在前天晚上以96∶80的成绩击败了芝加哥队，然后在早晨4点钟到达他们的印第安纳波利斯酒店。

"<u>最艰难的时刻是看电视播出的时候，他们第一个背过身去</u>（Ⅶ），"里费斯说道："8点开始，半个小时并不算什么，但是<u>当进行两个半小时或者三到四个小时的激战时</u>（Ⅷ），就是另一番感受了。但是每个人都挺了过来，不仅是我们。

印第安纳队确实很不错。我认为他们将会成为季后赛的球队。他们刚错失了<u>令人心碎的比赛</u>（Ⅸ），<u>最后篮球之神将会垂青他们</u>（Ⅹ），而因此，他们也将会成为一个很优秀的球队。"

（学生课堂练习）

【译文二】

步行者绝非泛泛之辈

沃尔瑟姆—凯尔特人可能没有把这一天看作是值得注意的一天。但是,他们应该强烈地意识到,今晚的对手印第安纳队是本赛季唯一一支已经大败他们的球队(Ⅰ')。

11月1日,步行者队以95比79获得胜利,这为凯尔特人不平凡的一周画上了令人沮丧的句号(Ⅱ')。这支队伍曾夺得第17届NBA的总冠军,且在此前也赢得过两次冠军(Ⅲ')。

但是,这场失利也为凯尔特人(赢17场输2场)敲响了警钟,这支本赛季最佳球队在此之前曾拥有赢15场输1场的战绩,并赢得过九连胜(Ⅳ')。

凯尔特人主帅里弗斯昨天表示:"我们知道他们赢了我们,我也认为他们表现得比我们出色。我们在攻防两端都表现的心有余而力不足。这让他们赢得了分数(Ⅴ')。只要看看他们的输球场次就会发现,他们输的押哨球比联盟中任何一支球队都多。"(Ⅵ')

"而我们则必须好好比赛,不能过分担心其他球队在做什么。我们必须要继续努力,加以改正,以打出更好的成绩。"

前一晚,凯尔特人以96比80的比分击败了芝加哥,之后于凌晨4点抵达他们在印第安纳波利斯的酒店。

里弗斯说:"这次的电视比赛是首次进行连续两场比赛,这就是困难之处(Ⅶ')。比赛从8点钟开始,一个半小时的赛时似乎并不长,但这真的够长了,尤其是当你打到赢21场输2场的时候(Ⅷ'),或是在经历了三个小时的飞行之后。但是每个人都要克服这种困难,不仅仅只有我们。"

"印地安纳队很棒。我认为他们会打进季后赛。虽然他们刚刚经历了一场令人心碎的比赛(Ⅸ')输了球,但最终篮球之神会眷顾他们的(Ⅹ')。而当那种情况出现,他们将是一支优秀的球队。"

(学生课堂练习)

【译文三】

步行者队被证明并不好对付/并非(鱼腩)不堪一击

沃尔瑟姆——也许,凯尔特人队并没有刻意强调今天这个日子的重要性/特别在意今天这个日子(也许,凯尔特人队并没有特意用红笔把今天的日期圈出来/并没有告诉自己今天是个什么样的日子)。不过,他们深知,今晚的对手印第安纳步行者队是本赛季唯一令人信服地击败过自己的球队。

在11月1日,步行者曾以95比79擒下了凯尔特人,使这支17次NBA总冠军得主此前两连胜的势头戛然而止。

不过,本场失利也吹响了/燃起了凯尔特人反击的冲锋号/号角/狂潮(目前的战绩为17胜2负)。经历此次失利之后,球队取得了15胜1负的傲人战绩,其中还包括一个9连胜,成为联盟中表现最为抢眼的球队。

凯尔特人队主帅多克·里维斯昨天表示,"我们当然知道/承认他们击败过我们,我想他们打得比我们好。当时,我们在攻防两端都疲于奔命。你必须承认,他们实力相当强劲。如果你看一下他们输掉的那些比赛,你会发现他们是全联盟中纠缠到终场哨响那一刻才输掉比赛场次最多的球队/压哨失利场次最多的。"

"对我们来说,重要的是打好自己的比赛,至于其他队伍的表现,并不在我们关注的范围。我们必须设法改进现在的不足,争取做得更好。"

凯尔特人队在前一天晚上以96比80击败了芝加哥公牛队,然后于凌晨4点抵达了印第安纳波利斯的宾馆。

里维斯说,"背对背的第一场比赛又遇上要电视直播,这可是个考验。虽然开球时间是8点——比非电视直播仅提早半小时——看起来并没有什么太大的差异,但是,当你经历了2个半至3小时的飞行,你会知道其实还是有差异的。当然,每支队伍都要经历这样的过程,也并非我们一家。"

"印第安纳是支很不错的队伍,我想他们会打入季后赛。他们刚输掉了几场伤心的比赛,但是,他们球队中的灵魂人物最终会找回感觉。当这一切发生的时候,他们将会变得非常强大。"

(本书作者译)

【点评】

本组英译汉的原文选自《波士顿环球报》的体育版面,内容是关于美国男子职业篮球联赛(NBA)的赛况,文中涉及的凯尔特人是波士顿当地的一支球队,也是美国男子职业篮球史上著名的球队。从译文一、二的情况来看,总体差别不算太大,有值得肯定的地方,也存在着一些缺陷。不过,译文二的表现要略好一些。至于反映出来的问题,主要集中在三个方面:一是准确性,二是精确性,三是专业性。

  准确性:这方面的问题比较多,关键是译者往往未能在译文中准确地还原原文作者所要表达的意思。以译文一为例,在第二段的最后部分"并且在过去的两天里赢了两次"中,"两天"一词就不准确,对照原文中的 previous days,应译为"此前几天"才较为理想。还有,针对原文中的 Give them credit,译文一的处理是"给他们得分",译文二为"这让他们赢得了分数",这两个翻译均不准确。译文三的处理"你必须承认,他们实力相当强劲"才较为接近原文的意思。还有,译文一的"如果你观看一下他们的失分状况,就可以发现从蜂鸣器响起的那一刻开始,他们就失去了比联盟的任何一个团队都多的赛事"也是一个误译,比较而言,译文二的"只要看看他们的输球场次就会发现,他们输的押哨球比联盟中任何一支球队都多"就要好得多。再来看一个例子,在译文一倒数第二段的开头部分有这样的句子:"最艰难的时刻是看电视播出的时候,他们第一个背过身去",这明显是一个误译。原文中的 TV games 和 the first of a back-to-back 都是篮球专业术语,前者是指"上电视直播的比赛",而后者现在一般译为"背靠背的比赛"。在这个句子的处理上,译文二显得更加准确一些("这次的电视比赛是首次进行连续两场比赛,这就是困难之处")。

  精确性:这方面的例子也不在少数,问题主要出在译文虽力求接近原文,却因理解和表达或其他种种缺陷而影响了整体的效果。比如,译文一第二个句子"但是他们越发强烈地感觉到今晚的对手印第安纳是在本赛季唯一一个令人信服地击败自己的团队"中的"击败自己的团队"就有瑕疵,准确的处理应该是"击败过自己的队伍"。别小看了一个"过"字,因为只有这个"过"字才能和原文的 has defeated them 吻合起来。再来看译文一的第三段:"但是这次击败为曾经有着 17∶2 的业绩的凯尔特人敲响了一个警钟,他们曾经获过 15∶1 的成绩,在本赛季的联赛中荣获九连胜,表现最好。"在这个只有一个句子的段落中,一上来的"击败"一词很不精确,如果不用"失利",至少也可以用"失败",因为这儿谈论的是凯尔特人队,是指其此前曾被步行者队所击败的事实。接下来的"业绩"一词同样不精确,或者说用得不恰当。要知道,这里谈论的是一支职业篮球队取得的成绩,而不是某个公司的销售业绩等。之后的文字看似没什么问题,实质也有欠缺。比如,"曾经获过 15∶1 的成绩"里的"曾经"就很成问题。它的原文是 have gone 15-1 since,但是,这个 since 应该译为"此后",也就是"自从遭受上次失利之后"的意思。而"九连胜"也是在那次输给步行者之后取得的,所谓"表现最好",严格意义上来说,应该是"迄今为止联盟中表现最好的球队"。

专业性:这方面出现的问题,其性质和精确性不足有点类似。比如,译文一第二段的"步行者们"就是一个不专业的称谓。原文虽然是一个复数(the Pacers),但是,翻译的时候却不能直译成复数。还有,所谓"画上了一个苍凉的结局"应该也不属于体育词汇的范畴。与此形成对照的是,译文二的"画上了令人沮丧的句号"看起来倒是一个不错的选择。不过,译文二也有不够专业的地方,像"这支队伍"就显得过于随意。还有,在翻译 and eventually the basketball gods will turn their way 的时候,两篇译文都不甚专业。不管是"最后篮球之神将会垂青他们",还是"但最终篮球之神会眷顾他们的",都和原文有出入。他们没有注意到原文中 god 一词是以复数形式出现的,此其一;第二点是,这儿的 god 一词只是一种比喻,并不是说凡出现 god 的地方,都非要翻译成"什么神",再说,也没有"篮球之神"一说。另外,在这个句子的前半部分,同样也有一个 game 的复数形式,只可惜两位译者似乎并未留意,结果造成他们的翻译不精确、不专业。

汉译英

【原文1】

国足1-5耻辱性不敌泰国,创对泰最大输球比分(1)

北京时间6月15日晚,国足在合肥进行了一场热身赛,对手是主要以U23球员组成的泰国国家队。比赛中国足开场后便突然崩盘,上下半场被对手连灌5球(2),以1-5惨败泰国,创下国足有史以来与泰国比赛的最大输球比分。王永珀在比赛中打入1个点球。现场球迷打出怀念高洪波的标语,同时怒不可遏高喊卡马乔下课。(3)

(齐鲁网,2013年6月15日)

【译文一】

Orangemen humiliating 1:5 defeat to Thailand,
The highest losing score with Thailand(Ⅰ)

On the night of June 15th (Beijing time), our national football team went on a warming-up match in Hefei with Thai's national team mainly made up of U23 players. Once the game began, our team suddenly collapsed. In the first and second halves, opponents got five scores (Ⅱ) and we got our waterloo with Thailand by 1∶5 at last. During the whole contest, Wang Yongbo scored a penalty. Fans in the field raised the slogan named "missing Gao Hongbo", at the same time, they flied into rages and cried out to let Camacho out (Ⅲ).

(学生课堂练习)

【译文二】

China football team lose to Thailand (1 - 5),
The worst score against Thailand ever (Ⅰ')

On the evening of June 15, the warm-up game had been held in Hefei between China football team and Thai national football team, which was mainly composed of the U23 players. China football team was defeated in morale after the game started for a while (Ⅱ'), losing 5 goals to Thai during the game. The 1 - 5 score is the worst ever against Thailand national football. Wang Yongbo scored a penalty in the game. During the game, the audience played the slogan (Ⅲ') "we are missing Gao Hongbo", while shouting furiously to ask Camacho to step down.

(学生课堂练习)

【译文三】

1 - 5: Chinese Football's Record-Breaking Loss to Thailand

On the evening of June 15, the Chinese National Football Team played a warm-up game against a Thai team composed mostly of under- 23 players in Hefei, Anhui province. After the whistle was blown, the Chinese National Football Team soon lost control, and they allowed their Thai counterparts to end up scoring altogether five goals during the game. Although Wang Yongpo scored a penalty kick, this defeat by Thailand was the worst ever in the Sino-Thai history of football confrontation. The fans that filled the stadium, mad with the result, shouted angrily to ask Jose Antonio Camacho, the head coach, to resign, while at the same time, they displayed banners urging for Gao Hongbo, the former head coach, to return.

(本书作者译)

【点评】

　　这组汉译英的原文选自齐鲁网,是有关中国国家足球队热身比赛的一则报道。篇幅虽较为精炼、简短,但要翻译得好却也不易,现在就译文一、二的情况,来探讨一下具体的优劣之处。

　　关于标题,两篇译文都存在一些缺陷。撇开其他方面的问题(包括词语和句式的选用等)不说,两者共同的一个问题是过于冗长,不适合用作标题。参考译文三的处理可以发现,在新闻标题的翻译上,简洁和凝练是一个十分重要的考量指标。而且,一般不宜以完整的句子形式出现,某些次要的成分往往可加以省略。

　　关于译文一,最大的问题还是语言的精确性和准确性不足。比如,一开头的 On the night of June 15th 中的 night,显然应为 evening。此后的 warming-up match 实则应为 warm-up game。在第三句中,got five scores 虽说过得去,但若译为 scored five goals 恐怕更好。在该句的后半部分中,by 1∶5 应该为 with a 1∶5。在随后的一句中,先是 whole 一词属于多此一举,再有 contest 可考虑以 match 或 game 取代才更为妥当。在最后的部分,还出现了搭配方面的问题。比如,raised the slogan 和 flied into rages。

　　译文二的问题与译文一大同小异。开首一句 On the evening of June 15, the warm-up game had been held in Hefei between China football team and Thai national football team, which was mainly composed of the U23 players. 中就有几处失误。一是不应在 warm-up game 之前使用定冠词 the, 二是不应在主句中使用过去完成式(句中已包含明确的表示过去的时间概念),三是与 game 搭配的动词 held 不甚理想(可考虑 played),四是"国足"的英译应为 Chinese National Football Team,而不是 China football team,五是 in Hefei 的位置不应提前至此,一般应置于句末。后一句中,was defeated in morale 好像太正式了,没有反映出原文体育新闻的特点;而 after the game started for a while 则既有语法方面的欠缺（应考虑 had started 而不是 started），也有意思表达方面的不足（对照原文，for a while 恐未能准确地表达出原文作者的意图）。

【原文2】

马拉松成中国地方政府经营城市窗口(1)

　　如果说纽约、伦敦、波士顿、柏林、东京等国际大都市有一个显著共同点的话，那其中一项必然有马拉松赛。这项历史悠久、参与人数动辄数万的城市马拉松赛事(2)已成为这些城市的耀眼"文化名片"，享誉盛名。

　　中国城市也在"快马加鞭"。近年来，方兴未艾的城市马拉松已成为不少地方政府"经营城市"的一辆重要"马车"(3)。

　　1981年，北京首次举办国际马拉松赛。随后，大连国际马拉松赛(创办于1987年)(4)、上海国际马拉松赛(创办于1996年)、厦门国际马拉松赛(创办于2003年)等相继出现(5)。2012年更被称为中国"马拉松年"，广州、深圳、兰州等城市"爆发性"加入马拉松队伍。

　　数据显示，中国城市马拉松赛事2011年有22场，2012年有33场，2013年有44场，连续3年，每年都以10场左右的数量在增加。

　　对于中国城市兴起的"马拉松热"，中国田径协会副主席王大卫认为这与马拉松的自身特点有关(6)，"马拉松运动具有强大的整合资源功能。举办马拉松赛可以向全国乃至全世界展示城市发展和市民风貌(7)。与此同时，举办马拉松赛所吸引到的资金以及带来的消费(8)，可以进一步推动城市发展"。

　　（新华社广州11月25日新媒体专电　新华社记者周强）

【译文一】

Marathon has become the city's business
window of Chinese local governments（Ⅰ）

　　If notable similarities are shared among international cities like New York, London, Boston, Berlin and Tokyo, marathon must be one. With a long history and tens of thousands of participants（Ⅱ）, it enjoys great popularity as "cultural card" of those cities.

　　Chinese cities are accelerating the speed of promoting marathon. In recent years, the growing city marathon has become an important leading carriage of managing cities for local governments (Ⅲ).

Beijing held the first international marathon in 1981. Then Dalian international marathon (established in 1987) (Ⅳ), Shanghai international marathon (established in 1996) and Xiamen international marathon (established in 2003) appeared in succession (Ⅴ). 2012 was even called "the Chinese Marathon Year" because Guangzhou, Shenzhen, Lanzhou and other cities quickly joined the trend of marathon.

The data showed, China had 22 marathon races in 2011, 33 in 2012 and 44 in 2013. During these three years, 10 more was held compared with the previous year.

When noted the marathon trend, vice president of Chinese Athletic Association David Wang said it owed to the characteristics of marathon itself (Ⅵ), "Marathon can integrate resources well. Holding marathon aims to show the world the rapid growth of cities and life of citizens. (Ⅶ). Meanwhile, the capital (Ⅷ) and spending can promote the further development of cities."

（学生课堂练习）

【译文二】

City Symbol for Chinese Local Government—Marathon (Ⅰ')

If there exists any significant thing in common among New York, London, Boston, Berlin, Tokyo and other international cities, then Marathon is a must to mention. Marathon, a time-honored and renowned competition with tens of thousands of participants at every turn (Ⅱ'), has become a dazzling "culture card" for these cities.

Chinese cities are also keeping up with this trend at their top speed. In recent years, the growing city marathons have become a great drive in "promoting cities".

In 1981, the first International Marathon was held in Beijing. Later, such competitions have been held in succession as Dalian International

Marathon (1987), Shanghai International Marathon (1996), Xiamen International Marathon (2003). The year of 2012 has even been known as China's "Marathon Year", since many cities such as Guangzhou, Shenzhen, Lanzhou joined the team to hold marathons.

Data shows that there are 22 Marathons held in China in 2011, 33 in 2012, 44 in 2013, growing by 10 each year in three consecutive years.

Speaking of the "marathon trend" in China, the vice chairman of Chinese Athletics Association Wang Dawei thinks <u>it has something to do with the inherent characteristics of marathon</u> (Ⅵ'). He says "marathon can integrate resources effectively. Organizing marathon can <u>demonstrate the outlook of urban development and citizens to the nation and even to the world</u> (Ⅶ'). Meanwhile, <u>the funds and resulting consumptions attracted by marathons</u> (Ⅷ') can further promote urban development."

(学生课堂练习)

【译文三】

Marathon in China: an Ideal Occasion for City Showcase

If one is to find some common features shared by cities such as New York, London, Boston, Berlin and Tokyo, he tends to think of the marathon race. To these major cities of the world, their marathon, <u>boasting a long history and attracting tens of thousands of participants every year</u>, is not just a sports event, but rather <u>a dazzling cultural festival</u>.

In recent years, this zest for the marathon has spread to China, where <u>the hosting of a marathon has been viewed as the golden opportunity to showcase the city's charm</u>.

In 1981, Beijing saw the opening of the first International Marathon Race in China. Later, in 1987, 1996 and 2003, Dalian, Shanghai and Xiamen <u>launched their own marathon races respectively</u>. In 2012, China's "Year of Marathon", Guangzhou, Shenzhen, Lanzhou and some other cities, one after another, declared themselves to be members of this growing marathon family.

Statistics show that China had 22 marathons in 2011, and this number increased to 33 in 2012, and 44 in 2013. For three consecutive years, there is the increase of at least 10 marathons every year in China.

According to Wang Dawei, Deputy Chief of Chinese Athletics Association, this "Marathon Fever" among Chinese cities <u>is not unrelated to what marathons can do as a sport</u>. He said, "The sport of marathons, often functioning as a powerful platform for the integration of various kinds of resources, is a unique channel through which <u>to enhance the image of the host city and its people</u>. Besides, <u>the money from the sponsors and the spending of those who come for the event</u> also helps to boost local economy."

(本书作者译)

【点评】

这组汉译英的原文为新华社刊发的有关马拉松比赛的一个专稿。现在先来讨论译文一,文中有一些较为成功的处理,但问题也不少。从标题来看,一是显得太冗长了;二是译者把它处理成一个完整的句子,这似乎违背了一般新闻文体翻译的原则;三是就这个句子本身而言,在 business window 后面跟了 of Chinese local governments 是不可取的(比较之下,译文二的标题翻译效果要好一些)。在第二段的翻译中,也有一些比较拘谨、刻板的例子。比如,所谓的 an important leading carriage of managing cities 属于典型的中式英语。还有,第三段的三个 established 以及此后的 appeared 则可归为选词不当。再来看最后一段的第一个句子,其前半句 When noted the marathon trend, vice president of Chinese Athletic Association David Wang said it owed to the characteristics of marathon itself 中至少包含了三个方面的问题:首先,从语法的角度看,开头的 noted 应为 noting;第二,即便改用了动词的 ing 形式,但是,此处的 note 也并非合适的单词(至少可考虑 commenting on 等);第三, it owed to 这个短语的使用不当。

至于译文二,它的总体效果比译文一有所改善。比如, Then Marathon is a must to mention; Chinese cities are also keeping up with this trend; many cities such as Guangzhou, Shenzhen, Lanzhou joined the team to hold marathons; Speaking of the "marathon trend" in China 和 marathon can integrate resources effectively 等应该算是较为理想的翻译。当然，失误也并非没有。像 Later, such competitions have been held in succession as Dalian International Marathon (1987), Shanghai International Marathon (1996), Xiamen International Marathon (2003) 这样的句子就令人觉着莫名其妙。还有，在 Organizing marathon can demonstrate the outlook of urban development and citizens to the nation and even to the world. 和 Meanwhile, the funds and resulting consumptions attracted by marathons can further promote urban development. 这两个句子中，也存在着一些问题。先是 outlook 一词被同时用来与 urban development 和 citizens 构成搭配是不恰当的。之后的一个 the funds 和 resulting consumptions attracted by marathons 也不专业。前者属于大而不当的用词，后面的 attracted by marathons 则属于死译、硬译。

总之，通过对上述种种问题和不足进行的一番简单分析、点评，我们认为，要真正做好体育竞技类文本的翻译并非易事，除了译者的态度和双语能力以外，还有一个关键点，那就是他必须具备扎实的体育专业知识和相关的背景知识。与此同时，翻译方法的选择也大有讲究。比如，在译前和译中广泛参考平行文本就是一个通常的做法。

第四章

旅 游 翻 译

4.1 旅游类文本的概念

旅游,是一个既古老又时新的话题。旅游业的兴起与人类文明的发展,特别是社会物质财富的积累和增加密不可分。在当今社会,随着科技的日新月异以及人类物质文明的高度提升,旅游业也迎来了一个全新的发展机遇。它不仅成为普通人追求的一种生活方式,更成为不少国家大力发展的一个支柱产业。旅游涉及的面很广,从自然科学到社会科学,从天文、历史、地理到各国各地的风土人情,甚至文化娱乐、吃穿用住,真可谓无所不包、无所不有。从广义上来说,旅游类文本可指与旅游活动相关的一切语言文字资料,比如,官方的旅游宣传手册、旅游节活动安排、旅行社线路推介、旅游景点介绍、旅游知识普及、民俗风情游览、掌故和传说、旅游告示标牌、古迹楹联解说、各类游记,等等。

旅游类文本主要属于应用文的范畴,其体裁多样、形式不一。一般而言,这一类的文本以说明为主,间或也会有描写和记叙的成分。比如,景区和景点的介绍、旅游告示标牌以及名胜古迹的说明文字等就是这方面的代表。同时,这一类文本往往内涵丰富,承载大量文化信息,具有比较明显的文化特征。从这个意义上来说,它也可以被视为一个国家历史文化对外宣传的窗口,甚或是其国家形象的一个重要组成部分。最后,这一类文本有时也体现出较强的文学性。以游记为例,不仅内容丰富多彩,自然、历史、人文等兼容并包,而且在行文风格上也讲究文采辞藻,是大众喜闻乐见的通俗读物。

4.2 旅游类文本的基本特征

旅游类文本是一种专门用途的写作形式，总体上属于非文学文本的范畴。不管其体裁如何变化不定、形式是否新颖或传统，也不管其风格是简洁还是繁复，它的终极目标是服务于游客。旅游宣传材料通过各种媒介，利用有形的视觉效果或劝服性的宣传途径发布和传播信息，目的在于吸引游客的注意力，诱发潜在旅游者对旅游目的地自然和人文景观产生兴趣，从而激发其购买旅游产品。换句话说，旅游类文本主要有两大功能：一是传递信息，二是诱导行动。通过广泛的市场调研和专题研究，在充分了解旅游者的消费心理与消费习惯以后，发布旅游宣传材料的主体便会以各种途径和手段，广泛宣传和推广其旅游产品，全方位地展现其旅游产品中的文化渊源和形象内涵，以期待诱发受众的旅游需求并促使他们最终采取行动。

因此，若对照莱斯的文本类型理论，旅游类文本既是信息型文本，同时又是感染型文本。可以说，在很多情况下，它更像是这两者的一个综合体，里面既包含大量必备的信息，又不乏劝说和说服的成分。这两个方面相辅相成、相得益彰，成为这一类文本不同于此前的时政民生、文化教育和体育竞技类文本的明显标志。

至于这一类文本的基本特征，除了游记往往展现较多的文学性以外，其余和旅游活动相关的语言文字材料一般具有简洁明朗、生动形象、富含多重文化色彩的特点。简洁明朗是所有旅游宣传材料的一大要件，这与此类文本以信息传达为根本的宗旨密不可分。既然是散布信息，自然必须做到要言不烦、简单明晰，这样才能迅速、及时地达到目标受众。比如，旅游活动安排、旅游景点介绍和旅游告示标牌等就可以被看作是最具代表性的。

当然，信息传播光有速度是不够的，它还必须具有有效性。也就是说，它必须是受众所乐于接受和易于接受的信息类型。否则，信息传播的速度再快也是徒劳，它不可能最终转化为潜在消费者的行动。这就引出了旅游类文本的第二个基本特征，即生动形象。生动形象的表现是全方位的，不仅反映在遣词造句和谋篇布局上，同时也反映在声音、颜色、图案的设计和搭配上，甚至还反映在特定传播媒介的精心挑选上面。

旅游类文本的第三个基本特征是它的文化附属性，即富含多重文化色彩。

旅游绝非简单的游山玩水,在现代社会,旅游的概念早已获得了无限的延伸,都市旅游、工业旅游、文化教育旅游、体育旅游、历史风情旅游、红色怀旧旅游等应有尽有。即便是纯粹的山水自然风光之旅,也超脱不了历史和文化的沉淀。因为有山有水的醉美之地必定也是文儒辈出的钟毓灵秀之地。从某种意义上来说,旅游实质上是一种对文化的感悟,而文化则构成了旅游的灵魂。对每个旅游者来说,在旅游观光的同时,他也在自觉或不自觉地接受某种文化的熏陶和影响。与之相对应,旅游类文本中除了表层的旅游专业术语和相关信息之外,往往还包含着大量若隐若现、或明或暗的文化内涵。比如,旅游观光手册、名胜古迹介绍里面经常出现的诗词歌赋、典故和传说等即是一例。

4.3 旅游类文本的翻译策略

在探讨旅游类文本的翻译策略、手段和方法之前,我们先来明确几条指导性的原则。

首先,准确性原则。既然旅游类文本的核心任务之一是向受众传达信息,那么,在实施翻译行为的过程中,对于准确性的考量必然居于首位。试想,如果译者在准确性和精准度上把握不好,导致原文中的信息在译文中发生了误差、偏差甚或丢失,则接下来的"感染"部分就无从谈起,其最终的"诱导行动"的目的也就无法达成。

其次,恰当性原则。这是指译者在翻译操作过程中须自觉意识到中英文之间的多重差异,充分照顾到目标读者、听众或观众独特的审美心理和审美习惯,无论是汉译英,还是英译汉,都应该追求以恰当的和受众喜闻乐见的方式把信息呈现出来。举个例子来说,英语的旅游类文本多从事实出发,行文简约透明,不太讲求辞藻堆砌;而在汉语方面则恰好相反,往往追求华丽的风格。这一点不仅与英汉两种语言本身的差异有关,同时也与这两个民族各自不同的文化传统、社会历史背景、审美思维习惯等密不可分。基于此,译者在翻译时除了要遵守准确性和忠实性的原则之外,还必须体现出相应的灵活性。他需要尽量使译文朝着符合目标语的文本和文化规约的方向靠拢,为此甚至可以不必拘泥于原文的形式和结构,并允许其对原文的内容和表达习惯等进行适度的调整,以便使译文能够雅俗共赏、为不同层次的受众所理解和接受。

第三，重视挖掘文化内涵原则。如前所述，旅游类文本往往包裹了或多或少、或明或暗的文化因子，类似古迹遗存、典故传说、名人轶事、诗词歌赋等内容都有可能隐身其中。这些柔性的东西看似虚无缥缈，却是旅游信息的一个有机组成部分，甚至是更为重要的一个部分。因为，旅游不仅是跋山涉水、登高望远，更是一种心灵的感悟和文化的体验。假设你在4、5月份的时候来到杭州，无疑立刻会被西湖的景致所吸引。但是，除此之外，你必定也会联想到白娘子的传说，会轻轻地哼起"淡妆浓抹总相宜"一类的诗句。可见，西湖的湖光山色和那些关于西湖的种种传奇和文坛佳话是浑然天成、不可分割的。再比如，英国西北部有一个著名的湖区，那里景色宜人，每年都要吸引大量的游客。但在历史上，这里也曾经是英国浪漫主义诗歌的滥觞之地，华兹华斯和柯勒律治等人曾常年在此流连吟唱，并因此获得了"湖畔派诗人"的名号。这两个例子显示了文化积淀和文化内涵对于旅游的重要性，而这一点也势必在旅游文本中有所反映。当然，旅游文本中的文化元素并非总是显性的，有时候只是隐性的存在，并且在实际翻译时恐较难处理。但不管是何种情形，译者都应该审慎对待，确保使之在译文中恰如其分地体现出来。

至于指导旅游类文本翻译的宏观策略，实际上仍然脱不开此前几章讨论中所涉及的一些基本策略，诸如文本类型理论、功能对等理论、接受美学理论或读者反应理论和互文性理论等或均可尝试采用。在此，我们来重点探讨一下具体的手段和方法问题。

1. 增译法

增译法在旅游文本翻译中比较常见，特别在英译汉时更为有用。我们已经知道，英语的表达讲究简单明晰、逻辑性强，行文忌重复堆砌。它不是单纯靠词汇出彩，而往往是通过句型结构的层层推进和前后呼应来实现写作意图，这一点在英语的旅游文本中也不例外。但另一方面，汉民族的审美习惯却多追求"语不惊人誓不休"。或者，即便达不到"惊人"的程度，至少也要向辞藻华丽、文采斐然靠拢。因此，出于照顾目标受众审美趣味和保持译文恰当性原则的需要，在英译汉的时候，译者就有必要作适当的调整，增加一些修饰性的词句和内容。请看这个例子：

Towers, domes, balanced rocks, and arches have been formed over millions of years of weathering and erosion, and the process continues, constantly reshaping this fantastic rock garden.

这句话是美国犹他州拱门国家公园（也称阿琪思国家公园）的网站主页上的介绍文字。拱门国家公园是一个地质宝库，以保存完好的 2 000 多座形态各异的天然石拱门闻名遐迩。不过，这些文字若按照汉语的标准来衡量，却够不上华丽的等级。如果把 balanced rock 中的 balanced 去除掉，整个句子只有一个修饰词，那就是 fantastic。因此，若要把它翻译成中文，必然需要添加一些修饰性的成分。

本书作者的试译："岁月沧桑、风化雨蚀，千百万年的超级洗礼造就了这里满山遍野的'高塔'、'穹顶'、'神来之石'和'耸立的拱门'。更令人叫绝的是，大自然神奇的表演仍未谢幕，这座美轮美奂的岩石花园时刻都发生着惊人的变化。"

2. 减译法

减译法大量用于中文旅游文本的英译，这是因为中文的写作多重视情景交融、虚实相生，反映在具体的行文中就是讲究四言八句、对仗工整，渲染的成分相对多了一些。基于此，在汉译英时就应注意化虚为实，化繁为简，从原文声情并茂、情感交融的语言表达中抽象概括出实质性的信息，以便更易于为目标受众所接受和理解。请看一例：

"元至元二十九年（1292 年），上海县正式设立，县治在上海镇。这时的上海也还不过是一个边陲小镇，名不见经传。然而历史前进的车轮很快就把她推上了世界的舞台。1843 年 11 月 17 日，上海正式开放为通商口岸。自此，上海开始以其襟江带海的地理位置，联系南北、沟通内外，各方面的发展突飞猛进，地位日隆，至民国时期，已经成为全国的经济、文化、工业中心。……"

此处，请特别注意最后一句中的几个修饰词："襟江带海"、"联系南北"、"沟通内外"。这三个词语实际上无非指上海拥有有利的地理位置，如果在英译汉全盘照搬把它们翻译出来，不仅有损于表达的简洁性，也不符合英文读者的审美意趣。故试译如下：

In the 29th year of Zhiyuan's Reign of the Yuan Dynasty (year 1292 by the Western calendar), Shanghai, then an obscure village, was officially announced to be the site of the newly established county-level administration. This marked the beginning of Shanghai's journey of legendary take-off. On November 17, 1843, Shanghai became the trading port for foreign business. Thereafter, Shanghai, the rising coastal town, taking advantage of its favorable geographic location, was soon able to carry itself to the frontline in China's national landscape. By the time when the Republic of China was founded, Shanghai was already developed into the country's important economic, cultural and industrial center.

3. 改译法

改译法在旅游类文本的英译汉和汉译英翻译中都会用到，这与英汉两种语言各自的文体规范及其背后的民族审美心理有关。就旅游文本本身而言，它通常只是一种大众读物，而翻译的目的则是提供相关的旅游信息，包括自然、地理、文化、风俗等方面的信息，让国外游客读懂、看懂并喜闻乐见。因此，译者在翻译时必须注重译文的实用性和可读性，注意内外有别。以汉译英为例，译者在实际操作过程中就应该注意兼顾英语的特点和英语读者的期待，否则他的译文难免文字诘屈，行文堆砌，与英语民族的审美心理和欣赏习惯发生冲突。请看下面的例子：

"旅客须知：旅客登记时，须凭足以证明本人身份的有效证件，并说明住宿原因。"

这是典型的中国语境下的文字，它的语气是命令式的、居高临下式的，更不必说它的内容也十分有趣，中国人早已经习以为常。但是，如果要把它翻译成英文，就势必要做出相应的变动和调整，以免英文读者感到费解、甚至心生反感。有人曾把它译为：

Guests Must Know: They are requested to show their own valid papers to prove their identities and to tell the reason for lodging when they check in at the hotel.

显然，这属于一种囫囵吞枣、全盘照搬的译法，既不可取，也不可能收到好的效果。现把它改译为：

Please note: valid ID required when check in.

这个改译的样本至少在三个方面对原文做出了调整：一是把原来强硬的"须知"和"须凭"改为语气平和的"请"；二是略去了可能会让英语读者感到莫名其妙的"并说明住宿原因"的部分；三是它整体的文辞和结构更趋于简洁明朗。应该说，改译后的文本更加符合英语读者的阅读习惯，也照应到了旅游文本翻译中的恰当性原则。

4.4 翻译实例及点评

英译汉

【原文】

Philadelphia Life: Tourism keeps the city vital and alive

PHILADELPHIA—"Major" Samuel Nicholas posed for a photo at a tourist's request. In a green tailcoat and under a black cocked hat, <u>he made a pompous look as if he were a real Continental Army officer</u> (1). The shutter clicked, and he resumed his position, strolling back and forth on the hallway of a visitor's center.

A historical impersonator, Nicholas' job is to interact with tourists and help them feel a real sense of US history. On any given day, he might chat with tourists, pose for pictures, <u>give directions</u> (2) or answer questions about the American Revolutionary War.

Nicholas, 37, works at the Independence Visitor Center, a 21st-Century modern building in Center City, <u>although he "lives" in the 18th century</u>. And while Nicholas himself is a single man from Mansfield, Pa., <u>his historical alter ego</u> (3) talks about his "lovely wife Mary Jenkins Nicholas" and their "five children."

Whenever Nicholas cracked a joke, visitors burst into laughter—a response he says he always loves.

"My presence makes their experience come alive," he said.

Nicholas, <u>who has worked for Historic Philadelphia for 15 years</u>, is one of the tens of thousands of employees in the multi-billion dollar tourism industry in Philadelphia, a city that would lose its vitality without funds tourism generates.

In Philadelphia, tourism brought in $5 billion in visitor spending and $8.2 billion in both direct and induced business sales in 2009, according to the Greater Philadelphia Tourism Marketing Corporation. Tourism in Philadelphia galvanizes local hotels, shops, restaurants, and markets. It also keeps double decker buses for museums, local farms and construction sites busy(4). Visitor spending in Philadelphia resulted in $1.2-billion tax revenue last year, helping schools, libraries and other public services stay afloat, GPTMC data showed.

(*Pavement Pieces*, by Kwanwoo Jun, December 20, 2010)

【译文一】

费城生活：旅游业使城市生机勃发

费城——应游客要求,"少校"塞缪尔·尼古拉斯摆造型拍照。他身着绿色燕尾服,头戴黑色三角帽,看上去很浮夸,宛若自己就是一个真正的陆军军官(Ⅰ)。按下快门后,他又回到了自己的角色中,在游客中心的走廊上来回走动。

尼古拉斯是一名表演历史的演员,他的工作就是与游客互动,帮助他们感受真正的美国历史。他可能会在任何时候与游客聊天,摆造型拍照,做出指导(Ⅱ),或回答有关美国独立战争的问题。

37 岁的尼古拉斯工作于"独立游客中心",虽然其中展示的是 18 世纪风格,但它却是一栋位于中心城市的 21 世纪现代建筑。虽然来自宾夕法尼亚州曼斯菲尔德的尼古拉斯还是单身,但他的古代角色(Ⅲ)却拥有"可爱的妻子玛丽·尼古拉斯·詹金斯"和"五个孩子"。

只要尼古拉斯开玩笑,游客们就会放声大笑,他说这是他永远都会很享受的反应。

"我的存在让他们的体验生动了起来,"他说。

尼古拉斯已在"历史费城"任职了 15 年,他也属于费城价值数十亿美元的旅游业中的上万名员工,而这座城市如果没有旅游业带来的资金,它就会失去其活力。

大费城旅游营销公司表示,2009 年,旅游业为费城带来了 50 亿美元的旅客消费和 82 亿美元的直接与间接销售额。费城的旅游业带动了当地酒店、商店、餐馆和市场。它还让双层巴士繁忙地往返于博物馆、当地农场和建筑工地(Ⅳ)。大费城旅游营销公司的数据显示,去年,在费城消费的游客带来了 12 亿美元的税收收入,这维持了学校、图书馆和其他公共服务的运作。

(学生课堂练习)

【译文二】

费城生活：旅游业让此地生机勃勃

费城——塞缪尔·尼古拉斯"少校"应一位游客的要求摆姿势拍照。身穿绿色燕尾服，头戴一顶黑色三角帽，他摆出<u>一脸高傲自大的表情好像自己真是大陆军的长官（Ⅰ'）</u>。拍照一结束，他又回到了工作岗位上，在一个游客中心的走廊里来回走动。

作为一位表演历史的人，尼古拉斯的工作是与游客互动并让他们有一种真正处于美国历史的感觉。每天他都会与游客们交谈，摆造型拍照，指路或者回答关于美国独立战争的问题。

37岁的尼古拉斯在独立游客中心工作，它是位于市中心的一座21世纪现代化的大楼，虽然尼古拉斯"生活"在18世纪。尽管他是来自曼斯菲尔德的单身男子，却总是以其扮演的历史人物的身份谈论着"可爱的妻子玛丽詹金斯·尼古拉斯"和他们的"五个孩子"。

尼古拉斯一讲笑话，游客们就放声大笑——他说这是他最爱的回应。

他说："我的装扮让他们的体验变得真实了。"

尼古拉斯已经在<u>历史中的</u>费城工作15年了，他是费城价值数十亿美元旅游业所拥有的成千上万员工中的一名。如果没有了旅游业的收益，费城将活力尽失。

据费城旅游市场营销公司说，2009年游客的支出给费城旅游业带来了50亿的收入，直接和间接的商业销售额为82亿。费城的旅游业刺激了当地宾馆，商店，餐馆和市场的发展。<u>也让开往博物馆，当地农场和建筑工地的双层巴士繁忙了起来（Ⅳ'）</u>。根据费城旅游市场营销公司的数据显示，去年游客们的消费让费城有了12亿美元的税收收入，用来维持学校，图书馆和其他公共服务的良好运营。

（学生课堂练习）

【译文三】

费城生活：旅游业使城市充满活力

费城——在一位游客的要求下，塞缪尔·尼古拉斯"少校"摆开架势，站到了镜头前。他头戴三角帽，身穿绿色燕尾服，<u>看上去派头十足，俨然一副当年</u>

内战时北方军军官的模样。等到快门闪过之后,他又恢复了原来的状态,在游客中心的走廊里来回走动。

作为一位历史人物的扮演者,尼古拉斯的工作是和游客进行互动以帮助后者真切地感受美国的历史。凡在上班的日子,他可能会和游客交谈,也可能摆出造型供人照相、为游客指路,或者,解答有关美国内战的问题。

尼古拉斯现年37岁,尽管他不得不"生活"在18世纪,但他上班的独立宫游客中心却是一幢位于市中心的21世纪现代化建筑。他是来自宾州曼斯菲尔德的一个单身汉,不过,在历史的语境中,他那遥远的另一个自我却要高谈阔论"漂亮的太太玛丽·詹金斯·尼古拉斯"以及他们的"5个孩子"。

每当尼古拉斯开起玩笑,游客们便忍不住哈哈大笑。对此,他颇感自得。

他说,"我的出现为他们的体验增加了色彩"。

尼古拉斯已经在历史名城费城的旅游部门工作了15年,他是成千上万服务于这个城市的旅游行业的一员。旅游业是费城的活力之源,它为这个城市带来了几十亿美元的利润。

根据大费城地区旅游营销公司的报告,在2009年,费城的旅游业创造了50亿美元的游客消费额和82亿美元的直接和间接商业销售额。旅游业带动了费城当地宾馆、商店、餐馆和各类市场的发展。它也使得穿梭于各大博物馆、郊区农场和尚未改造竣工的热点旅游景区之间的双层巴士异常繁忙。大费城地区旅游营销公司的统计数字显示,去年因游客消费而创造的税收达到12亿美元,为当地学校、图书馆和其他公共服务设施的良好运行提供了有力的保障。

(本书作者译)

【点评】

本组英译汉的原文是关于美国费城旅游业的一个情况介绍,文章通过讲述一个名叫塞缪尔·尼古拉斯的旅游业从业人员的例子,概述了旅游业对于费城的重要性。从译文一、二的表现来看,总体上比较理想。主要表现在:① 准确性基本得到保证;② 恰当性方面也相对较为成熟和牢靠。

就译文一而言,如果我们对准确性的要求不那么严格的话,它仅有两三处明显的失误:一为第二段的"做出指导"(原文为 give directions),二为第三段的"虽然其中展示的是18世纪风格"(原文为 although he "lives" in the 18th century)。至于译文二,如果也按照这样宽松的标准来衡量,我们甚至可以说基本找不出什么明显的缺陷。

当然,这是在对此两篇译文十分宽容的前提下得出的结论。事实上,若要细察和深究的话,我们还是会发现在某些细节上存在着一定的不足,这就引出了恰当性的话题。比如,针对原文第一段中的 Continental Army officer,译文一译为"陆军军官",译文二的处理是"大陆军的长官",可以说两者均不理想,也不恰当。这个词与美国内战有关,如何翻译,是有约定俗成的规矩的,不能随便翻译。译文三给出了正确的译法"内战时北方军军官"。再比如,同一个句子中的一个形容词 pompous,译文一译作"浮夸",译文二译作"高傲自大",两者均含有一定的贬义。但是,从这个句子的整体来判断,原文作者在使用 pompous 这个词的时候,恐怕并没有贬低尼古拉斯的成分。如果把它翻译成"气度不凡"、"气宇轩昂"、"十分气派"或"派头十足"等,效果应该会更好一些。在接下来的部分,针对原文的 his historical alter ego,译文一是"他的古代角色"。这里的"古代"一词似略嫌夸张,对照译文三的处理,"在历史的语境中,他那遥远的另一个自我"显然更为合理。还有,在翻译 Nicholas, who has worked for Historic Philadelphia for 15 years 中的 Historic Philadelphia 时,译文二的"历史中的费城",也有点令人看不懂。比较而言,译文一的"历史费城"要好一些。最后,关于 It also keeps double decker buses for museums, local farms and construction sites busy 中的 construction sites 一词,译文一、二的处理似乎也都显得过于随意和简单。它们只是根据原文照直译为"建筑工地",问题是,载着游客的双层巴士去博物馆和当地农场还可以理解,可它们为什么要去"建筑工地"呢?这不是有点牵强和违背常识吗?

汉译英

【原文1】

蔡元培故居

蔡元培先生被毛泽东同志赞誉为"学界泰斗,人世楷模",是中国近代最著名的教育家、哲学家、政治家、记者、心理学家、诗人、宗教家之一(1)。当您漫步在保持原样的故居间,观赏精心设计的先生生平陈列(2),瞻仰先生生前使用过的打字机、行李箱等文物,听听仍居住在故居里的伟人之后娓娓道来的故事,足以感悟到"应使翰墨常留香"的含意(3)。上海蔡元培故居是一幢独立式花园洋房,它是蔡先生在上海的最后一处住所,亦是国内保存最完好的一处故居(4)。

地址:上海市华山路303弄16号(近巨鹿路路口)

开放时间:周二—周日,上午9:00—11:00;下午1:00—4:00

公共交通:15、927、49、40、93、94、830、148、地铁1号线

(蔡元培故居简介)

【译文一】

The Former Residence of Cai Yuanpei

As one of the most celebrated educationists, philosophers, politicians, journalists, psychologists, poets and religionists, Mr. Cai Yuanpei was acclaimed as "the Academic Dean, the World Model" by Comrade Mao Zedong(Ⅰ). When you roam around the former residence (Ⅱ) which is still original, you can enjoy the exquisitely designed exhibition in his life (Ⅱ), look at such cultural relics as his used typewriter and luggage with reverence and listen to his stories vividly told by his descendants who are still living in the former residence. By all of these, you will fully comprehend the hidden meaning of "Calligraphies should be kept fragrant" (Ⅲ). Shanghai Cai Yuanpei's Former Residence is an independent garden villa, which is also his last residence in Shanghai and one of the best preserved residences in China.

Address: No. 16, 303 Lane, Huashan Road, Shanghai (near to the crossing of Julu Road)

Opening Time: Tuesday to Sunday, 9 a.m.—11 a.m., 1 p.m.—4 p.m.

Public Transportation: 15, 927, 49, 40, 93, 94, 830, 148, Line 1

(学生课堂练习)

【译文二】

The Former Residence of Cai Yuanpei

As one of the most renowned educators, philosophers, politicians, journalists, psychologists, poets and religionists, Mr. Cai Yuanpei was highly praised by Comrade Mao Zedong as "the Academic Dean, Model of the World", which means Mr. Cai has obtained high achievements in the academics being the model of the world (Ⅰ'). When you wander around the well-kept old residence (Ⅱ'), you will fully comprehend the hidden meaning of the sentence "Calligraphy should hold fragrance." (Ⅲ') by watching carefully-designed display of his daily use (Ⅱ') such as his used typewriter, luggage and other artifacts and listening to his life stories vividly told by his descendants who are still living there. Shanghai Cai Yuanpei's former residence is an independent garden-style villa, which is also one of the most preserved residences (Ⅳ') in China, is his last residence in Shanghai.

Address: No.16, 303# Huashan Road Shanghai (near to Road Julu)
Open Time: From Tuesday to Sunday, 9 a.m.—11 a.m., 1 p.m.—4 p.m.
Public Transportation: 15, 927, 49, 40, 93, 94, 830, 148, Line 1

（学生课堂练习）

【译文三】

Former Residence of T'sai Yuan-pei

T'sai Yuan-pei, "a leading figure in the academic circles and a role model for the entire world" as late Chairman Mao Zedong praised him, is one of the most celebrated educationists, philosophers, statesmen, journalists, psychologists, poets, and religion experts in modern Chinese history. His former residence, kept as it was in the original, allows visitors to have a genuine taste of the dazzling charm of this great intellectual figure. The pictures hung on the wall, the typewriter he used to work with, the suitcases he carried, and even the anecdotes told by those who still live here, all serve as reminders of the wondrous accomplishments Mr. T'sai once achieved. An ideal place to muse about tradition, heritage, culture and continuity, this detached garden house, is Mr. T'sai's last residence in Shanghai, and it is also the best-preserved among all of his former residences in the country.

Address: No.16, Lane 303, Huashan Road

Open Hours: 9:00—11:00, 13:00—16:00/Tuesday to Sunday.

Transportation: Bus # 15, 927, 49, 40, 93, 94, 830, 148; Metro Line No.1

（本书作者译）

【点评】

　　一般说来，汉译英要比英译汉更具挑战性。这也解释了为什么在汉译英的时候所暴露出来的各式各样的缺陷和问题会比较多，包括译文的准确性和恰当性以及其他方面的问题等。尽管时下令人眼花缭乱的翻译指导方针、翻译策略和手段十分热门，但是，毕竟纸上谈兵是一回事，实际操作并呈现出来的效果又是另一回事。

　　现在来谈一谈具体的翻译情况，本组汉译英的原文是一则旅游景点（名人故居）的介绍，属于旅游类文本中常见的一种。它的翻译难点体现在两个方面：一是原文的某些词句有点文绉绉的，翻译时恐不易把握其准确含义；二是如何译出此类文本固有的风格，即简明、精确，需要译者动一番脑筋。

　　先来看译文一、二的开头第一句，两篇译文虽有所差异，但在句式选用上却出现了同样的问题。从原文的行文以及逻辑关系来判断（包括从一般常识来判断），"蔡元培是中国近代最著名教育家、哲学家、政治家、记者、心理学家、诗人、宗教家之一"这个部分在整个句子中应该是主要部分，而此前的"蔡元培先生被毛泽东同志赞誉为'学界泰斗，人世楷模'"则可以被看作是一个次要的修饰部分。这样的主次安排，从英文的角度考虑更应如此。可惜，这两篇译文恰好把主次关系颠倒了。

　　另外，译文一把原文中的"学界泰斗，人世楷模"翻译成"the Academic Dean, the World Model"恐也多有不妥。特别是 the Academic Dean 很容易会被外国读者误以为是哪所大学里某个学院主管学术的院长（或副院长）。还有，对"应使翰墨常留香"的翻译也是个叫人头疼的难题。所谓 "Calligraphies should be kept fragrant" 恐怕不是合格的翻译。且不说 calligraphy 不应该以复数出现，它简直就是盲目的对位填词，英语读者是不会明白的。实际上，这里就涉及翻译中的改译法，也可以说是综合法。这里的"应使翰墨常留香"一般可以理解为"应该发扬光大前人开创的文化和传统，不使其失传"，或者是

"应该努力让过去年代的光荣和传统薪火相传"的意思,照着这样的思路去组织和安排翻译文字才不至于走偏。

译文二的情况也大致如此,除了一些零星的小失误(比如,carefully-designed display of his daily use 和 one of the most preserved residences 等)以外,它对于"应使翰墨常留香"的翻译也不理想。至于它的第一个句子,不仅在主次关系上颠倒了,其后的 which means Mr. Cai has obtained high achievements in the academics being the model of the world 更显得多此一举。最后,针对原文中的"当您漫步在保持原样的故居间",其中的"漫步"一词其实是有很大的欺骗性的。一般来说,人们会"漫步街头","漫步沙滩"或者"漫步乡间的小道"等,也就是说,他们都会选择在空旷而开阔的场所"漫步"。可是,两位译者却没有进一步展开思考并做出变通,于是,就有了 roam around the former residence 和 wander around the well-kept old residence,这两种动词词组与名词的搭配方式都显得十分不协调,甚至刺眼。

【原文 2】

西 摩 教 会 堂

<u>上海保存时间最长、在远东地区规模最大的犹太教会堂</u>(1)。该会堂是当年生活在上海的犹太人宗教信仰活动的中心,<u>始建于 1917 年,1920 年竣工</u>(2)。<u>建筑呈典型新古典主义风格,同时折射出浓厚的犹太民族建筑特色和民族风情</u>(3)。<u>立面三段划分,南门主入口以通贯二层的一对柱子和一对方形壁柱形成门廊</u>(4)。<u>大堂内有 10 根廊柱,空间近 600 平方米,可供 500 人进行宗教活动</u>(5)。<u>入选 2002 年世界纪念性建筑遗产保护名录</u>(6)。

地址:上海市陕西北路 500 号

公共交通:公交 136、24、112、23、738

(西摩教会堂简介)

【译文一】

The Ohel Rachel Synagogue

Established in 1917 and completed in 1920(Ⅱ), the Ohel Rachel Synagogue, as the religious center of Jewish people living in Shanghai at that time, is the Synagogue <u>which is the longest preservation in Shanghai as</u>

well as the largest scale in the Far East (Ⅰ). <u>Its building is a typical neo-classical style, and meanwhile reflects the strong architectural features of the Jewish nation and ethnic customs</u> (Ⅲ). The facade of the building is divided into three sections, <u>with the main southern entrance hall formed by a pair of pillars access to the second floor</u> (Ⅳ) and a couple of quadrate pilasters. There are <u>10 pillars</u> in the hall, with the space of nearly 600 square meters, <u>available for 500 people to hold religious activities</u> (Ⅴ). It was taken into the directory of <u>2002 Annual Global Protected Memorial Buildings by World Monuments Fund</u> (Ⅵ).

Address: #500 North Shaanxi Road, Shanghai

Public Transportation: Bus No.136, No.24, No.112, No.23, No.738

(学生课堂练习)

【译文二】

Seymor Church

It is the largest synagogue in the Far East and <u>was kept for the longest time in Shanghai</u> (Ⅰ'). This church, <u>with its construction began in 1917 and completed in 1920</u> (Ⅱ'), is the religious activities centre of the Jewish people living in Shanghai at that time. This kind of typical neoclassic style of architecture <u>reflects the strong architectural characteristics and national features of the Jewish nation</u> (Ⅲ'). The facade is divided into three parts and at the main entrance of the South Gate, <u>there is a colonnade consisted of a couple of pillars</u> (Ⅳ') leading up to the second floor and a couple of square pilasters. With <u>10 colonnades</u> (Ⅴ') in it, the church hall is nearly 600 square meters and can accommodate 500 people to conduct religious activities. This church has been chosen into the <u>2002 World Memorial Architectural Heritage and Conservation List</u> (Ⅵ').

Address: No.500, North Shaanxi Road, Shanghai

Public Transportation: Line 136, 24, 112, 23, 738 (Bus)

(学生课堂练习)

【译文三】
The Ohel Rachel Synagogue

The Ohel Rachel Synagogue on Seymour Road (now Shaanxi Road) is the longest-preserved Jewish church in Shanghai, and also the largest in the Far East region. The synagogue, whose construction began in 1917, and was completed in 1920, became the center of religious activities for the Jewish people living in Shanghai at the time. It was a typical neo-classical building with a suggestion of obvious Jewish architectural features and ethnic traditions. The facade of the building is divided into three sections, with the main southern entrance forming its porch with a pair of pillars leading up to the second floor and a pair of quadrate pilasters. There are 10 columns in the lobby which is 600 square meters in space and can accommodate 500 people for religious activities. The synagogue was accepted onto the 2002 World Heritage List of Monumental Architecture.

Address: No.500, North Shaanxi Road, Shanghai

Traffic: Bus ♯ 136, 24, 112, 23, 738

(本书作者译)

【点评】

这一组汉译英在性质上与此前的"蔡元培故居"翻译基本相同，只不过，文中有若干关于建筑本身的描述性术语。因其专业性，这个部分恐会对译者构成一定的挑战。

比如，针对原文中出现的"廊柱"一词，译文一使用了 pillar，译文二选用的则是 colonnade。colonnade 实际上是意为"柱廊"，也就是"由一排柱子连成的走廊"的意思。显然，在这个环节的处理上译文二的精准度存在问题。再比如，原文中"立面三段划分，南门主入口以通贯二层的一对柱子和一对方形壁柱形成门廊"。因为描述具体细致，且包含好几个专业词汇，两位译者在翻译过程中顾此失彼，出现了语法上的疏漏。

人们都说"细节决定成败"，此处让我们也来关注几个细节。"始建于1917年"，译文一是 Established in 1917，而译文二是 with its construction began in 1917，比较起来，后者更加合理一些，因为这里的"始建"即"开始建造"，而不是

"成立"的意思。"可供500人进行宗教活动",译文一的翻译是 available for 500 people to hold religious activities,而译文二的翻译是 can accommodate 500 people to conduct religious activities。虽然后者略显啰嗦(若能译为 can accommodate 500 people for religious activities 更好),但它至少是规范的英语句子。还有,在翻译"建筑呈典型新古典主义风格"时,译文一的 Its building is 应改为 This building has,而译文二的处理比较明智。不过,在翻译随后的"折射出浓厚的犹太民族建筑特色和民族风情"时,译文一、二都犯了不注重细节、盲目追求中英文一一对应的毛病。

第五章

广告翻译

5.1 广告类文本的概念

广告,古已有之,自从有了商品生产和交换,广告即随之出现。作为一种营销的工具和手段,从本质上来说,广告最基本的功能是传播信息和诱导消费。虽然现在恐无法确证世界上最早的广告究竟是谁做的,它又出现在哪里和哪一年,不过,随着社会的进步和发展,特别是在人类进入21世纪后,广告及其巨大的影响力已深入到社会生活的每一个角落,成为一种独特的商业文化现象。

广告的种类和样式繁多,从路边高高竖立的巨型广告牌到建筑物和车身上的图案和文字,从报纸、杂志封面或内页的广告到专门印制的精美宣传推广手册,从广播、电视广告到如今互联网上铺天盖地的滚动式广告,等等,不一而足。广告是为了某种特定的需要,通过相应的媒介或载体,公开而广泛地向公众传递信息的宣传手段。它一般都有明确的目标指向,期望通过信息的传播起到促进、说服、提示和增强的作用。换言之,广告的目的是希望通过信息的传播来改变受众的消费观念和消费心理,并最终影响其消费行为和消费习惯。

对广告类文本来说,准确性之重要是不言而喻的。我们甚至可以说,信息的真实、准确是它的立身之本。凡涉及广告的写作,不管是精炼的广告语,还是具有一定篇幅的广告文案,都应该避免夸大其词、无中生有。因为巧言取悦绝非成功之道,蒙蔽和欺骗受众到头来只会自食苦果,尤其是在消费者的消费心理和消费行为日趋成熟的情况下,更是如此。不过,广告作为一种竞争性的商业行为,其最终目的毕竟仍然是争取消费者。因此,在一定程度上,广告文本的撰写不可避免要投消费者所好，以打动他们的心弦，促成其最终实施消费行为。这就引出了广告文本的另一个要素，即语言的优美和凝练，也就是国外广告商追求的所谓 KISS(Keep it sweet and simple)原则。此外，伴随着社会形态的变化以及广告业自身的发展，现在广告文本的内涵已大大超出了经济和商业的范畴，它往往还反映出特定时期人们独特的社会价值观念、思维方式和生活追求等，这也使得它多了一份相应的文化含义。

5.2 广告类文本的基本特征

根据美国市场营销协会(American Marketing Association)给出的定义，"广告通常是由特定的广告主以有偿的方式，通过各种传媒途径对产品、服务或理念等实施的非个人化且具有劝说性质的信息推介活动"。(Advertising is the nonpersonal communication of information usually paid for and usually persuasive in nature about products, services or ideas by identified sponsors through the various media.)广告的核心是信息，而信息传播是否成功有效，关键在于广告文本的内容和形式。有人曾经说过，一则成功的广告文本应该是集专业知识、市场调研、消费心理和语言艺术于一体的完美综合体。这句话具有高度的概括性，大体上总结出了广告类文本的一些主要特质。所谓"专业知识"，指的是广告类文本应该体现出的专业性或专业精神。"市场调研"和"消费心理"可以合起来看，这两者应该是指此类文本所包含的浓郁的商业气息和商业元素。至于"语言艺术"，当然是指此类文本在语言运用上应该达到的美学境界。如果说可以再补充一点的话，那就是此类文本还应该体现出相当的文化内涵和意蕴。众所周知，广告现在已不仅仅是一种商业现象，它已经成为一种社会文化符号。而且，不同的文化环境对于广告文本的设计和撰写也会产生一定的影响。因此，在强调广告文本所具有的文化内涵的同时，还应当留意因地域和文化背景不同而造成的文化差异性。

现在让我们撇开广告类文本的专业性、商业性和文化性特点，单从语言的角度来对此作一番初步的探讨。英国语言学家杰弗里·利奇(Leech)在论述有关语言交际功能时曾经指出，语言有五大交际功能，即信息功能、表情功能、指示功能、美学功能和酬应功能。对照这一理论，再细察广告文本语言运用的种种表现，我们会发现广告文本的语言实际上兼具了信息和美学两大功能。

信息功能指向的是文本的内容,而美学功能指向的则是文本的形式。而且,这两大功能相辅相成、互为补充、缺一不可。具体来看,它在语言运用方面的基本特征可以概括如下。

1. 词汇特点

多使用通俗简明的词汇以便于信息迅速有效的传播;多使用委婉语和模糊性词语以营造朦胧的审美意境;也常使用自创的新词以突出产品的新、奇、特,满足消费者追求新潮、标榜个性的心理;使用动词的频度较高以利于刺激消费者实施消费行为;使用缩略词和复合词的比例也较高,目的是既增强语言的感染力,又可以节约广告篇幅、降低成本。总之,广告类文本的语言可以说是"雅""俗"并存、各有其用武之地。举一个例子,感恩节之后的 Black Friday 以及此后的圣诞假期是美国商家传统的促销旺季。在美国中部奥马哈市的一家大型商场里,就曾有过一则仅出现一个单词的广告:Giftopia。这个 Giftopia 显然是由 Gift 和 Utopia 合成的,是专为促销而自创的一个新词。它新颖、独特,表达的意思也十分明确。还有,在另一家商场出现的 Jingle More Bells 也是一例。

2. 句法特点

多使用主动语态和一般现在时,不仅给人一种直接感,更暗示了商品的持久和永恒特性;多使用简单句以便消费者在尽可能短的时间内把广告内容看完;多使用设问句以烘托气氛、调动广告受众的好奇心,从而为其采取行动埋下伏笔;多使用祈使句以增加强烈的鼓动色彩,鼓励消费者购买其所宣传的产品或服务。来看一个例子,在美国内布拉斯加州林肯市的机场候机厅里,一家餐饮店的边上有这样一行文字:Something light for your flight.这则不起眼的广告简单、温馨,凡是看到这行文字的人们,假如不急着赶飞机,很可能禁不住走进去点上一个三明治、喝上一杯咖啡。这里的 light 和 flight 两个词读起来音乐性很强,而且,light 一词用得也恰到好处,因为身在机场,即使饥肠辘辘,恐也不可能奢求大吃一顿吧。

3. 修辞特点

多使用双关语或带有谐音的词语,不但以文字的张力营造出独具一格的美感,更提升了广告产品或服务的层次;多使用比喻和拟人化的手法,一方面使广告的产品和服务显得更为生动形象,同时也拉近了和消费者之间的距离;多引用谚语、名人名言和典故等以增强广告的文学色彩和历史厚重感;多使用简短的排比句式,结构规整、层层推进,使广告受众产生身临其境的现场感。再看一个例子:英国的劳埃德银行曾经推出过一个很有名的广告:Money doesn't grow on the trees. But it blossoms at our branches.这则广告就成功地运用了双关语,其中的 branches 表面意思是树枝,实质指该银行遍布各地的分支机构。而且,由 money, trees 和 branches 串联起来的整个意象既风趣幽默,又令人印象深刻。

5.3 广告类文本的翻译策略

如前所述,广告是一种独特的文体。在广告类文本中,其设计者往往运用多样化的语言手段以促发广告受众对文本意义的多层次解读。因此,广告不但具备信息价值,同时还承载着审美诉求。

根据翻译目的论,翻译的策略由语篇所要实现的目的或其功能来决定。也就是说,翻译行为所要达到的目的决定了整个翻译行为的过程。既然广告文本不仅具有信息功能,还具有美学功能,它的最终目的是通过创造性的审美手段实现信息迅速有效的传播,那么,对于此类文本的翻译就必须兼顾内容和风格的统一。所谓内容,当然是指信息本身。内容表达是否准确、是否忠实于原文,这是衡量翻译是否成功的标志。不过,从某种意义上来说,风格是否得以恰当表达同样不可小视。风格多与历史积淀、民族心理、文化氛围和审美意趣相关。不同的民族因社会历史文化和经济上的巨大差异往往造成对风格的理解和追求不尽相同,反映在广告文本中,就有可能出现内容虽相同而表现形式却截然不同的情况。奈达(Nida)在提出功能对等理论(functional equivalence)时曾强调,理想的译文除了追求在语言层面(音韵、词法、句法、修辞等)有效再现原文特征外,还必须充分考虑双语间的文化及民族心理差异等因素,只有这样,才可称为真正的对等。基于此,我们认为,对于广告类文本的翻译应遵循三条基本原则,第一,注重原文风格和译入语风格之间贴合的原则;第二,注重译入语读者反应和接受度的原则;第三,最大限度地保留和发挥原广告内在审美价值的原则。

现在我们来讨论一下具体的翻译手段和方法。关于广告文本的翻译,一般所采用的无非是直译、意译、直译和意译相结合(或称创造性译法)、增译和节译(或称删减法)等方法。至于究竟该如何使用不同的方法,则主要取决于文本本身。

1. 直译

这种方法多适用广告口号或标题的翻译，同时篇幅较长的广告文本中某些词汇和句法结构简单、明晰，意义较为明确的句子也可适用。它的特点是只要按原文字面意思直接翻译即能同时表达其表层意思和深层意思。如法国航空公司的一则广告语 Winning the World 即可被直译为"赢遍天下"。需要指出的是，直译的方法往往更适合英文广告的中译。

2. 意译

这种方法使用的面较广，从精致凝练的广告语到具有一定篇幅的广告正文，从英译汉到汉译英都可能会用到。意译是相对直译而言的，它的特点是译文处理较为灵活、自由，翻译过程中译者通常会照顾到译入语读者因文化差异而产生的阅读困难，提交的译文从读者角度看显得比较地道，可读性强，但对原文的忠实度则有所不足。换言之，意译强调的是忠实于原文本的内容。当内容与形式无法兼得，为了追求内容的完整和准确，则可能舍弃原文本的形式。请看两个例子，先是麦当劳曾经用过的一句广告语 Every time a good time! 现试译为：畅享每一刻。这个翻译简洁、明朗，易于上口。虽然并非完全直译，却体现出了它的神韵。第二个例子是建设银行龙卡的广告语："衣食住行，有龙则灵。"这个广告语并不容易翻译，单说"衣食住行"就包含了日常生活的四个方面，还有"有龙则灵"也是有出处的，若要直译出来，难度可想而知。而且，这是一则广告语，翻译时显然不允许拖泥带水。有人把它译为：Longcard settles your everyday payment in a flash. 看起来不错，也是采取了意译的办法。但是，这个处理的效果如何呢：*Longcard* Has It All!

3. 直译和意译相结合（或创造性译法）

这种方法的使用面也很广，英译汉和汉译英都有可能会用到。它的特点是在实际操作中更灵活、更自由，看似只是直译和意译的融合，但往往还包含了译者独具创造性的延伸和拓展。这种译法的目的是为了求得译语与源语在功能或效果上的对等与契合，以便译文更容易为译语读者所接受。当然，这种译法也并非任意或天马行空式的创作，应该说，这是在充分考虑文本本身的内容、源语和译入语的文化及审美要求基础上由译者所作出的恰当而又必要的调整。举个例子来说，2010年上海世博会的口号是："城市，让生活更美好！"对于这个宣传口号，上海世博会官方的英文翻译是：Better City, Better Life. 这就是一个典型的采用直译和意译相结合（或创造性译法）办法的翻译,在这个英译里面,我们看到了"城市",看到了"生活",也看到了这两者之间的关系。虽然并非直译,却取得了比直译更好的效果。

4. 增译

所谓增译,顾名思义,即是对原广告内容进行适当的补充。比如,对原文的某些关键字词进行挖掘、引申和拓展,以便使原文的深层意思更完整地凸显出来,从而实现信息的有效传播。比如,福特汽车在美国的一句广告词是:Built Tough. 翻译成中文的时候,不妨可以考虑增补的手法"福特汽车:生性强悍、纵横天下"。

5. 节译（或删减法）

所谓节译（或删减法）,顾名思义,即是去除原广告中多余的部分或不符合译入语要求的部分,以达到删繁就简、突出信息和迎合译入语读者阅读趋向的目的。比如,国内某机场的候机大厅有这样一条公益广告标语:"为了您和家人的健康,吸烟请到吸烟区。"对于这个句子,如果不做必要的调整,直接把它翻译成英文,很有可能处理为 For the health of yourself and others, passengers who smoke, please go to the smoking area. 这样处理不但造成句式冗长,而且可能会让外国人产生去吸烟区吸烟不会影响身体健康的错觉。因此,还是要做一些灵活的变动,可以把它译为:(This is) Not a Smoking Area.

5.4 翻译实例及点评

英译汉

【原文】

Here's to the crazy ones (1). The misfits. The rebels. The troublemakers (2). The round pegs in the square holes (3). The ones who see things differently (4). They're not fond of rules. And they have no respect for the status quo. You can quote them, disagree with them, glorify or vilify them. About the only thing you can't do is ignore them. Because they change things. They push the human race forward. And while some may see them as the crazy ones, we see genius. Because the people who are crazy enough to think they can change the world are the ones who do.

（美国苹果公司于1997年推出的产品广告）

【译文一】

专为疯狂的人们而来（Ⅰ）。为那些特立独行者。为那些叛逆者。为那些惹是生非者（Ⅱ）。像方孔里的圆钉子，格格不入（Ⅲ）。他们用不同的眼光看世界。他们讨厌循规蹈矩。他们不愿安于现状。你可以引用他们的话，持反对态度，赞扬或贬斥。唯独不能无视他们。因为他们改变了事物。他们引领人类社会进步。有人把他们当疯子，我们把他们当天才。只有疯狂到认为自己能改变世界的人才能真正改变世界。

（学生课堂练习）

【译文二】

这是一群疯狂的人类（Ⅰ'），他们中有孤僻者、叛逆者、麻烦制造者（Ⅱ'）。如放在方孔中的圆形钉子一般（Ⅲ'），这群很不合时宜的人类看待事物也是鹤立独行（Ⅳ'）。他们不喜欢规则，不尊重现状。你可以引用他们，可以不同意他们，可以美化或丑化他们。但是你唯一不能做的是忽视他们。因为他们让事情发生改变。他们推进人类向前。然而有些人把他们看作疯狂的一类，我们称他们为天才。因为疯狂到足够认为他们可以改变世界的人类是真正改变世界的那一类。

（学生课堂练习）

【译文三】

致那些疯狂的人们：那些与周围的一切格格不入、崇尚叛逆的人士，那些无法安分守己、始终桀骜不驯的另类人群，那些目光独到的异质禀赋者。他们讨厌规则、藐视现实的存在。你可以认同他们，也可以否定他们；可以为他们唱赞歌，也可以把他们贬得一文不值。唯有一点，你无法忽略他们。因为他们改变着世界，推动着人类向前迈进。也许，有人认为他们是疯子，我们却视他们为天才。我们相信：那些自认为疯狂到足以改变世界的人们真的能够改变世界。

（本书作者译）

【点评】

　　这一组英译汉的原文是美国苹果公司于1997年推出的极具创意的产品广告,当时曾经在美国的电视和纸面媒体风行一时。它以产品所针对的人群为重心,语言精准犀利,句式上多采用简短的排比句,给人以卓尔不群和气势逼人的感觉。

　　从总体效果来评判,译文一和译文二都还算不错。译文一唯一明显的失误是对原文第一个句子的处理。对于 Here's to the crazy ones,要想译得准确,关键在于理解里面的 to 是什么意思。应该说,这个 to 相当于"致某某人"或"为某某人而写"或"谨以……献给某人"等;也就是说,它类似于写信时信封上标注的 To ×××。也许还可以理解为"(这个产品)是专为某类人而开发生产的"。但是不管怎样,把它译为"专为疯狂的人们而来",应该是没有反映出原文作者的意图。当然,译文二译作"这是一群疯狂的人类",效果也不理想。译文一的不足还有两点:一是对标点符号的处理完全照搬原文,似乎与中文的使用习惯以及读者的阅读期待有所出入;二是 The round pegs in the square holes 最好不要直译为"像方孔里的圆钉子",应该对此作一番更灵活的处理。

　　至于译文二,除了对开头第一句的翻译问题之外,在对 The round pegs in the square holes 的翻译上,也犯了与译文一同样的错误,即没有采用意译的办法。另外,它的一些用词不够谨慎。比如,"孤僻者、叛逆者、麻烦制造者"和"鹤立独行"。"孤僻者"和"麻烦制造者"明显带有贬义,基于原文文本内容的性质,译者至少应考虑采用具有中性色彩的词语才较为妥当;而"鹤立独行"则属于译者自己编出来的词,汉语中只有"鹤立鸡群"一说。当然,它在标点符号的使用上并没有盲从原文,这是其可取之处。

汉译英

【原文1】

　　雅倩深层保湿美容膏
　　要演好一个角色
　　由内而外都要充分发挥(1)
　　正如皮肤保护一样

内外都要得到均衡滋润(2)

我用雅倩(3)

全新雅倩深层保湿美容膏

特有保湿修护素

能迅速渗透至肌肤深层

平衡肌肤水分及养分(4)

用雅倩,肌肤时刻都清爽润泽,娇美动人

自然有好表现啦

雅倩深层保湿美容膏

表里如一,娇美动人(5)

(雅倩护肤品广告)

【译文一】

ARCHE deep-moisturizing cream

To play a role well

Performing internally and externally is a must（Ⅰ）

As skin care does（Ⅱ）

Nourishment has to go to the surface and deep skin

I prefer ARCHE（Ⅲ）

New ARCHE deep-moisturizing cream

Rich in moist repairing essence

Quickly penetrating into deep inner skin

Helping balance skin's moisture and nutrients（Ⅳ）

Choosing ARCHE

Your skin maintains moist and radiant

You will do a better job

ARCHE deep-moisturizing cream

External appearance corresponds to inside, shining and gorgeous（Ⅴ）

(学生课堂练习)

【译文二】

Arche deep-care moist cream

<u>To be a good actor,</u>

<u>You should let your inside out fully.</u>（Ⅰ'）

Just as skin care，（Ⅱ'）

You should keep your skin in an equilibrium moisture condition.

Arche is my choice.（Ⅲ'）

The new Arche deep-care moist cream contains extra-strength moisturizing essence,

<u>able to penetrate into the skin rapidly and deeply,</u>

<u>and give you a balanced skin with moisture content and nutrients.</u>（Ⅳ'）

Arche brings you a fresh and moist skin at all times,

making you more beautiful and charming.

Arche deep- care moist cream

<u>Out from within, beautiful and charming.</u>（Ⅴ'）

(学生课堂练习)

【译文三】

Arche, Deep Moisturizing Beauty Cream

<u>For acting, the best to be expected of an actor is perfection from inside out.</u>

<u>Likewise, for skin care, the best to look for in a product is miraculous change that works its way from within. / the effect most desired is for the miraculous change to work its way from within.</u>

Arche, the all-new deep moisturizing beauty cream, <u>with its special moisture repair, penetrates deep into the skin and is highly effective in restoring moisture and helping to maintain skin elasticity.</u>

Try Arche today, and you'll have your dream come true for the youthful glow of your skin.

Arche, the deep moisturizing beauty cream that performs miracles from within.

（本书作者译）

【点评】

　　本组汉译英的原文是一则典型的化妆品广告，包含了此类文本特有的基本元素，包括"清爽润泽"、"表里如一"和"娇美动人"等四字成语，一开头出现的类比修辞手法、重复的手段和简洁明快的句式，等等。当然，也不乏常见的专业或准专业术语，如"保湿修护素"、"渗透至肌肤深层"和"平衡肌肤水分"等。因此，若想把它翻译成较为理想的英文，除了要具备一定的专业知识以外，还需熟谙此前提到的一些指导方略、手段和方法。从译文一、二的表现来看，有令人感到欣喜的地方，也存在着一些不足和缺憾。

　　首先，两篇译文都把原文的前四行理解为一个意思的停顿，这是可取的（尽管原文并没有使用标点符号）。而且，两者在开头部分都采用了类似的句式，一为 To play a role well ...，另一为 To be a good actor ...，这也属于恰当的选择（当然，具体的选词和搭配方面还存在着一点问题）。但是，译文一的第二行，即 Performing internally and externally is a must 与其前面的部分不匹配。相比较而言，译文二显得更加合理。不过，两篇译文的第三行，即 As skin care does 和 Just as skin care 部分却把主次关系弄反了。原文固然是"正如皮肤保护一样……"，但是，翻译成英文的时候，译者应考虑做一些必要的调整，把"正如要演好一个角色，由内而外都要充分发挥"移到前面去，因为"演好角色"在这儿只是一个铺垫，而"皮肤保护"才是句子的重心和整个文本的重点。换句话说，如果真要使用 As 或 Just as 之类的词语，那也应该将它们提前到该句句首才比较恰当。可惜两位译者未能就此作出合宜的变通，可见其对中英两种语言之间的差异还缺乏深层次的认识，才导致出现了这样的硬伤。

　　第二，关于原文第二句的句意，两位译者把握得不错，都划分至第一层次后面的五行。但是，和此前的情况一样，在具体的翻译过程中还是暴露了一些问题。其他的暂且不说，译文一最后一句中的 Helping 至少应改为 Helps。同样地，假如我们忽略掉译文二中的一些小失误，然后把 able to 改为 is able to，再在 give 后面加一个 s，那么就会更完美一些。

第三，关于人称指代，两篇译文中既有 you 和 your，同时也出现了 I 和 my，看起来有些混乱、不统一。假如译者能够吃透原文，并在此基础上多一些自主灵活的变通，则译文效果会更好。

【原文2】

并非所有的人都能真正懂得它所代表的含义

面对火箭升空，<u>人们更多的是陶醉于它那扶摇直上的雄姿、雷霆万钧的气势，只有少数人从火箭每一米的上升高度，来测量人类创造力的无限，感受科技进步的美妙</u>(1)。<u>24小时之内</u>(2)，<u>作为中德科技多年合作的辉煌结晶的另一种创造力与进步的代表</u>(3)，它就要出现在你的面前了。<u>也许你已经焦急地等待了好几天，那么现在你真的可以暂时放下手边的事，平心静气，拭目以待——一个振奋人心的时刻，它的到来已经进入倒数计时了</u>(4)。

(上海大众汽车桑塔纳2000型汽车广告)

【译文一】

Not everyone understands what it stands for

Seeing the rising of the rocket, people are mostly intoxicated in its soaring and thunderous manner and <u>only a few of them measure the infinity of human beings' creativity and experience the beauty of technological improvement from every meter's rising height</u>（Ⅰ）. As the representative of another kind of creativity and progress（Ⅱ）which are the brilliant achievements of many years' cooperation between Germany and China in science and technology, it will appear in front of you <u>within 24 hours</u>（Ⅲ）. Maybe you have waited it for several days, but now you can temporarily leave the matters in your hands aside and be calm to see it. It's an exciting moment（Ⅳ）and it has already entered the countdown timer.

(学生课堂练习)

【译文二】

Not all people can understand the real meaning of it

Thinking of a rocket launch, <u>people tend to be enchanted by the</u>

imposing sight of its rapid rise and its lightning speed（Ⅰ'）. Only a few people, noticing the lifting height of a rocket per meter（Ⅰ'）would admire the immeasurable creativity of human beings and is affected by the wonder of technological progress（Ⅰ'）. Within 24 hours（Ⅱ'）, there will be another representative of the creativity and progress made by the multi-year Sino-German cooperation（Ⅲ'）in science and technology. Perhaps, you have been waiting anxiously for several days. But now, you really can put aside your work temporarily and wait and see. An exciting moment is about to come!（Ⅳ'）

（学生课堂练习）

【译文三】

Not Everyone Knows What It Stands for

When people follow the path of a rocket flying high into the sky, most are fascinated merely by its velocity and the thunderous sweep. Only a few see the great creative potential of the human race and the wonder of scientific advancement in every meter the rocket gains in height. Now as the result of years of scientific and technological collaboration between China and Germany, another kind of power surprise is to be brought to you within the next 24 hours. You may have been waiting anxiously all these days, but now is the time to put aside whatever is at hand. Just hold your breath and begin the countdown to welcoming this grand moment—the premier of Santana 2000.

（本书作者译）

【点评】

　　这组汉译英的原文是上海大众发布的桑塔纳2000型汽车广告。篇幅虽短,但气势不凡,它以火箭升空所包含的尖端科学技术做铺垫,引导读者对即将登场的新款轿车的技术含量展开丰富的联想。文本中出现"扶摇直上的雄姿、雷霆万钧的气势"等词语,显得力量感十足。此外,"平心静气,拭目以待"和"它的到来已经进入倒数计时"等表达方式的使用,也制造了一种急迫感和悬念丛生的感觉。对于此类文本的翻译，除了考虑一般的原则和策略以外，还要特别注意整体风格的把握。

从译文一、二的总体表现来看，译文二要略好一些。它对某些关键点上的处理显得相对更为成熟和合理，因此也能较好地反映出原文的风貌。比如，它开头第一个句子中的 tend to be enchanted，读起来柔和而有弹性。随后的一个句子中，句式的选用，特别是中间插入的 noticing the lifting height of a rocket per meter 这个部分，使整个句子的层次感丰富了起来（当然，若要真正深究，应该说还有进一步提高的空间）。还有，最后部分的三个句子 Perhaps, you have been waiting anxiously for several days. But now, you really can put aside your work temporarily and wait and see. An exciting moment is about to come! 对于事件发生时间的先后顺序把控得比较好。在这里，先是出现了一个现在完成进行时的运用，之后的 But now 又与此形成了对照和时间上的反差，而最后的 is about to come 则把将来的时间概念明晰化了。这一系列较为成功的处理是建立在对原文文本的仔细解读和翻译方法的灵活运用之上的。反观译文一，它在这方面的表现就要平淡得多，虽然看似也并无太大的不妥，但难免给人以直白和呆板的感觉。比如，它的最后部分是这样的：Maybe you have waited it for several days, but now you can temporarily leave the matters in your hands aside and be calm to see it. It's an exciting moment and it has already entered the countdown timer. 在这里，尤其扎眼的是 It's an exciting moment，它比译文二的 An exciting moment is about to come! 要低了一个层次。

当然，撇开这些相对宏观的方面不说，两篇译文在细节上其实都还有不少瑕疵，这是要引起重视的。像译文二的 is affected by the wonder of technological progress 和 another representative of the creativity and progress 等，显然属于盲目的直译，并没有经过很好的思考过程。译文一的情况也是如此，像 measure the infinity of human beings' creativity, from every meter's rising height 和 As the representative of another kind of creativity and progress 等基本就是译文二同类问题的翻版。还有，针对原文的"24小时之内"，两篇译文都翻译成 within 24 hours，而更加准确和精确的翻译应该是 within the next 24 hours，这样才符合原文所要表达的意图以及英文的表达习惯。

第六章

学术翻译

6.1 学术类文本的概念

学术类文本指政治、经济、军事、历史、地理等领域的学术专著、论文或论文集、书面报告等，也包括各领域的人物传记。学术文本的翻译并不是一种机械地将原文本中的源语符号切换成译入语语言符号的行为，而是一种积极的、以信息意义的交流为宗旨的活动。

英国学者彼得·纽马克(Peter Newmark)认为翻译文本的功能可以分为三类：表达功能(expressive function)、信息功能(informative function)和呼唤功能(vocative function)。他将严肃文学(纯文学)、权威性的陈述(演说或声明)、个人信件或私密性的写作归为表达功能一类；将新闻、期刊、科技论文、一般教材以及大部分非文学类作品(事实重于风格)归为信息功能一类；将广告、宣传、辩论性作品("主题文学")、流行文学(畅销书)这类试图说服读者的文本以及通知、说明、规章制度这类试图指导读者的文本归为呼唤功能一类。

莱斯提出不同类型的文本需要不同的翻译策略，能够解决所有文本类型的翻译方法并不存在，翻译批评应考虑到这一点；而奈达等学者则有将某种文本类型的翻译方法(如圣经翻译等)推广至所有文本类型的翻译方法的不足。莱斯认为，一个文本可能有多种功能，但会有一个最主要的功能。她将文本按其功能划分为三种基本类型(但不排除有这三种类型的混合形式的文本)：信息型(informative)、表达型(expressive)、感染型/操作型(persuasive/operative)。信息型文本重在内容的交际，表达型文本则按艺术手法组织文本内容的交际，感染型/操作型文本包含说服、劝说成分的交际。莱斯认为，在通常情况下(若追求译文和原文在功能上的对等),文本类型决定整体的翻译方法,文本体裁要求翻译考虑语言和语篇结构的惯例。在通常情况下,学术翻译任务的发起者、委托者或赞助人都希望通过翻译实现译文和原文在功能上对等,并最终达成原作者和译入语读者之间的有效交流。

学术类文本的功能以纽马克和莱斯所说的"信息功能"为主,但在传递信息(书中内容)的同时,原作者通过描述、推理、论证等方式表达自身的观点与立场,并试图说服、感染或影响读者。从这个意义上来说,学术类文本兼具纽马克或莱斯各自言说的文本的三种功能,即信息功能、表达功能和呼唤功能或是信息型、表达型与感染型/操作型兼具的文本。与此对应的是,学术类文本的特征是专业性与学术性兼具、逻辑性和文学性并存。

6.2 学术类文本的基本特征

1. 专业性和学术性

学术著作往往涉及相关学科、交叉学科乃至跨学科的专业知识,译者需要有一定的专业学识并被希冀通过阅读提高自己的专业学识。在专业性之外,学术著作还有一个本质属性"学术性"。学术著作的原文本和译文本的行文、引文、注释等都应符合其所处历史阶段的学术规范;译者在翻译时也应遵循该领域的学术规范。各领域的人物传记往往涉及书中人物所从事的一种或几种行业的相关内容,不可避免地涉及相关行业的行业知识和专业信息,体现出一定的"专业性";译者需要了解人物传记涉及的相关行业的专业知识。一般而言,各领域的人物传记的"学术性"比不上各领域学术专著的"学术性",但是优秀的人物传记仍是读者(包括专业读者和普通读者)了解乃至研究某个行业著名人物的不可或缺的参考资料,从这层意义上来说,人物传记也具备一定的学术参考价值。

2. 逻辑性

在学术著作中,无论原作者是致力于提出、分析、解决某个学术问题,还是针对某一学科、某一阶段、某个问题进行综述性著述,或是对其他学者的观点提出商榷与反驳,都需要较强的逻辑性,这也使得学术类文本呈现出较强的逻辑性。而在人物传记中,原作者也围绕传记的基本核心展开描写或叙述,也体现出较强的逻辑性。

3. 文学性

"文学性"(literariness)一词由罗曼·雅各布森(Roman Jacobson)提出，但至今学界对于"文学性"并没有达成一个统一的认识。李龙在《文学性问题研究——以语言学转向为参照》一书中指出，"以雅各布森为代表的俄国形式主义主要将其理解为语言的诗性功能；结构主义者则试图找到共同的叙述模式和文学性规则；而解构主义者则将语言的修辞功能发挥到了极致"。王东风赞同俄国形式主义的观点"文学性并不是来自于内容本身，而是这内容的表达方式"，并提出："这样的表达方式并不仅仅只是微观层面上的遣词造句，宏观层面的变异和陌生化也同样有着深刻的诗学促动，而且更加挑战译者的诗学识别能力。"史忠义在2000年第3期的《中国比较文学》中撰文"'文学性'的定义之我见"，指出西方学者对"文学性"这个概念至今尚未找到令人满意的定义，而他本人认为："文学性存在于话语从表达、叙述、描写、意象、象征、结构、功能以及审美处理等方面的普遍升华之中，存在于形象思维之中。形象思维和文学幻想、多义性和暧昧性是文学性最基本的特征。文学性的定义与语言环境以及文化背景有着密切的联系。"

本书更赞同史忠义的观点，不过学术类文本的文学性与文学作品的文学性还是有所区别的。学术著作的文字表述应明确、清晰，不应追求语义暧昧而误导读者。但是，学术著作的语言因原作者源语写作功底不同，仍然存在不同程度的"文学性"，体现在原文本的表达、叙述、描写、结构等中。人物传记除了拥有学术著作所体现出来的"文学性"特征，在文字效果的"召唤和情感功能"、"多义性和暧昧性"方面束缚更少。

一般说来，面对学术专著、论文、书面报告，译者需要对原文本所涉及的学科知识、理论脉络等具有更多的专业性；而人物传记的翻译虽然也需要译者掌握传记中人物的背景知识及其所从事行业的相关知识，但与学术著作的翻译相比，在学理上的难度要低一些。商务印书馆译作室副主任陈小文曾指出："即使按照最低的标准来衡量——专业知识不闹笑话、对外文的基本文法理解不出错误、中文表述基本符合习惯，如果说大多数翻译作品的翻译质量是不合格的，可能有的人会提出异议，但是如果说至少有一半的学术翻译质量不合格，我想，是不会有反对意见的。"这也为未来从事学术翻译的人们敲响了警钟。

6.3 学术类文本的翻译策略

学术类文本的特征决定了学术类文本的翻译文本的特征,并相应地决定了这类文本的总的翻译原则是:以专业性、学术性、逻辑性为主,以文学性为辅。在专业性方面,译者不仅需要把握术语翻译的准确性、避免讹误,也要注意用译入语表达原文本中学科知识、理论著述等方面的专业性。学术著作的翻译还需要注意遵循译入语语言文化的学术规范、出版规范等,而人物传记的翻译也要符合译入语语言的写作出版规范。此外,译文也需要具有较强的逻辑性,并反映学术文本原文本中一定的文学性。

学术类文本的翻译文本,以及学术翻译还需要实现非文学翻译的一个整体特征:实现信息的有效交流。具体而言,是实现原作者或原文本与译入语读者之间信息的有效交流。

译者在翻译学术文本前,通常需要做以下准备工作:

(1) 在某个待译的学术类文本的语篇之内,读懂、读透原文。

(2) 在某个待译的学术类文本的语篇之外,了解该文本所涉及的背景知识、关键的学科流派、理论发展脉络等,以更好地把握学术文本本身的理论观点、术语表达等。

(3) 阅读有代表性的、优秀的平行文本。"平行文本"(parallel text)指不同语言文化中起到相同或相似功能的文本。20 世纪 50 年代以来,平行文本经常用于译员培训,以帮助学员译出自然和地道的译文。事实上,阅读优秀的平行文本对译者而言是多多益善的;但考虑到现在职业翻译时间限制比较紧,译者不可能在短时期内读完所有的平行文本,也不可能将所有的时间放在阅读平行文本而不是放在翻译上,所以译者在翻译时可以挑选一些比较有代表性的、优秀的平行文本来阅读,以增加自己对用译入语表达待译文本的语感和所需遵循的译入语学术文本写作规范的认识。

在做好这些准备工作后,译者在开始翻译原文本中的人名、地名、书名、文章名和专业术语等方面时,才能够更加专业、更为业内读者所接受。翻译后,译者还需要核查原文与译文,对译文进行纠错与改善。在面对数字与不同语言文化度量衡单位翻译时,译者更要耐心仔细。有时原文在行文中也会有人名拼写、数字或数量单位等方面的失误,此时,如果译者通过自己的学术素养、相关阅读或者运用 Google 等互联网工具查找发现原文的错误,则可以在译文中更正并加以注译。

学术类文本的翻译方法主要有以下几种:

1. 译文与注释相结合

在面对人名、地名、书名、篇名、刊名和专业术语等时,译者应查阅相关资料,避免讹误,并对全文中的同一译名保持前后统一(原文中一词多义者另当别论)。如果业界已经有约定俗成的表达方式,可以予以采用;如果译者对现有的翻译不满意或发现现有的翻译有讹误,可以自行翻译,但要做到准确无误并保持全文前后一致。此外,当人名、地名、书名、篇名、刊名、专业术语第一次在学术类文本的译本中出现时,译者应采用插注或脚注的方式标明其原文表达方式,以方便读者的理解、查证或今后按图索骥对相关源语资料进行研究。在翻译学术类文本时,还有一种情况要注意。有时原作者采用外文写作讨论中国问题,并委托译者或翻译机构将其翻译成中文。在这种情况下,原文本中的人名、地名、书名、篇名、刊名和专业术语等需要译者准确地还原成中文语境中的说法,而不能似是而非地音译过来,造成读者阅读理解上的障碍。例如,如果将原文本中的 Mencius(孟子)音译为"门修斯"或"孟修斯",反而会让读者云里雾里,摸不着头脑。

对于译入语读者不太熟悉,而在文本中起奠基作用或对文本的理论表达起到关键性作用的理论术语,译者除了在译文中译出译名、插注原文表达方式,还可以在脚注或章末尾注中简要注明该理论术语的含义、主要内容或核心观点,以方便学术类文本的翻译文本的传播与理解,并实现源语文本与译入语读者之间信息的有效交流。此外,学术类文本原文本中的注释最好予以保留并翻译,当注释中涉及人名、专业术语等信息时,译者在翻译之余还可以注明原文的表达方式。另外,学术著作中的参考文献也应该保留。源语参考文献的信息可以翻译成译入语并保留原文(或至少保留原文),这可以方便专业读者日后查找资料;译入语参考文献的信息(但原作者在原文本中译成源语形式)应还原成译入语,并最好还原成其在译入语语言文化系统中原有的表达形式。

在翻译关于历史朝代、历史人物的名词时,如果业界已经有约定俗成的表达方式,应予以采用;如果没有,可以采用音译或音译意译相结合的方法。而无论采用何种翻译方法,都应在译文表述后面补充说明朝代或人物任期历时公元年份,使译入语读者对其有更直观、更明晰的时间概念。如果具体年份不清楚,在译文行文中可以简要说明从第几世纪到第几世纪或某个年代到某个年代。

2. 直译与意译相结合

能够直译的地方直译,不能直译的地方意译或采用直译意译相结合的方法。茅盾曾经说过,"直译的意义若就浅处说,只是'不妄改原文的字句';就深处说,还求'能保留原文的情调与风格'。所谓'不妄改原文的字句'一语,除消极的'不妄改'而外,尚含有一个积极的条件——必须顾到全句的文理。西文里同一字的意义,用在某段文中的和注在字典上的,常常有些出入;换句话说,某字的活动的意义,常随处变动,而字典中所注的只是几个根本的意义,字典势不能将某字随处活动的许多意义都注了上去。所以直译时必须就其在文中的意义觅一个相当的字来翻译,方才对;如果把字典里的解释直用在译文里,那便是'死译',只可说是不妄改某字在字典中的意义,不能说是吻合原作"。

事实上,直译、意译的方法在翻译实践中由来已久。与玄奘同时代的翻译理论家道宣就极为推崇玄奘的翻译,因为"玄奘明于佛法,兼通梵汉语言,译笔谨严,多用直译,善参意译,世称'新译'"。到了 20 世纪 20—30 年代,鲁迅、瞿秋白等左翼学者主张直译,提出翻译可以帮助创造新的中国的现代言语,造出新的字眼、新的句法、丰富的词汇和细腻精密正确的表达;并认为意译派的做法是蒙蔽读者,使读者不能够知道作者的原意。赵景深、陈西滢等右翼学者则主张意译,认为直译派的做法使译文佶屈聱牙。抛开这场论争的阶级立场与硝烟,一些学者的论述仍不乏真知灼见。茅盾曾指出:"直译在理论上是根本不错的,惟因译者能力关系,原来要直译,不意竟变做了死译,也是常有的事。或者因为视直译是极容易的,轻心将事,结果也会使人看不懂。积极的补救,现在尚没有办法;消极的制裁,唯有请译书的人不要把'直译'看做一件极容易的事。"林语堂则在《论翻译》一文中归纳了四种不同程度的翻译:直译、死译、意译和胡译。他认为死译是直译极端的结果,例如将"the apple of my eye"(掌上明珠)译为"我目的苹果",而胡译是意译的"过激党"。如今,在这一问题上我国的翻译界和翻译学界已经基本达成共识。比如,王东风在《异化与归化——矛与盾的交锋?》一文中就指出,"直译不是死译、硬译、呆译,意译不是胡译、乱译;在保证原文语义不流失的情况下尽量直译,也就是说,能直译时直译,不能直译时意译;直译和意译并行不悖,任何译本都是直译和意译相结合的结果"。

3. 不主张死译、硬译,也不主张过于自由、背离原文的翻译

死译、硬译包括过于囿于原文字序、被原文字面之义所束缚,而没有译出原文真正含义或言外之意的翻译,以及虽然勉强传递原文之义,但因完全不符合译入语语言、事理逻辑导致不能被译入语读者所接受的译文。过于自由、完全背离原文的翻译则与原文相去甚远。无论是死译、硬译,还是胡译、乱译都无法实现原文作者或原文本与译入语读者之间信息的有效交流。

需要说明的是,在学术问题的讨论上,许多问题的确存在争议或尚无定论,不同学者可能有不同的学术立场与理解。如果译者有自己的想法与观点,或试图补充其他学者的观点以扩充读者的学术视野,译者可以在脚注或章末尾注中简要说明,但不宜将其杂糅在译文的正文中并把它作为原作者的观点表现出来。如果这样的文字篇幅较长,可以放在译著的"前言"或"译后记"中予以阐述或述评,而不宜放在译著正文中。

在学术翻译中,还有一个比较容易出现失误的地方,即对原学术著作中引文翻译的失误。张亚权博士在《论学术翻译的文献回译——以梅尔清〈清初扬州文化〉中译本为例》中把这些失误归结为以下几种:"① 原著直接引文,译著擅改为间接引文或意译原文;② 原著全引,译著擅改为节引;③ 原著节引,译著擅改为全引;④ 译著回译直接引文所据版本与原著不同;⑤ 译著回译直接引文标点、文字有误;⑥ 译著想当然臆译直接引文。"这些失误的表现形式是过于自由、偏离原文的翻译,究其根本原因恐怕是译者对于学术翻译所需要遵循的学术规范的严谨性这一点认识不足。对于学术翻译的专业读者或潜在的专业读者来说,当他们不精通源语或时间精力有限未能全文阅读源语文献的情况下,他们有可能将学术翻译的译文当作其从事相关研究的专业文献和参考资料并从中析出资源、摘抄有用引文等。因此译者在翻译时对原学术文本中引文的擅自改动都有可能误导未来的专业读者,所以危害极大。在职业翻译中,如果译者由于翻译任务委托方的硬性要求删改学术译文中的引文,可以在引文后添加脚注予以说明和提醒读者。需要补充说明的是:由于政治语境的原因,对原作大幅度的改译、编译、扭曲或重塑原文本学术形象的翻译不在本文讨论范围之内。因为那样的翻译严格意义上来说已经不是学术翻译了,而是一种政治翻译。

译者翻译学术类文本时的具体翻译技巧有：增词、减词、合并、转译、前置、倒置、拆离、重组和重译等。

6.4 翻译实例及点评

英译汉

【原文】

Terms differ from words in that they are endowed with a special form of reference, namely that they refer to discrete conceptual entities, properties, activities or relations which constitute the knowledge space of a particular subject field (1). In order to differentiate between general and special reference in linguistic parlance (2), a distinction is established between terms which have special reference within a particular discipline, and words which function in general reference over a variety of subject fields. And, to increase the specificity of reference, agreements are concluded on (3) the precise meaning and expression forms of lexical items by means of processes of regularization, harmonization and standardization (4) (See TERMINOLOGY, STANDARDIZATION). We thus have conscious processes of term selection and creation in the sense of adopting characteristics of artificial languages (5).

Special subjects are therefore differentiated from general knowledge primarily by the nature of reference, and also by the fact that they contain additional concepts. This difference is one of degree, and it is therefore more appropriate to speak of general reference and special reference as two extremes within which language can and does vary (6). As we can actually see in scientific papers, university textbooks and popular science and newspaper articles, the distinction between general and special knowledge takes the shape of a cline in practice (7).

As far as terms are concerned, we can say that behind each term there should ideally be a clearly defined concept which is systematically related to the other concepts that make up the knowledge structure of the text or discourse in question. The choice of the term should reflect this concept effectively and unambiguously, and the outward form the term takes should be generally acceptable. Another important difference between terms and words is that a term keeps its life and its meaning only for as long as it serves the system of knowledge that gave rise to it. In actual usage, terms are influenced by the same factors as words. If they are long, they are usually shortened in discourse among specialists, with different variants emerging according to the social, formal or <u>even geographical stratification of occurrences of texts</u> (8). In practice, therefore, we encounter variants of a term without always knowing precisely which of these forms is more widely accepted than others, or which could be considered the unmarked, neutral form to be used as a safe option. There are also cases where a term has no parallel variant in a target language of translation. Translators are therefore basically always dealing with variants, except where a concept has only one designation. <u>They need to undertake their own research to establish in which setting a variant is or is not acceptable</u> (9).

(Sager，2009：261)

【译文一】

术语与词语的不同之处在于前者拥有一层专业的含义,也就是,<u>它们所代表的一些相互独立的概念、特性、活动或关系,能够构建出某一特定学科领域的知识空间</u>(Ⅰ)。为了<u>从语言用语上</u>(Ⅱ)对普通含义和专业含义加以区别,<u>我们决定</u>,术语是指在特定学科中含有特殊含义的词,而词语是指在多个学科领域中其词义仍保持普通含义的词。并且,为了增加其含义的特殊性,<u>人们同意</u>(Ⅲ)对术语的精确含义及表达形式进行<u>常规化、和谐化及标准化处理</u>(Ⅳ)(见"术语"、"标准化")。<u>因此,我们有意识的对术语进行选择,人为地将一些语言特色加入术语创造中</u>(Ⅴ)。

这样一来,专业学科与普通知识主要便通过含义本身进行分别,而前者包含的额外含义也是二者的不同之处。<u>两者的差别是含义程度上的差别,我们可以视其为两个端点,而两者中间过渡部分所使用的语言是可以且确实是有差别的</u>(Ⅵ)。<u>从学术论文、大学课本、科普书籍到报刊文章,我们可以清晰地观察到知识的专业性呈现了递减趋势(Ⅶ)。

既然谈到术语,我们认为,在理想状况下,每一个术语背后都应包含一个明确的概念,它与其他概念系统的联系起来,共同组成讨论的文本或话题的知识结构。选择的术语应该能有效地、明确地体现这一概念,且其外在形式应为大家普遍接受。术语与词语的另一重要区别是,一个术语的价值和意义只有在服务创造它的知识体系时才体现出来。在实际应用中,影响术语与影响词语的因素相同,如果术语过长,专家在讲到它时通常会将其缩短;文章写作的社会背景、形式甚至地理层次的不同都会导致术语的多种变体出现。因此在实践中碰到一个术语的变体时,我们无从知晓哪一种形式才是为大家普遍接受的,也无法得到哪一种是未受影响的、中性的词,可以用作我们的保守之选。有些情况下,某个术语的变体在翻译成目标语时没有对应的词。所以,译员基本上总在处理一些变体词(一个概念只有一个名称的情况除外)。他们需要自己进行调查,以确定在何种场合下,一种变体可以或不可以被接受。

(学生课堂练习)

【译文二】

术语和词汇的差别在于术语具有特殊的指代功能,即<u>术语可以指代分立的概念实体,特性,活动和关系,从而构成一个特别学术领域的知识空间(Ⅰ')</u>。我们可以利用语言学词汇泛指和特指的概念来解释术语和词汇的差别。术语是某个学科专有词汇的名称,是特指。而词汇可以应用于不同学科之间,是泛指。通过对词条的规则化,和谐化和标准化处理,我们可以得出词条的精确的含义和表达,从而提高词汇的特指度。<u>这就是我们对术语的严谨的挑选和创造过程(Ⅴ')</u>。

专业学科和普通知识的差别主要在于他们指代的本质区别,而且专业学科包括更多的概念。这种差别的程度不同。可以说泛指和特指是两种极端,语言表达因此而不同。我们从实际上可以从科学论文,大学教科书,<u>流行科学(Ⅶ')</u>和报纸文章中看出,普通知识和专业知识的差别常<u>以变异群的方式(Ⅷ')</u>表现出来。

每个术语都应该有一清楚的定义,这个定义与其他定义系统的联系在一起,共同构成文章和会话中的知识框架。术语的选择应该能有效清楚的体现术语定义,并且术语的外部构成要被大众所接收。术语之于词汇的另一个重要差别在于,术语同它的含义存在的寿命长短取决于它能为产生它的知识体系服务的时间长短。在实际运用中,术语和词汇受相同因素的影响。如果术语很长,专家们会在会话中运用他们比较短的变体。术语因文章中出现的社会,正式甚至<u>地理阶层的分化</u>(Ⅷ')有不同的变体。所以,实际上我们在遇到术语的变体时,并不能清楚地知道哪种变体更能被广泛接受,哪种变体形式是最好的选择。我们在翻译中经常会遇到在目标语中没有与源语相对应的术语的例子。因此,译者总是会遇到变体问题,除非定义只有一个术语名称。<u>他们需要自己调查,变体的建立能否被接受</u>(Ⅸ')。

(学生课堂练习)

【译文三】

　　<u>术语与词语的区别在于两者指称对象不同,即:术语指称的对象是某学科知识空间内具有独立概念的实体、属性、活动或关系</u>。<u>为区分语言学用语中的泛指和特指</u>,可以说术语用于指称某学科内的特殊对象,词语则用于指称<u>不同学科内的普通对象</u>。为了增强术语表达的准确性和专业性,<u>需要通过术语管理、术语统一和标准化过程对术语的确切含义和表达形式达成一致意见</u>(参见"术语学"、"标准化")。因此,就<u>吸收人造语言特点而言</u>,我们在有意识地<u>选择和创造术语</u>。

　　由于指称对象性质的不同及其所包含的附加概念,专门学科知识不同于一般知识。<u>这种差异是程度上的差异,因此把泛指和特指看作两个极端更为恰当,在两者之间,语言有且的确存在差异。正如我们在科学论文、大学教材、科普读物和报纸文章中所看到的那样,专业知识和一般知识的应用呈渐变状态。</u>

　　就术语而言,每个术语理想中都有一个清晰定义的概念,与构成所讨论的文本或话语知识结构的其他概念系统地联系在一起。术语的选择应清晰有效地反映它对应的概念,表达形式也必须能被普遍接受。术语和词语之间另一个重要区别是:术语的生命和含义只在产生它的知识系统内有效。在实际使用中,术语与词汇受到一些相同因素的影响。在专业人士的表述中,长术语通常被缩略,并随文本所处的不同社会场合、正式程度<u>甚至地域分布产生不同的变体</u>。当我们在实践中遇到术语的不同变体时,有时候并不知道哪个变体是广为接受的,或者哪种变体是无标记的、中性的、安全的术语表达。有时术语在译入语中并没有平行变体。因此,除非一个概念只有一个术语名称,否则译者都在与术语的不同变体打交道。译者需要自己研究某个变体的可接受性。

(本书作者译)

【点评】

  这组英译汉的原文具有相当的专业知识性,内容虽看似平淡,但要译得好却非易事。就译文一和译文二所呈现出来的效果评判,并不是十分理想。问题主要集中在三个方面:一是准确性有所欠缺;二是专业性不够强;三是逻辑不够严密。

  从准确性有所欠缺的角度来看,两篇译文都可以找出不少这方面的例子。比如,译文一第一句后半部分的"它们所代表的一些相互独立的概念、特性、活动或关系,能够构建出某一特定学科领域的知识空间"就有很多问题。且不说一些字和词的选用失当(如"相互独立的概念"),开首的"它们"就有死译和硬译的嫌疑。更加要命的是,译者在这里所采用的搭配和句式(如"构建出……的知识空间")完全颠覆了原文作者的意图,使得原本十分清晰的意思表达变得含混不清。对于这个部分的处理,译文二的表现略好一些。当然,它最后的"从而构成一个特别学术领域的知识空间"的表述也不准确。此外,所谓"分立的概念实体"也叫人摸不着头脑。再对照一下译文三的译笔,应该说高下立判。还有,译文一第二段的第二句和第三句以及译文二第一段的最后一个句子等也都存在信息还原不准确的缺点。之所以会出现以上种种情况,归根结底恐还在于译者对原文的理解和把握存在较大的出入,并没有真正读懂和吃透原文。

  接着来谈一下专业性不够强的问题,这方面的例子也不在少数。比如,译文一第一段中的"从语言用语上"、"我们决定"、"人们同意"以及"常规化"、"和谐化"等就属于此列。在译文二中,"词条"、"流行科学"、"变异群"和"地理阶层的分化"等也可归为同样性质的问题。上述所举例子还只是词汇层面的不足。在句法层面也多有欠缺。仅以译文二第三段最后一句为例:"他们需要自己调查,变体的建立能否被接受。"这个表达就很不专业,不利于原文信息的准确和有效传播。

  至于逻辑性不强、意思表达不严谨和不明确的缺点,实际上是上述两个问题的叠加。从某种程度上来说,这样的情况在两篇译文中相当普遍。仍以译文一开首的第一句为例:"术语与词语的不同之处在于前者拥有一层专业的含义,也就是,它们所代表的一些相互独立的概念、特性、活动或关系,能够构建出某一特定学科领域的知识空间。"这个处理可以说已经使原文的意图变得支离破碎,把一个关于术语的本来清晰、简单的定义搞得既复杂且混乱了。

汉译英

【原文】

身份的焦虑

"英伦才子"(1)阿兰·德波顿写过一本书,书名就叫《身份的焦虑》。中国的经济在改革的浪潮推动下,一浪高过一浪,打破了改革之前几乎所有家庭生活平均化而无差别的格局(2)。

初期曾身在国企的职工们看不起那些小商小贩和个体户,而当卖大碗茶的收入超过了官员与教授的收入时,人们的观念开始发生了变化(3)。当国企职工下岗、干部下海之后,社会开始拉大了贫富差别。金融服务业的产生和民企的上市再一次引发了经济地震,《福布斯》的排行掀起了一阵阵波浪(4)。让这个社会在改革开放中不断改变着评价的标准和身份的定义。数千人争夺一个公务员名额的招考,全民炒股的动员,商人排行榜与精英的选拔,超女和明星的价值提升,教授专家们的走穴,以及留学人员与海归,这一切都在改变着这个世界(5)。

可怕的并非是中国出了李彦宏、马云等精英(6),引发身份焦虑的不是每个人与比尔·盖茨的对比,而是同龄人之间、同学之间、同事之间的生活与地位的变化,最熟悉的人群之间的对比。

(任志强,2010:185)

【译文一】

Status Anxiety

Alain de Botton, the famous "British wit" (Ⅰ), once wrote a book, called "Status Anxiety". Driven by the higher and higher wave of reform, China's economy has broken the pattern that almost all families live in average, without difference (Ⅱ).

Earlier, employees of the state-owned enterprises looked down upon those small peddlers and individual households, but the concepts of people have started to change, when the earnings of those who just sold stall tea exceeded the income of the officials and professors (Ⅲ). After the employees were laid off from state-owned enterprises and officials went into business, the gap between the rich and the poor has been widened. An economic earthquake was caused in that the financial service industry generated (Ⅳ) and private enterprises were listed in the market. The Forbes ranking also raised a flood of waves after another that people rushed to make a fortune. All of these have made the standard of evaluation and the definition of status constantly change in the process of reform and opening up. Thousands of people compete for one civil servant enrollment. People speculate on stocks. Wealthy merchants are ranked on the rich list and the elites are selected. The social status of the "super girls" and stars are promoted. Professors and experts begin to moonlight for extra income. The number of overseas returnees is rising, all of these are changing the world (Ⅴ).

What is terrible is not the rising of such elites as Li Yanhong and Ma Yun. What causes the status anxiety is not the comparison between the ordinary people and Bill Gates, but the changes of the living standard and social status among peers, schoolmates, colleagues, and the comparison between people and their most familiar companions.

(学生课堂练习)

【译文二】

Status Anxiety

Alain de Botton, one of the Great British Wits (Ⅰ'), has once written a book *Status Anxiety*. Pushed by the wave of reform, China's economy is gradually boosting, which breaks the average and undifferentiated situation of nearly all the families in China before the reform (Ⅱ').

Once the workers of the state-owned enterprises looked down upon the small business operators and the self-employed, however, when those pretty dealers earned more than officials and college professors, people began to change their stereotypes. The gap between the rich and poor became much wider when SOE workers lost their jobs and officials resigned but to start their own business. The economic earthquake was once again triggered by the financial services' coming into being and the private enterprises' appearing on the market (Ⅳ'); meanwhile, the rankings made by the *Forbes* caused the society, under the waves of reform, to continuously change its standards of evaluation and the definition of status. And this society was changed by the tricky situations, such as thousands of people applied for one single position in the Civil Service Sector, nearly everyone rushed into the stock market, business people were fond of being rated in certain leader boards, elites had to go through strict selections, the social status of star drafts and pop stars was skyrocketing (Ⅴ'), experts or professors started their moonlighting, more and more people went abroad for further study while those who had already studied abroad now went back to motherland.

The appearance of elites, such as Li Yan-hong and Ma Yun in China, is never scaring (Ⅵ'); what caused the status anxiety is not the comparison between normal people and Bill Gates but the contrast between oneself and those who he is familiar with, including the change of life and status among peers, students, and colleagues.

(学生课堂练习)

【译文三】

Status Anxiety

A gifted English writer Alain de Botton has written a book named *Status Anxiety*. Driven by waves of reforms, Chinese economy has become increasingly developed, breaking the pre-reform pattern in which almost all families shared and shared alike.

Originally, staffs in state-owned enterprises despised tradespeople and those self-employed; but people have changed their minds as stall tea sellers earned more than officials and professors.

When state-owned staffs were laid off and officials went into business; the gap between the rich and the poor began widening. Financial service industry emerged and private-owned enterprises came into the market, triggering a new economic earthquake. *Forbes* set off one wave after another. During the process of reform, the society has consistently changed its evaluation standards and the definition of status. Thousands compete for one position in Civil Service Examination; the public are mobilized to speculate in stocks; the value of stars and winners of the show "Super Girls" (which is a singing competition) is enhanced; professors and experts start their sideline occupations; the business ranking lists, the selection of talents, overseas students and returnees all help changing the world.

Elites like Li Yanhong and Ma Yun are not dreadful. What triggers status anxiety is not the contrast between individual and Bill Gates, but that among the closest people: the changed life and status of peers, classmates and colleagues.

（本书作者译）

【点评】

本组汉译英的原文从内容上看并非很"学术"，里面基本找不到专业性的词语，其表达体系也相对通俗和大众化。不过，就译文一和译文二的表现而言，还是存在较多失误和不尽人意之处。在这些问题中，既有选词和用词失当、搭配失误、句子结构混乱、颠三倒四等，也有对原文理解出现偏颇的情况。从具体翻译手法的角度来考察的话，则还存在死译和胡译两种情况。

现在先来讨论一下译文一。在第一段的两个句子中，问题更多地集中在后一句。比如，以 Driven by the higher and higher wave of reform 来翻译"在改革的浪潮推动下，一浪高过一浪"颇有点死译的味道。在接下来的部分，pattern 后面不应该以 that 接续，这涉及搭配问题。此后的 live in average, without difference 则属于想当然的翻译，翻译腔太浓。在第二段中，各类问题也不少。一是选词用词的失当。比如，以 earlier, individual households 和 compete for one civil servant enrollment 来翻译原文的"初期"、"个体户"和"争夺一个公务员名额的招考"，显然不够精准。另外，The number of overseas returnees is rising 中的 is rising 宜改为 is on the rise。二是某些句子时态的使用有些混乱，还有一些句子则因为语法或逻辑的缺陷让人感觉莫名其妙。比如，开头一句中，译者在前半部分使用了过去时态，对照原文，这应该是合理的选择。但是在后半句中，其主干部分却出现了现在完成时态（the concepts of people have started to change），并且此后的 when 后面又再一次出现了过去时态，整个句子的时态选用显得随意和不统一。紧接着的第二句中，前半部分的从句使用过去时态，而后面的主句则是现在完成时态。还有，An economic earthquake was caused in that the financial service industry generated ... 这个部分读来也十分令人费解。上述种种情况不仅影响了译文表达的效果，也必然不利于准确反映原文作者的意图。三是对原文的理解过于僵化和刻板。比如，针对原文中的"《福布斯》的排行掀起了一阵阵波浪……全民炒股的动员，商人排行榜与精英的选拔，……这一切都在改变着这个世界。"译者先后译为 The Forbes ranking also raised a flood of waves after another that people rushed to make a fortune. People speculate on stocks. Wealthy merchants are ranked on the rich list and the elites are selected. 和 ... all of these are changing the world. 撇开语法、用词等方面的失误不说，这些译文最大的不足是对原文意图的误解和曲解。"掀起了一阵阵波浪"很可能是指引起公众的热议或关注，但是译者却硬加上了 rushed to make a fortune。随后的"全民炒股的动员，商人排行榜与精英的选拔"等，从结构上来看应该是一个并列的部分，但是，译者却把它们分开来单独处理。不仅如此，就其译文本身而言，这两个句子都属于无意义陈述。原文第二段末尾的"改变着这个世界"，从上下文来看，应该理解为"改变着这个国家（即中国）"，但显然译者未能做出灵活的变通。

译文二与译文一的情况大致相同。比如，以 one of the Great British Wits 来翻译"英伦才子"显然不恰当。熟悉英国文学史的读者或许听说过"大学才子派"，它的英文倒是 the University Wits。只不过，"大学才子派"（一个专有名词）岂能拿来和这里的"英伦才子"相提并论（译文一的 the famous "British Wit" 与此不相上下,也属不妥)?再看 the financial services' coming into being and the private enterprises' appearing on the market,与译文一在同一点上的处理同样令人费解。还有 business people were fond of being rated in certain leader boards, elites had to go through strict selections, the social status of star drafts and pop stars was skyrocketing,其中的 be fond of 用错了,leader boards 有点滑稽,had to go through strict selections 与原文意图不相符,star drafts 究竟指什么让人摸不着头脑,而 skyrocketing 一词用得过头了。最后,The appearance of elites, such as Li Yan-hong and Ma Yun in China, is never scaring 中的 never scaring 使用不够准确(原文是"可怕的并非是中国出了李彦宏、马云等精英……")。

第七章

科技翻译

7.1 科技类文本的概念

科学包括自然科学和社会科学,哲学是两者的概括和总结。本章所讨论的科技类文本指自然科学和应用技术类文本,不包括社会科学类的文本。具体来说,科技文本包括几乎所有理工常见学科(如数学、物理、力学、天文、地理、生物、化学化工、冶金、环境、矿业、机电、航空、交通、水利、建筑、能源、医药、卫生、电子技术和信息科学等学科)的科学论文、科普文本等,还包括产品说明书和专利说明。

7.2 科技类文本的基本特征

科技类文本首先具有很强的信息性和专业性。科技类文本中的科学论文往往重在对科学原理的阐述、实验设计和操作过程的说明、推理论证过程的呈现等,信息含量大并具有极强的专业性;其目标读者是专业人士群体,因此往往用词较难、术语较多、公式与图表较多。科普文本的目标读者是普通读者群体,因此在专业知识语言、术语运用方面与科学论文有所区别,更注重其对普通大众的可读性和可接受性,用词、句式更简单。产品说明不重在阐述科学原理与专业推理论证,更少用科学术语,但重视对产品安装、使用、维护、故障、安全方面的说明并在这些方面表述专业、信息性强。

科技类文本的词汇可以分为三种:第一种是专业词汇,以专业术语为主,因科技领域的不同而不同;有些词汇尽管在不同科技领域都出现,但其在每个领域的具体含义可能因其所在领域的不同而不同。第二种是半专业词汇，由一些普通词汇逐渐转变而成，但其含义与其在普通用语中的含义不同，并也可能在不同的学科里有不同的含义。译者在翻译科技文本时特别要注意这类词汇。第三种是普通词汇，具有与其在普通用语中相同的含义，并将专业词汇和半专业词汇串联成句。总体来看，普通词汇在科技文本中仍然占据一定篇幅，这为译者的理解和翻译提供了便利。

科技类文本的第二个特征是逻辑性和客观性。如前文所述，科学论文注重对科学原理的阐述、实验设计和操作过程的客观说明、推理论证过程的客观呈现，具有极强的逻辑性，并注重语言表述的客观性。科普文本、产品说明与专利说明尽管在专业知识与术语运用方面有别于科学论文，但仍注重语言表述的逻辑性和客观性。总的来说，科技类文本属于书面语体，语法结构严密、文字严谨，表述力求客观准确。行文中一般避免使用第一、第二人称，多用无主句或第三人称。此外，科技类文本语中还有将要表达的内容全部字面化的特点，英语的科技类文本中经常从句套从句，充分运用不定式、分词短语、定语从句、状语从句等结构将要表达的内容阐述清楚。英文科技类文本还经常使用强调句、被动语态等，有时将重要内容前置或后置、句型扩展，总之句子成分之间关系复杂、逻辑严谨。

科技类文本的第三个特征是文字既严谨翔实又简洁规范。一方面，科技类文本经常翔实地说明实验步骤或操作步骤，在叙述说明时严谨地将要表达的内容全部字面化以避免歧义；但另一方面，科技类文本的表述又力求简洁、规范，在要表达的内容之余不会有其他主观性的阐述或与主题无关的文字。例如，某家用电器的使用说明中有这样的语句：This appliance is designed for domestic use only, specifically for the storage of edible foodstuffs. It is not intended for commercial or industrial use. 译为"该电器仅适用于家庭用途，专门用于储存可食用的食品，不适用于商业用途或工业用途。"在此组句中，原文与译文详细地说明了该电器的适用范围是家庭用途，而非商业用途或工业用途，且专门用于储存可食用的食品（而不是其他物品）。又如：Do not store any flammable materials, such as spray cans, fire extinguisher, refill cartridges etc. in the appliance. 译为"电器内严禁存放易燃物品，如喷雾罐、灭火器、填充墨盒等。"

7.3 科技类文本的翻译策略

按照翻译目的论,翻译的目的不同,翻译的策略与方法也不尽相同。在科技翻译中,一般有全译、编译和摘译。全译需要从头到尾翻译原文,而编译和摘译主要根据客户的具体要求翻译出原文主要信息和内容。下面主要讨论全译的翻译策略、方法与技巧。

1. 宏观策略

科技类文本的功能主要属于纽马克和莱斯所说的"信息功能",因此科技翻译的首要目标是将原文的信息准确、清晰、无误地传递给译文读者,帮助他们了解与掌握原文的科技信息与内容。

其次,科技翻译还需要用符合译入语的语言规范与表达方式的语言来表达,这有助于译出的信息更好地被译文读者理解与接受。

最后,科技翻译的译文需要保持原文的专业性、逻辑性和客观性,并保留原文严谨而又简洁规范的语言风格。保持原文的专业性指的是译者在翻译科技类文本时应密切关注原文本中所涉及的科技专门知识与术语表达,并以职业和专业的表达方式在译文中呈现出来。比如说,科技术语的翻译要符合业内人士的表述,并在译文中保持前后一致。此外,科技类文本往往是客观的描述或记录,不涉及作者的主观情感,译者在翻译时也要注意译文的客观性,行文表述要做到逻辑严密。

2. 科技术语的翻译

翻译科技术语时,译者可以借助专业词典、网络搜索工具乃至翻译软件的术语库,或查阅相关书刊中的专业表达,或者阅读以译入语写作的平行文本与已经翻译成译入语的科技文本的翻译文本,查找行内对于某个术语约定俗成的翻译,以供借鉴。从翻译方法上来说,科技术语一般采取音译、意译、音译意译相结合或字母与释译相结合的译法。例如,liter 意译为"升",milliliter 则音译意译结合译为"毫升",deciliter 译为"分升(十分之一公升)"。meter 音译为"米",millimeter 则音译意译结合译为"毫米",decimeter 译为"分米、公寸(十分之一米)",kilometer 译为"千米"。gram 译为"克",decigram 译为"分克(十分之一克)",kilogram 译为"千克"。El Nino 音译意译结合译为"厄尔尼诺现象"。对于原文包含字母的术语,翻译时可以采用字母与释译相结合的方法。

例如：Z-iron 译为"乙字铁"，Z-bar 译为"乙字钢"，X-ray 译为"X 射线"，T-square 译为"丁字尺"，Herring bone gear 译为"人字齿轮"。对于一些原文以缩写字母构成的术语，科技译文中有时可以保留原文缩写字母的术语形式。例如：PS/2 and UNIX are available for PCs. 译为"PS/2 和 UNIX 可用于 PC 机"。

3. 直译与意译相结合的翻译方法

许多人对于直译的理解是这种翻译方法不仅传递原文的内容，还要传递原文的形式（乃至原文的句子结构）。但是对于科技类文本来说尤其要注意的一点是：不是说一定要与原文本中的句子结构对译才是直译。在传递原文含义的同时，更要注意用符合译入语语言习惯的句子结构来表述；科技翻译有时需要译者在译文中部分调整乃至全部调整待译语句的句子结构，变更句子成分，转换词性等。

4. 具体翻译技巧

译者译前需要读透原文，在第一遍阅读时不用急于查找专业术语的翻译，可以只求获得原文的大致印象；第二遍阅读时可以确定难点，结合上下文来理解或查找专业词典与翻译软件的术语库或网络搜索工具。在线翻译的网络翻译工具与全文翻译的翻译软件可以帮助译者获得译文的初步印象；而翻译软件中的术语库或记忆库可以为译者提供术语翻译的参考。

从句型来看，英语单个句子较长，汉语单个句子较短。英语中由于从句套从句或者带有分词、不定式、介词短语等结构，一个完整逻辑关系的句子可以很长；而汉语中每个单句一般不会那么长。

科技类文本的翻译技巧主要有：一，从大的句型结构处理方面有四种：顺译、逆译、分译和合译；二，从小的词汇方面调整的有四种：增词、减词、转译（译文中转换原文某些词汇的词性、语法成分等）和插入译法（用括号内容或破折号后面内容译弦外之音或说明解释类文字）。下面从大的句型结构处理方面举例，而小的词汇调整技巧（增词、减词、转译、插入译法分析）则穿插在大的技巧译例中。需要注意的是，翻译技巧不等于翻译公式，不一定每句翻译都要套用这些技巧，译者可以灵活运用各种翻译方法与技巧，传递原文信息。

（1）顺译。当英文原句的语序与汉语的语序习惯较一致时，可以大致按原文语序顺译。例如：After the discovery of electromagnetism in the first part of the nineteenth century, inventors strove to utilise it for the transmission of messages by electricity. 原文时间状语从句在前,主句在后,比较符合汉语的语序习惯,可以顺译为"19世纪上半叶人们发现电磁后,发明家们力争用电来传递信息"。原句时间状语从句除了上述增词(增译主语)的处理之外,还可以译成无主句及被动态"19世纪上半叶发现电磁后,发明家们力争用电来传递信息"或"19世纪上半叶电磁被发现后,发明家们力争用电来传递信息"。又如:Heat travels in any of the three different ways: by radiation, convection or conduction. 译文1:"热的传播有三种不同的方式:辐射、对流和传导。"译文2:"热的传播方式有三种:辐射、对流和传导。"译文1和译文2都采用顺译,在词汇调整方面则采用减词、转译处理,省略原文介词by,将原文动词travels转换词性处理为名词"(热的)传播"。

(2) 逆译。逆译是部分颠倒或全部颠倒原文句子的顺序来进行翻译。英译汉时常常把原文中的后置定语逆译放在其所修饰的名词前。例如:Captive trajectory testing is a technique utilized in wind tunnels to predict and generate the trajectories of air-launched stores from parent aircraft. 译为"捕获轨迹试验是风洞中采用的一种试验技术,用来预估并生成外挂物在空中从母机上投射时的飞行轨迹"。原句中utilized in wind tunnels 做 a technique 的后置定语,译文逆译为前置定语,其余部分采用顺译。需要说明的是,英译汉时并非所有定语从句都采用逆译的方法,有时定语从句较长,可以将定语从句另译成一个句子以叙述先行词的情况,构成补语或译文谓述成分中的一个部分。

逆译也适用于一些主句在前,(时间、原因或条件)状语从句在后的原文,此时可以颠倒原文主、从句的顺序来翻译。即原文是先果后因、先结果后条件时,译文可以调整为先因后果、先条件后结果的顺序。例如:It is not for nothing that scientists are in such a footrace to get the human genome mapped. 译为"科学家以这样一种赛跑的速度来绘制人类基因组图并非是没有目的的"。原句先说结论,再介绍具体的事项。译文逆译为先介绍事项再阐述结论。

逆译还可适用于以 it 作形式主语,后面用不定式短语或 that 从句做真正主语的句子,如 it is + adj.(for sb) to do sth. 例如:It may be economically sound, in the long run, to subsidize their initial production, even at prices above the projected market for natural hydrocarbon fluids, in order to accelerate the deduction of dependence on oil imports. 译为"从长远来看,资助开发这类产品的生产,即使价格高于自然碳氢化合液的市场价格,但为了加快减少对进口石油的依赖,在经济上可能还是合算的"。原文开头的 It may be economically sound 在译文中逆译放在句尾"在经济上可能还是合算的"。此外,该译文还使用了转译(转换词性)的翻译技巧,原句不定式短语 to subsidize their initial production 做主语,译为"资助开发这类产品的生产";此处原文中的形容词 initial 转译为动词"开发"。

(3) 分译。分译指对单词、短语、单句、复句的分译。此外,原文(无论是单句还是复句)有时讲到几件事,不同事情又各自有不同的表述内容,仿佛一棵树长出几个主要枝干,每个枝干上又分为几个小的枝干。此时,译文可以重新提纲挈领来表述。

单词的分译。可以将某些评论性的动词、形容词、副词或名词等从原句中分离出来译成短语或短句。例如:Significant increases in CPU are expected to continue for some time in the future. 译为"预计在将来的一段时间内,CPU 的运行速度会继续大幅提升。"原文中的动词 are expected 被分离出来,与时间状语 for some time in the future 合译为"预计在将来的一段时间内"。

短语的分译。可以将原文中的一些短语分离出来译成短语或句子,必要的时候可以增词、减词、转换词性等。例如:Cold water is heavier than warm water and goes under it, pushing the warm water up. 译为"冷水比暖水重并沉到暖水下面,迫使暖水上升。"该句分译了原文的分词短语 pushing the warm water up。以 with 引导的介词短语也非常适合分译。例如:Hydrogen is the lightest element with an atomic weight of 1.008. 译为"氢是最轻的元素,原子量为 1.008"。此外,一些名词短语也适合分译。例如:An acid can react with a base to form a salt, a substance with quite different properties from those of acids or bases. 译为"酸和碱反应会生成盐,盐的性质迥异于酸或碱"。原文中的名词短语 a substance with quite different properties... 被分译为一个单独的句子"盐的性质迥异于酸或碱",并用具体的主语"盐"代替原来的 a substance。

单句的分译。原文单句较长,表达了较为丰富、复杂的内容时,可以对原句进行适当断句,分译表达;有时可以重新组织主谓宾、重新提纲挈领来翻译。例如:Computer languages may range from detailed low level close to that immediately understood by the particular computer, to the sophisticated high level which can be rendered automatically acceptable to a wide range of computers. 译为"计算机语言有高低级之分。低级语言比较详细烦琐,接近于特定计算机直接能懂的语言,高级语言比较精密复杂,适用范围广,能自动被许多计算机所接受"。原文单句较长,主干是 Computer languages … range from … low level … to high level,而 low level 和 high level 各自有一个后置定语。译成中文如果采用原句语序,单句过长,也较佶屈聱牙。译文采用分译,先译原句的主干"计算机语言有高低级之分",再分别叙述"低级语言……"和"高级语言……"的情况。这样的话,译文脉络分明、条理清晰、易于理解。

复句的分译。复句有并列复句和包括主语从句、表语从句、宾语从句、同位语从句、定语从句、状语从句在内的各种主从复句。并列复句有时用分号断开,有时由 and,or,but,yet,so,for,while 等并列连词引导。例如:It is very good, yet it can be better. 译为"这很好,但还能精益求精。"有时一个句子既包括并列句,又包括主从复句,例如:There have been no revolutionary inventions; what has occurred is a very important steady improvement in materials, and in the techniques of both manufacture and installation, which has made strain gauges far more reliable, accurate, and versatile. 译为"虽然其间没有什么革命性的发明创造,但在材料、加工方法和安装方法方面都已有了重大的、扎实的进步,这使得应变仪更加可靠、更加准确和更加多样化"。原文是用分号隔开的并列句,第一句简单明了,第二句是一个主从复合句,包括一个主语从句和一个非限制性定语从句。译文将原句的两个并列分句分开翻译,并将第二个并列分句中的非限制性定语从句也分离出来翻译,转译成一个结果分句,使译文表达更符合汉语习惯。又如:Many man-made substances are replacing certain natural materials because either the quantity of the natural product can not meet our ever-increasing requirement, or, more often, because the physical properties of the synthetic substance, which is the common name for man-made materials, have been chosen, and even emphasized, so that it would be of the greatest use in the fields in which it is to be applied. 译为"人造材料正在代替天然材料,这或者是因为天然材料的数量不能满足日益增长的需要,或者更多时候是

因为人们选择了合成材料(人造材料通称为合成材料)的一些物理特性并加以强化而造成的,以最大限度地发挥其在拟用领域中的作用"。该译文将原文主干(即原文主要事项)分译为第一句,后面分译两个原因,并采用插入译法,添加括号,将补充说明类文字放入括号内,将原句中修饰 synthetic substance 的非限制性定语从句"which is the common name for man-made materials"译为"(人造材料通称为合成材料)"。由于汉语中并没有非限制性定语从句这种结构,此处如果按原文翻译而不添加括号采用插入译法的话容易干扰句子主干,影响读者理解。

(4) 合译。合译经常与减词处理出现在一起,例如省译原句某些介词、名词、代词和连词等。但是合译要谨慎,不能损失原意;英译汉时,原文时态不能一律省译,因为这有时会影响到科技文本表述的精确性。例如:The rivers which run to the east are usually longer than the ones which run the west. 译为"往东流的河通常比往西流的河更长。"译文中省略了原句的两个关系代词 which,但并未伤及原意。

7.4 翻译实例及点评

英译汉

【原文】

　　Electronics is still a relatively young science. It was introduced by the invention of the electron tube (1). Within the last two decades, however, the electron tube has been largely replaced by the transistor — that wonderful electronic device that can do practically anything the electronic tube can do, and more (2).

　　Transistors are made from semi-conductors. But all semi-conductors are not really useful for transistors. Among them, only germanium and silicon prove to be the most suitable (3). In fact, pure semi-conducting materials conduct electricity only to a very limited extent. To make them suitable for electrical purposes, minute quantities of impurities must be introduced. With different impurities added, semi-conductors are made into two types — the N-type, which is ready to give up electrons, thus having a negative character, and the P-type, which is liable to accept electrons, therefore being of a positive character (4). In practical use, an N-type and a P-type are created side by side in the same semi-conductor crystal, forming a P-N junction (5). It is this P-N junction that forms the basis for the transistor (6).

(严俊仁,2010:236)

【译文一】
　　电子产业仍是相对新兴的科技,它的提出得益于真空管的发明(Ⅰ)。然而,在过去的 20 年里,晶体管的出现大量地取代了真空管的应用,作为一种完美的电子设备,晶体管几乎可以实施任何真空管的操作,而且可以做得更多(Ⅱ)。
　　晶体管是由半导体制成。但并不是所有的半导体都对晶体管都有用。其中,只有锗和硅是最合适的(Ⅲ)。事实上,纯半导体材料只能在非常有限的范围内导电。为了使它们导电,纯半导体材料必须加入微量的杂质。加入的杂质不同,生产出的半导体分为两种:N 型和 P 型。前者易排斥电子,因此具有消极作用;后者易接受电子,因此具有积极作用(Ⅳ)。在实际应用中,人们将 N 型和 P 型混合在一起制成 P-N 节。这种 P-N 节是晶体管的基本组成部分。

(学生课堂练习)

【译文二】
　　相对而言,电子学仍然是一个新兴科学。它源于电子管的发明。在过去的 20 年来,电子管的绝大部分用途已经被晶体管所取代,这种精妙的电子元件几乎包含了电子管的所有功能,在此基础上功能还扩大了许多。
　　晶体管由半导体制成。但并不是所有的半导体都能制作晶体管。经证明,只有锗和硅是最合适的制作材料。事实上,纯半导材料的导电能力非常有限。为使得它们易于导电,必须在其中加入微量杂质。根据添加的杂质不同,半导体被分成两类——N 型,即不吸引电子因此呈阴性,和 P 型,即吸引电子因此呈阳性(Ⅳ')。在实际运用中,在同一半导体晶体内创造紧挨着的 N 型和 P 型半导体(Ⅴ'),从而形成一个 P-N 结。晶体管就建于这种 P-N 结的基础之上(Ⅵ')。

(学生课堂练习)

113

【译文三】

电子学仍是一门相对年轻的科学，它是随着电子管的发明而产生的。然而，在最近20年里，电子管多半已为那种奇妙的电子装置——晶体管所取代了。实际上晶体管具有电子管的一切功能，甚至更多。

晶体管由半导体制成，但并不是所有的半导体都能制成晶体管。在它们之中，只有锗和硅被证明是最适合的。事实上，纯半导体材料的导电能力十分有限，只有加入少量杂质后才能用于导电。由于添加的杂质不同，半导体被分成两类：N型半导体和P型半导体。N型半导体准备释放电子，呈现负极的性质；P型半导体易于接受电子，呈现正极的性质。在实际应用中，N型半导体和P型半导体并排列于同一半导体晶体，形成P-N结，这种P-N结是构成晶体管的基础。

（严俊仁，2010：236，有所改动）

【点评】

本组英译汉属于典型的科技类文本，内容简明、晓畅，词法、句法以及整体的行文均体现出较强的专业性。从译文一和译文二的表现来看，译文二的效果明显好于前者。

译文一的问题涉及几个方面，有对原文意义理解不够准确的，有表达不精确、不规范或缺乏专业水准的，也有逻辑不严密的。比如，第一段的开头一句：Electronics is still a relatively young science. 原句意思十分明晰，却被处理成"电子产业仍是相对新兴的科技"。其中把electronics和science分别译为"电子产业"和"科技"显然太随意了。类似的错误还包括把electron tube译为"真空管"，把having a negative character和being of a positive character分别译为"具有消极作用"和"具有积极作用"等。这些问题的出现有可能是译者的语言能力所限，才导致译文意思发生偏差。不过，也有可能是译者对待译文的态度比较随意和草率。再来看第一段最后部分的译文"作为一种完美的电子设备，晶体管几乎可以实施任何真空管的操作，而且可以做得更多"。在这里，所谓"完美的电子设备"、"几乎可以实施任何……的操作"以及"可以做得更多"在意思上虽不可谓不准确，但是，若要论表达的精准度、规范性和专业水准，那就差了不少。至于逻辑不严密的问题，只须看一下第二段开头的译文即可。在这个部分，原文是三个英语简单句，译者也给出了三个句子对应的译文。从表面上看,这样的处理方式似乎也无可厚非。但问题是,按照中文表达习惯,它的第一句和第二句宜合而成为一个句子,中间再以逗号相分隔。此外,第三句中的"只有锗和硅是最合适的"意思也不明确,与上一句中的"并不是所有的半导体都对晶体管都有用"之间的联系不紧密、不顺畅。如果把它处理成"只有锗和硅被证明最适合用来制成晶体管",显然更合理,也更能够清晰地还原作者的意图。

关于译文二,总体效果较为理想,通篇仅有两到三处误译和表达欠妥。比如,把 negative 和 positive 分别译为"阴性"和"阳性",以及"创造紧挨着的 N 型和 P 型半导体"和"晶体管就建于这种 P-N 结的基础之上"中的"创造"一词和"建于……基础之上"等。

汉译英

【原文】

把两块金属焊接在一起的最简单方法称为压焊(1)。用火焰把每块金属的端部加热到白热状态——铁的焊接温度应当为 1 300℃ 左右。在这种高温下,金属变成塑性体(2)。然后,再把接头强压在一起或锤击在一起,最后把接缝弄光滑(3)。必须注意,首先保证焊件接头表面十分清洁(4),因为污物会减弱焊缝强度。此外,把铁或钢加热至高温时会引起氧化作用,从而在加热表面上形成一层氧化膜。为此,要把某种助焊剂用在加热金属上(5)。当达到焊接的高温时,助焊剂融化,并将氧化物同其他可能有的杂质一起溶解在其中(6)。再将金属表面强压在一起,助焊剂就被从焊缝中间挤压出来(7)。焊接的形式可有多种多样,但对于较厚金属件,通常应采用 V 形焊接(8)。它比普通的对接焊接强度高得多。

(严俊仁,2010:228)

【译文一】

The easiest method to weld two piece of metals together is pressed welding(Ⅰ). Heat the ends of each metal to white since the welding temperature of iron is about 1,300 degree centigrade. In this state of high temperature, metal becomes plastic body. Their joints then are forced or hammered together, and finally polish the juncture (Ⅲ). It should also note that make prior ensure that the surface of the joints should be very clean (Ⅳ) because the dirty substance can reduce weld strength. Besides, Oxidization must be aroused when the iron or steel is heated to high temperature and form a layer of oxide on the heated part. In this case we should use some chemical substance to help welding on the heated metal (Ⅴ). When it reaches the welding temperature, the chemical substance would melt altogether with other presumable impurities (Ⅵ). Force the metal's surface together once more and squeeze the chemical substance from the inside juncture (Ⅶ). There are diversities of welded shapes, for relatively thick metal parts, it is usually adopted V-shaped welding (Ⅷ) which is much stronger than general butt joint or welded joint.

（学生课堂练习）

【译文二】

　　The simplest way to weld two metals together is the so-called bonding (Ⅰ'). At first, you need to heat the bottom of both metals until they are white-hot — iron, for example, should reach about 1,300℃ before being welded. Under such a high temperature, the metal turns into plastic character (Ⅱ'). Then, you pressure the junctions together, to make it more effective, you can turn to a hammer (Ⅲ'). Finally, you smooth the seam. During this process, you need pay attention to the following points (Ⅳ'): firstly, you should make sure that the surfaces of the junctions are clear and tidy, because dirt would attenuate the function of the seam. Secondly, seeing that iron or steel would be oxidated when it is heated into a high temperature, as a result, there would be oxidation film on the heating surface, so you need to add some scaling powder to the heating metal (Ⅴ'), so that when the metal reaches the required temperature, the scaling powder would melt, and the oxide and other possible dirt would also dissolve in it (Ⅵ'). And when the surfaces of the metals are pressured together, the scaling powder would be extruded from the seam (Ⅶ').

There are plenty types of welding, but for thick metal, we usually use V-type, which is much more powerful than the ordinary one (Ⅷ').

(学生课堂练习)

【译文三】

  The simplest method of welding two pieces of metal together is known as pressure welding. The ends of metal are heated to white heat in a flame. The welding temperature of iron should be about 1,300℃. <u>At this temperature the metal becomes plastic</u>. <u>The ends are then pressed or hammered together, and the joint is smoothed off</u>. <u>Care must be taken to ensure that the surfaces are thoroughly clean first, for dirt will weaken the weld</u>. Moreover, the heating of iron or steel to a high temperature causes oxidation, and a film of oxide is formed on the heated surfaces. For this reason, <u>a flux is applied to the heated metal</u>. At welding heat, the flux melts, and <u>the oxide particles are dissolved in it together with any other impurities which may be present</u>. The metal surfaces are pressed together, <u>and the flux is squeezed out from the center of the weld</u>. <u>A number of different types of weld may be used</u>, but for fairly thick bars of metal, <u>a vee-shaped weld should normally be employed. It is rather stronger than the ordinary butt weld</u>.

(严俊仁,2010:228)

【点评】

  本组汉译英的原文具有典型的科技类文本的特征,不仅包含较多专业词汇,其句式结构以及总体的行文风格也趋于简明扼要、不事修饰。比如,在文中多处出现了"压焊"、"塑性体"、"氧化作用"、"氧化膜"、"氧化物"、"助焊剂"和"V型焊接"等术语或准术语的表达。在句式方面,多选用简单句和祈使句,有时候则出现两者合二为一的情况。此外,整体意思的表达显得较为流畅、合理,并且注重逻辑的严密性。对此,句子与句子之间出现的"首先"、"然后"和"最后"以及"当……时"、"并将……"和"再将……"等就足以证明。

  针对科技类文本的翻译,若想取得好的效果,除了要具备扎实的语言基本功和认真踏实的态度以外，还须特别注意两点：一是应掌握（或尽量设法掌握）相应的专业知识；二是在具体的遣词造句方面应力求与原文的风格相符合。从译文一和译文二的表现来看，两者均存在相当多的不足之处。以译文一为例，把"压焊"译为 pressed welding，把"再把接头强压在一起或锤击在一起"译为 Their joints then are forced or hammered together，以及把"某种助焊剂"译为 some chemical substance 等都是不够专业的体现。另一方面，它的句式选用也有不恰当和混乱的情形。比如，对于"为此，要把某种助焊剂用在加热金属上"，译文一处理为 In this case we should use some chemical substance to help welding on the heated metal. 这与它前后的句式不相匹配，也与此类文本一般应采用的句式不符（此处不宜以 we should ... 主导全句，而应该考虑使用被动句式）。还有一个比较严重的问题，那就是译者在语言能力方面的不足。诸如 two piece of metals，It should also note that make prior ensure ...，Oxidization must be aroused when the iron or steel is heated，There are diversities of welded shapes，以及 it is usually adopted V-shaped welding 等涉及用词、搭配和语法上的缺陷，应尽量避免。

　　译文二的情况与译文一大致相当，也存在不少需要改进的地方。译者固然已作出了相当大的努力，但就其最终所呈现出的效果来评判，在专业性、准确性和逻辑合理性等方面仍有待进一步提高。此处仅举几个处理欠妥的例子：two metals（此似可理解为"两种金属"，而文中的"两块金属"则宜译为 two pieces of metal）；... is the so-called bonding（此不但和原文意思有出入，且 bonding 一词也令人费解）；the metal turns into plastic character（尤其 character 一词可谓莫名其妙）；Then, you pressure the junctions together（此处的 pressure 和 junctions 都属于用词不当，而以 you ... 主导全句则属于句式选用欠妥）和 you need pay attention to the following points（此处也有句式问题，而 need 后面则应该加上 to）等。

第八章

法律翻译

8.1 法律类文本的概念

法律类文本包括法律、法规、条例、裁决书、合同、章程、契约、协议等,还包括证明文件如结婚或离婚证明、公证书、判决书等。

法律类文本不同于自然科学的文本,自然科学没有国别之分,而法律有国别之分,并因所属国家或地区不同而千差万别。因此,翻译法律类文本时,要特别注意不同国家(或司法管辖区)不同的法律制度、法律文化与法律术语。译者不仅要有扎实的源语和目标语的语言功底,还须对源语国家的法律体系与目标语国家的法律体系都有深入的了解,才可能较好地翻译法律类文本。

8.2 法律类文本的基本特征

1. 严肃性

法律类文本用词严肃、庄重、正式,是比较典型的书面语。比如,在法律文本中,通常用 provided（that …）代替日常用语 if,来表示"如果"、"假如"、"在……条件下"或"条件是……"。例如,We will buy everything you produce, provided the price is right. 译为"若价格合适,我们会采购你们的全部产品"。又如：Provided that you have the money in your account, you can withdraw up to £100 a day. 译为"只要账户存款足够,每天可提取不超过100英镑"。又比如,provide that + 从句的表达在法律类文本英译汉时通常译作"规定",而不是"提供"。例如：The final section provides that any work produced for the company is thereafter owned by the company. 译为"最后一节规定,为公司创作的一切产品均为该公司所有"。又如:In no event shall any arbitration award provide a remedy beyond those permitted under these Terms and Conditions, and any award providing a remedy beyond those permitted under this Agreement shall not be confirmed, no presumption of validity shall attach, and such award shall be vacated. 译为"在任何情况下,仲裁裁决规定的救济不得超出本协议条款和条件允许的范围;超出本协议允许范围规定的救济不予确认,亦不得推定为有效,且该等仲裁裁决应予以撤销"。

2. 程式性

法律类文本,尤其是一些合同条款,在句式、格式、内容上往往都有一定的程式性,有许多沿用的行话和套话。例如,在我国的合资经营合同(Equity Joint Venture Contract)中,合同的前半部分一般随合同的具体内容不同而不同,但合同的后半部分一般是关于适用法律(Applicable Law)、违约(Breach of Contract)、保密(Confidentiality)、不可抗力(Force Majeure)、侵权(Infringement)、竞业禁止(Non-compete)、通知(Notice)、争议的解决(Settlement of Disputes)等事项的原则性规定,一般被称为标准条款(Boilerplate Clauses),稍加修改便可适用于许多不同的合同。

法律文本的程式性还反映在它经常使用的一些术语上。例如,法律英语中至今仍有许多以 here, there 和 where 与介词合成的词。here 一般理解为"本法律文件"、"本合同"、"本协议"等。there 通常情况下指"前文刚刚提及的事物",有时则指"本法律文件外的"、"本合同外的"其他文件。whereas 比较特殊,译为"鉴于",一般用于正式文件的开头或句子的开头;whereby 相当于"凭此、借以"。

here 与介词合成的词一般有:

hereafter: (in legal documents) in the rest of this document 以下部分,以下文件/合同中;

hereby: (as a result of this statement) 特此,借此,谨此,兹;

herein: in this place, in this document 在此处,于此;于此文件(声明、合同)中;

hereof: of this, of this document 关于此;在本文件中。例如:a period of 20 days from the date hereof 译为"从本文件日期起的 20 天的时间"

hereto: to this (document/contract) 至此;于此;到此为止;

hereunder：在下文；依此；在本合同中。例如：In the event that any of the conditions referred to in Clause X is not fulfilled on or before the Cut-off Date, then the Purchaser may by notice to the Vendor terminate this Agreement whereupon all obligations and liabilities of the parties hereunder shall cease and determine. 译为"如果在截止日期或之前，X 款提到的任何条件未得到满足，买方可以经通知卖方终止本协议。协议一旦终止，各方在本协议项下的所有义务和责任即刻终止"。（原文靠近句末的"hereunder"翻译为"在本协议项下"。）

herewith：with this letter/document/contract ① 随同此信/文件/合同；随函；② 借此，据此。例如：I enclose herewith a copy of the policy. 译为"我随信附上一份保险单"。

There 与介词合成的词一般有：

therefrom：from the thing mentioned 由此，在那里。例如：The committee will examine the agreement and any problems arising therefrom. 译为"委员会将审查这项协议和由此引起的问题。"

therein：in the place, document, etc. just mentioned 在那里，在其中（刚刚提及的地点、文件等）。例如：The insurance policy covers the building and any fixtures contained therein. 译为"保险单为这座大楼及其中所有的设施保了险"。

thereof：of the thing mentioned 在其中，由此。例如：Is the property or any part thereof used for commercial activity? 译为"这一房产或其中任何部分有用于商业活动吗？"

thereunder：under the thing mentioned 在其下，据此。例如：This savings plan is only available under the Finance Act 1990 and any regulations made thereunder. 译为"这项储蓄计划只根据《1990 年金融法案》及其下规定提供"。

thereafter：其后。

3. 严谨性

法律类文本非常注重表述的严谨性，力求精确、周密。法律文本在拟定一些条款和规定时，需要考虑到问题的每个方面，并顾及条款实施的依据、前提、条件、例外情况等。例如，合同条款中通常有关于发生不可抗力时的通知时限条款：If one Party has been prevented from performing its responsibilities stipulated in the Contract because of an Event of Force Majeure, it shall notify the other Party in writing within fifteen（15）days after the occurrence of such Event of Force Majeure, and both Parties shall use reasonable endeavors to mitigate damages, to the extent possible. 原文中用文字和阿拉伯数字两种方式表述发出通知的时限，译文也如此。译文1："如果一方因不可抗力不能履行其在合同中被规定的责任，应从不可抗力事件发生后十五(15)天内书面通知另一方，双方应尽合理努力，以尽可能减少损失。"译文2："若一方因不可抗力无法履行本合同所规定的责任，该方应从不可抗力事件发生起十五(15)天内书面通知另一方，双方应采取合理措施，尽量减少损失。"这两种译文大致相当。译文1中，within fifteen（15）days after the occurrence of …译为"从不可抗力事件发生后十五(15)天内"是目前业界比较常用的译法。译文2则将 within fifteen（15）days after the occurrence of …译为"从不可抗力事件发生起十五(15)天内"，在时限表述上更为严谨，也更符合英文 within 的原意。

最后，法律类文本还有一个重要特征，即表述追求客观公正，不带主观色彩。因此，法律类文本中较多运用第三人称主语如"甲方"、"乙方"，英文分别是 Party A，Party B，而较少采用第一人称和第二人称主语。此外，英文的法律类文本中经常出现被动态和名词化表达。

8.3 法律文本的翻译策略

法律类文本总的翻译原则是：文字严谨、表述专业、逻辑严密。

法律文本的翻译目的一般有两种：一种是参考用途，仅供客户或读者了解另一国（或地区）的法律法规，此时的译文并不具有法律效力；另一种是法律用途，即译文是具有法律效力的法律文件，例如中外合资企业的合同和章程等。而无论译文是作何种用途，译者都需考虑译文对于读者的影响与后果，都需谨慎严谨，避免以讹传讹或给客户带来损失。因此，法律类文本的首要翻译原则是严谨。其次，一般源语国家与目标语国家的法律制度、法律文化和法律术语普遍存在一些差异，因此在翻译法律类文本时，要注意译文表述的专业性，要用专业的译文表达准确表述原文的信息，并做到逻辑严密、不出差错。

下面介绍法律类文本的具体翻译技巧：
1. may, shall 和 will 的翻译技巧

根据规则内容规定的不同，法律规则分授权性规则与义务性规则。

授权性规则是指规定人们可为或不可为一定行为以及要求其他人为或不为一定行为的规则。授权性规则可以分为职权性规则和权利性规则：① 职权性规则，是规定国家机关职权的规则。国家机关的职权对于国家机关而言，既是其权利（职权），也是其义务（职责），必须行使和履行；② 权利性规则，是规定自然人、法人或者其他组织权利的规则，此种权利，自然人、法人或者其他组织一般可以行使，也可以不行使。授权性规则在法律条文中，多以"可以"、"有权"、"享有"、"具有"等词来表达。

义务性规则是指规定人们应为或勿为一定行为的规则。义务性规则可分为命令性规则和禁止性规则：① 命令性规则是规定人们应为一定行为的规则；② 禁止性规则是规定人们勿为一定行为的规则。

在英文的法律类文本中，一般用 may 表达"权利"（rights），多用于权利性规则中，汉语译文一般为"可以"、"有权"、"享有"等词。shall 用来表达"义务"（obligations）或"职责"（responsibility）时，多用于义务性规则中，可译为"应"、"应当"、"必须"等词；其否定形式 shall not 可译为"不……"、"不得"、"不准"、"不允许"、"禁止"等词。will 则多用来表达当事人的意愿，可译为"将……"或根据语境省略"将"字；其否定形式 will not 则译为"不……"等词。示例如下：

例1：原文：Client acknowledges and agrees that Consultant may, in performing its obligations pursuant to this Agreement, be dependent upon or use data, material, and other information furnished by Client without any independent investigation or verification thereof, and that Consultant shall be entitled to rely upon the accuracy and completeness of such information in performing the Services.

译文：客户确认并同意，顾问根据本协议履行其义务时，可以依赖或使用客户提供的数据、材料和其他信息，而无须进行任何独立的调查和合适，且在履行服务时有权依赖该等信息的准确性和完整性。

例2：原文：Party A shall bear all responsibility for any losses or damages suffered by Party B as a result of any mistakes, errors or omissions caused by

Party A in connection with the processing and packing of the Products.

译文：因甲方加工和包装产品出错、失误或疏漏而使乙方遭受损失或损害时，甲方应承担一切责任。

例3：原文：The company appreciates that whilst the Sponsor will use its reasonable endeavors to discharge its duties as sponsor to the Company and provide the Company with advice and assistance as described above, it remains the primary responsibility of the directors of the Company to ensure that the Company will comply in full with and discharge its responsibilities under the Growth Enterprise Market ("GEM") Listing Rules and other relevant laws and regulations applicable to the Company.

译文：公司理解，虽然保荐人将尽合理努力履行其作为公司保荐人的职责，并向公司提供以上所述的建议和协助，但确保公司完全遵守并履行《创业板上市规则》和适用于公司的其他有关法律和法规规定的责任，仍然是公司董事的主要责任。

2. 复叠词的翻译技巧

法律类文本中有时会有两个近义词或短语放在一起形成复叠词或词组的情况。在翻译时，可以翻译为目标语中的两个近义词或词组，也可以只译成一个词或词组。

例如：原文：During the term of this Agreement, Party A shall undertake, renew and maintain for its *benefit and interest*, and at its own *cost and expense*, the following primary insurance policies.

译文1：在本协议期间，甲方应为自身裨益和利益自费购买、续买和保持下列主要保险。

译文2：在本协议期间，甲方应为自身利益自费购买、续买和保持下列主要保险。

3. 人称代词和物主代词的翻译技巧

英译汉时要注意，并不是每一个英文的人称代词或物主代词都必须并可以译成中文的人称代词或物主代词。例如，英文的非限制定语从句和限制性定语从句中包含先行词和关系代词；可中文译文若因为人称代词和物主代词较多又缺乏原文先行词和关系代词在句型结构上的形式照应，就可能出现指代不清的情况，译者需要酌情处理人称代词和物主代词的翻译。一般说来，除了按原文译成人称代词和代词的处理办法之外,译者有时候可以将原文中的人称代词和物主代词译成其所指代的名词内容,有时可以译成"其",有时可以根据上下文语境省略不译。

例如:原文:Party A shall be responsible <u>at its own cost</u> for the timely provision of <u>all utilities and related installations</u> to such locations close to the boundary of the areas comprising the Expressway, the Ancillary Facilities, the Service Facilities and the Adjacent Land Parcels as designated by Party B and the Operator <u>that</u> may, in the opinion of Party B and the Operator, be required for the development, operation and maintenance thereof, provided that <u>Party B shall pay Party A its normal and reasonable costs</u> in providing the electricity and water consumed in the performance of such development, operation and maintenance works.

译文:甲方应负责及时提供乙方及经营者指定的、紧靠构成高速公路、附属设施、服务设施及毗邻地块的区域边界各地点的所有公用事业设施及配套安装,费用由甲方承担;这些公用事业设施及配套安装,在乙方和经营者看来,可能是高速公路、附属设施、服务设施及毗邻地块的开发、运营和维护所需要的;但条件是:乙方应向甲方支付其在从事上述开发、运营和维护工作中提供所消耗的水、电的正常和合理的费用。

在上述例子中,有几处需要注意。首先,句子开头的 Party A 虽然不是人称代词,却是法律类文本中经常出现的人称表达方法,译文译成相应名词"甲方",Party B 则译作"乙方"。第二处是句首 Party A 后面不远处的 at its own cost,此处的 it 指代"甲方",译文为避免混淆也译出了 it 的具体指代内容,并将原文中的短语分译成短句"费用由甲方承担"。第三处是原句中间位置的关系代词 that,其指代内容是原句中的先行词 all utilities and related installations,译文仍译出此处 that 的具体指代内容"这些公用事业设施及配套安装"。最后一处是 Party B shall pay Party A its normal and reasonable costs in doing sth 中的物主代词 its,代指 Party A's,即"甲方的";此处可以译成"其",也可以译成其具体指代的内容"甲方(的)",即"乙方应向甲方支付甲方在从事上述开发、运营和维护工作中提供所消耗的水、电的正常和合理的费用。"这样译文更为严谨周密,不会产生任何混淆或歧义。

当然,因为英文是一种"形合"的语言,注重语言的结构上的照应,而中文是可以"意合"的语言,有时候一些人称代词或物主代词可以省略不译。在下例中,原文的 it("一方")可以省略不译。

例如:原文:When a Party wishes to transfer all or part of its registered capital contribution to a third party, <u>it</u> shall provide a written notice to the other Party.

译文:一方欲将其全部或部分注册资本出资额转让给第三方时,应向另一方提供书面通知。

4. 被动句的翻译技巧

英文法律类文本中被动句较多,英译汉时可以根据具体情况和中文表达习惯译成主动句,也可以保留被动语态,但不一定都译为"被……",有时可以译为"受……"、"由……"、"予以"、"得以"、"得到"、"达成……"等表达方式。

(1) 译成主动句。

例1:原文:This Agreement <u>is executed</u> in Chinese. If necessary, it <u>may be translated</u> into English.

译文:本协议<u>以中文文本签署</u>。需要时,<u>可译成英文</u>。

例2:原文:The document <u>must be delivered</u> to the office of the secretary of state for filing. Delivery <u>may be made by</u> electronic transmission if and to the extent <u>permitted by</u> the secretary of state. If <u>it is filed in typewritten or printed form</u> and <u>not transmitted</u> electronically, the secretary of state may require <u>one exact or conformed copy to be delivered</u> with the document (except as provided in sections 5.03 and 15.09).

译文:文件<u>必须交付</u>州务卿办公室备案。如果州务卿同意,<u>且在州务卿允许的范围内</u>,文件<u>可以通过电子传输的方式提交</u>。如果文件是<u>以打字或印刷的形式提交备案</u>而不是电子传输<u>的方式提交备案</u>的话,州务卿可以要求随文件一起提交一份相同的或一致的副本(第5.03节和第15.09节另有规定的文件除外)。

(2) 译成被动句。

例1:原文:The formation of this Contract, its validity, interpretation, execution and settlement of disputes in connection herewith <u>shall be governed by</u> the laws of the People's Republic of China ("PRC"), but in the event that there is no published and publicly available law in the PRC governing a particular matter relating to this Contract, reference shall be made to general international commercial practices.

译文：本合同的订立、效力、解释、履行及合同争议的解决，均受中华人民共和国（"中国"）法律管辖。中国正式颁布的法律对本合同相关的某一事项未作规定的，参照国际商业惯例。

例2：原文：If an amount due to the Lender from the Borrower in one currency（the "first currency"）is received by the Lender in another currency（the "second currency"），the Borrower's obligations to the Lender in respect of such amount shall only be discharged to the extent that the Lender may purchase the first currency with the second currency in accordance with normal banking procedures.

译文：如果贷款人以另一货币（"第二货币"）收到借款人到期应付给贷款人的某一货币（"第一货币"）的款额，则借款人对上述贷款人的上述款项的债务应在贷款人可以按正常的银行程序用"第二货币"购买"第一货币"的范围内予以解除。

5. 否定句的翻译技巧

英文文本中表示全部否定的方式，除了在情态动词或助动词后面加 not（如法律类文本中常见的 shall not）外，还有：never（决不），none（谁也不，一点也不），nothing（什么也没有），nowhere（什么地方都不），nobody（谁也不、没有人），neither（也不，两者都不），nor（也不），neither … nor …（既不……也不……，都不）之类的表述。

例如，原文：Neither more than ten（10%）of the aggregate amount of all the purchases, nor more than ten（10%）of the aggregate amount of all the sales, of the Company are obtained or made from the same supplier.

译文：公司总采购量或总销售量中，向同一供应商或客户购买或销售的量均不得超过百分之十（10%）。

需要注意的是，英文文本中还有些由 all，both，always，every，each，much，many，often 等与 not 结合构成的否定句表示部分否定。在英文文本中，not 如果放在上述词之前，部分否定的逻辑合乎汉语的逻辑，不易引起误解。但是，英文文本中有时 not 可以放在上述词之后、谓语中，这种表述与汉语的逻辑习惯相差较大,比较容易造成误解。

例1：原文：Both the windows are not open.

译文：并不是两扇窗户都开着。

例2：原文：All that glitters is not gold.

错译：闪闪发光的东西都不是金子。

正译：闪闪发光的东西并不都是金子。

但在汉译英时,译者宜采用较不易引起歧义的表述方式来翻译否定句。

例如：原文：董事会会议应当有三分之二以上董事出席方能举行。少于六(6)名董事亲自、通过电话或委托代表出席的会议通过的决议无效。

译文：Two-thirds of the Directors constitutes a quorum for Board meetings. Resolutions adopted at a meeting where less than six（6）Directors are present in person, telephonically or by proxy are invalid.

8.4 翻译实例及点评

英译汉

【原文】

1. If any one or more of the provisions contained in this Agreement or any document executed in connection herewith shall be invalid, illegal, or unenforceable in any respect under any applicable law (1), (i) the validity, legality and enforceability of the remaining provisions contained herein or therein shall not in any way be affected or impaired and shall remain in full force and effect (2); and (ii) the invalid, illegal or unenforceable provision shall be replaced by a valid, legal and enforceable provision that comes closest to expressing the true intent of such invalid, illegal or unenforceable provision (3).

2. If any of the provisions of this Agreement is held invalid or unenforceable and unless the invalidity or unenforceability thereof does substantial violation to the underlying intent and sense of the remainder of this Agreement, such invalidity or unenforceability shall not affect in any way the validity and enforceability of any other provisions of this

Agreement except those which the invalidated or unenforceable provisions comprise an integral part of or are otherwise clearly inseparable from (4). That invalidity or unenforceability shall not affect any valid and enforceable application of the remaining provisions, and each such provision shall be deemed to be effective, operative, made, or entered into in the manner and to the full extent permitted by law (5).

（孙万彪，2002：179 - 180）

【译文一】

1. 根据任一适用法律的任一方面，本协议中包含的一个或多个条文，或与此协议相关的任何执行文件无效，非法或不可执行（Ⅰ），(i) 本协议其他条款的有效性、合法性和可执行性不得以任何方式被影响或损害（Ⅱ），并依然全面生效；及(ii) 该无效、非法或不可执行条款由最接近其真正意图的有效，合法和可执行的条款所取代。

2. 本协议任一条款被裁定为无效或不可执行，除非该无效或不可执行条款严重违反了本协议其余条款的基本意图（Ⅳ），该无效或不可执行条款不得以任何方式影响协议中其余条款的有效和可执行性，包含或与无效或不可执行条款明确相关的条款除外在法律允许的最大范围内（Ⅴ），该无效或不可执行条款不得影响其余条款的有效和可执行，严格订立的其余每一条款被视为有效。

（学生课堂练习）

【译文二】

1. 若该协议或其他相关文件中有一项或多项条款无效、非法或在现行法律框架中无法强制执行，(i) 该协议或其他相关文件中其他条款的有效性、合法性和强制性不受影响或损害，依然保有完全的效力；(ii) 有效、合法、有强制力的条款应替换无效、非法、无强制力的条款，并且能同样表达这些无效、非法、无强制力条款的真正意图（Ⅲ'）。

2. 若该协议中的任何条款被认为是无效或无法强制执行，则该协议中其他条款的有效性和强制性不受影响，以下两种情况除外：(i) 这些条款的无效性和无强制性严重破坏了该协议中其他条款的潜在意图和意义；(ii) 其他条款是这些无效、无强制力条款中不可或缺的组成部分或它们之间存在明显密不可分的关系。其无效性和无强制性不影响其他有效、有强制力条款的实际应用,这些其他条款都视为合法有效,已成定例,能在法律框架中发挥最大的效力(V')。

(学生课堂练习)

【译文三】

1. 如果本协议或涉及本协议而签署的任何文件中某条或数条条款,根据任何适用法律在任何方面是无效的、不合法或不能强制执行的,则(i)本协议或涉及本协议而签署的任何文件中的其他条款的效力、合法性和可强制执行性不受任何影响或损害,并仍然有效,(ii)该无效、不合法或不能强制执行的条款应被最能表达其本意且有效、合法和可强制执行的条款所取代。

2. 如果本协议任何条款被认定为无效或不可执行,除非该等无效或不可执行性实质性地违反本协议其余部分的根本意图与含义,否则该等无效或不可执行性不得(以任何方式)影响本协议任何其他条款的有效性或可执行性,但由无效或不可执行的条款构成其不可分割的一部分的条款或不能与无效或不可执行的条款明显分离的条款除外。该等无效或不可执行性不得影响其余任何条款有效的和可强制执行的应用,且每条有效的和可执行的条款应被视为是以法律允许的方式和在法律允许的全部范围内生效、实施、制定或订立的。

(孙万彪,2002:186 - 187)

【点评】

从内容上看,这组英译汉的原文应是某个合同或协议的一部分,涉及该协议的有效性以及在何种条件下方可终止执行的条款等。文中包含较多此类文本常见的复叠词和同义反复词语,如 one or more of the provisions contained, this Agreement or any document executed, invalid, illegal, or unenforceable, validity, legality and enforceability, herein or therein, be affected or impaired, remain in full force and effect, be deemed to be effective, operative 等。总的说来,中译难度不算太大,至少在原文的理解上一般不会对译者构成太大的挑战。真正有难度的是,如何确保以严密的逻辑

和专业的表述把它转换成恰当的中文。从译文一和译文二的表现来看,恐怕还存在着较大的不足,尤其是前者问题更多一些。

译文一以"根据任一适用法律的任一方面"来开头,且不说措辞不够精确,关键是与原文的侧重点有偏差。该句译文中随后的"执行文件"、"非法"和"不得以任何方式被影响或损害"等也不是专业、严谨的法律用语或表述。它的第二个长句中,前面出现的"裁定"和"基本意图"也有表达失当的嫌疑。"裁定"的确可以说是法律用语,一般用于仲裁或法庭的裁决等。但问题是此处对应的原文是 is held invalid or unenforceable,译者应考虑把它翻译成"被认定"才更为合理。至于"基本意图",甚至难称地道的中文,更不能说符合法律文本的语言特征了。还有,在该句的后半部分出现的"包含或与无效或不可执行条款明确相关的条款除外在法律允许的最大范围内",句子不仅不具备规范性,连基本的通顺都成了问题。

译文二的情况相对要好一些,仅有个别表述,如"潜在意图和意义"以及"无效性和无强制性"等需提高和改进。不过,译者在整个文本的处理中,做了两处较大的调整:一是第一句的后半句,二是第二句中"以下两种情况除外"以后的部分。这些调整涉及原文的结构和句式,因此,也必然对原作者所要表达的意图或侧重点有所影响。从效果来看,至少第一处的调整显得并无必要。而且,按照一般的翻译原则,除非迫不得已,译者在考虑对原文的结构和句式等进行调整之前需慎之又慎。

汉 译 英

【原文】

甲方确认,乙方根据本协议向甲方交付的一切技术文件以及与系统的设计、开发、构形、使用、安装、操作和维修相关的一切其他信息,构成乙方的机密信息或专有信息(1),且乙方确认(2),甲方可以根据本协议向乙方提供机密信息或专有信息(合称"机密信息")(3)。各方同意仅为本协议预期的目的而不是其他的目的使用从对方收受到的机密信息。除本协议规定外,本协议并不授予,亦不通过机密信息的转让授予任何其他明示的或暗示的权利,包括但不限于执照、商标、发明权、著作权、专利权或任何其他知识产权。所提供的机密信息不得以任何形式加以复制,但为实现本协议的意向和根据本协议的条款需要复制的除外。除非本协议有规定或另有书面规定(4)，一切机密信息(i)始终为披露方的财产(5)，(ii)且在收受方所需要的使用期届满后必须退还披露方或予以销毁。应披露方要求，收受方应提供经收受方的一名董事或授权的主管人员签字的证明，证明未退还披露方的机密信息已被销毁。

（孙万彪，2002：55－57）

【译文一】

　　Party A confirms that all the technical documents and the system design, development, pattern, use, installation, operation and maintenance related to all other information Party B consigns to Party A under this agreement constitute the secret information or proprietary information of Party B（Ⅰ）. And under the confirmation of Party B（Ⅱ）, Party A can provide secret information or proprietary information (altogether called the "secret information")（Ⅲ） to Party B according to this agreement. Both parties agree that the secret information provided by each other can only be used for intended purpose of this agreement not for other purposes. In addition to the rights specified in this Agreement, this Agreement does not grant rights by the transfer of secret information, including but not limited to licenses, trademarks, inventions, copy rights, patents or any other intellectual property rights are granted under this Agreement. Secret information provided may not be reproduced in any form except the requirements for the intention of the Agreement and in accordance with the terms of the Agreement. Unless otherwise provision or specified in writing（Ⅳ）, all confidential information (i) keeps as the property of offering party（Ⅴ）, (ii) should be returned to the offering party or be destroyed by the receiving party after the using term. Asked by the offering party, the receiving party should offer document signed by one director or one executive to promise that unreturned secret information have been destroyed.

（学生课堂练习）

第八章 法律翻译

【译文二】

　　Party A confirms that, in accordance with this Agreement, <u>all the technical documents and all the other information</u> (Ⅰ') related to the system (including the design, the development, configuration, usage, installation, operation and maintenance) delivered by Party B, are confidential or are Party B's proprietary information. And Party B confirms that according to this Agreement Party A can provide confidential information or proprietary information (hereinafter <u>collectively referred as</u> " Confidential Information") (Ⅲ'). Both parties agree that the received Confidential Information is used for the intended purpose of this agreement, not for any other purposes. <u>Except the provisions of this Agreement</u>, this Agreement does not grant or transfer any other rights (both the expressed and the implied) through Confidential Information, including but not limited to the licenses, trademarks, inventions, copyrights, patents or any other intellectual property rights. The provided Confidential Information cannot be duplicated, excluding the intention used to achieve this Agreement and *the cases* needed to be replicated in accordance with the terms of this Agreement. Unless it is regulated in this Agreement or is written in this Agreement, all the Confidential Information (i) remains the property of the disclosing Party, (ii) and after the expiry, the receiving Party must either return the Confidential Information to the disclosing Party or destroy it. In accordance with the request of the disclosing Party, the receiving Party must prove that the not-returned Confidential Information has been destroyed by providing the document signed by one director or one authorized manager of the receiving Party.

（学生课堂练习）

【译文三】

　　Party A acknowledges that all technical documents delivered to Party A by Party B hereunder, and all other information relating to the design, development, configuration, use, installation, operation and maintenance of the System constitutes confidential or proprietary information of Party B, and Party B acknowledges that Party A may provide confidential or proprietary information to Party B hereunder (collectively referred to as "Confidential Information"). Each Party agrees to use Confidential Information received from the other Party only for the purpose contemplated by this Agreement and for no other purposes. Except as specified in this Agreement, no other rights express or implied, including but not limited to licenses, trademarks, inventions, copyrights, patents, or any other intellectual property rights whatsoever, are granted hereunder or by the conveying of Confidential Information. Confidential Information provided is/shall not to be reproduced in any form except as required to accomplish the intent of, and in accordance with the terms of, this Agreement. Except as provided herein and unless otherwise specified in writing, all Confidential Information (i) remains the property of the disclosing Party, and (ii) must be returned to the disclosing Party or destroyed after the receiving Party's need for it has expired. At the request of the disclosing Party, the receiving Party shall furnish a certificate signed by a director or authorized office of the receiving Party certifying that Confidential Information not returned to the disclosing Party has been destroyed.

(孙万彪,2002:55-57)

【点评】

汉译英的情况往往比英译汉更具挑战性,尤其像此类法律类文本的翻译,因其对语言使用的严密性和规范性有特殊的要求,所以常令译者苦恼不已。译文一和译文二的译者虽已尽了很大的努力,但是,效果仍难以令人满意。译文一中的字、词和句等不同层面的各种疏漏和破绽较多,在此仅举几例略作说明。比如,以 secret information 和 offering party 分别翻译原文的"机密信息"和"披露方"显然不够严密和严谨。作为一般场合中使用的日常用语,secret information(在译文中多次出现)或许并无不妥,但问题是此处涉及的是合同文本,要求就不一样了。至于 offering party,则还存在和原文意思不相吻合的问题。一个 offer 恐难以还原原文的"披露",译文三中的 disclose 才称得上精确。再比如,译文一开头的 and the system design, development, pattern, use, installation, operation and maintenance related to all other information Party B consigns to Party A ... 应译为 and all other information relating to the design, development, configuration, use, installation, operation and maintenance of the System 才算通顺,而且也能更好地表达原文的意思。还有,under the confirmation of Party B 中的 under 应改为 with 才可行;而 Unless otherwise provision or specified in writing 中的 provision or 应予删掉才合乎表达习惯等。

　　比较而言,译文二的质量要高一些,基本可以被接受。当然那些需要改进的细小地方也不在少数。比如,all the technical documents 中的 the 应略去。在 collectively referred as "Confidential Information"中,在 referred 和 as 之间应该加上 to。还有,Except the provisions of this Agreement 也并非合理的表达,等等。

第九章

商务翻译

9.1 商务类文本的概念

商务类文本包括商务沟通、商务活动、商务管理中涉及的各种文本,如:企业介绍、项目介绍、产品描述、行情报告、招商引资公告、商业信函、合同协议等。随着我国改革开放的进程,对外商贸活动日益增加,跨境电子商务逐渐兴起,商务翻译的需求也随之增加。

9.2 商务类文本的基本特征

商务类文本的基本特征是程式化、规范化和专业化。许多商务类文本如商业信函、信用证、商业合同等在格式、句型、内容上都有程式化的特点,具有某种比较统一的风格和特征。例如,商业信函末尾常用"如蒙早日回复,将不胜感激。"英文对应句子一般为: Your early reply will be highly appreciated. 或 Your early reply will be very much appreciated. 随后是大家耳熟能详的结束敬语 Yours sincerely 或 Sincerely 加上落款(中文一般为"……谨上")。又如,在通过询盘、报价初步建立关系后,商业信函主题的标题前经常有 Re:(译为"事由:")或 Subj:(译为"主题:")的字样;信末也常有 Encl.:(译为"随信附上:")的字样。

国际贸易中关于价格的术语: FOB 或 F. O. B. 指 Free on Board(不包括运费和保险费),译为"离岸价、船舷价或船上交货价";C. I. F. 指 cost, insurance, and freight,译为"成本、保险费加运费";而 CFR 或 C&F 指 cost and freight(不包括保险费),译为"成本加运费"。

国际贸易中关于各种单据的表述例如:发票(invoice),提单(Bill of Lading),海运提单(Ocean Bill of Lading),海运保险单(marine insuance),装箱单(packing list),重量单(weight list 或 weight memo),商品检验证(inspection certificate),货物原产地证书(certificate of origin)(出产国领事馆的证明 consular statement of the country of origin),信用证(letter of credit 或 L/C),跟单信用证(documentary letter of credit)等。而表示每种单据一式几份时一般也有以下说法:一式两份(in duplicate 或 in two copies),一式三份(in triplicate 或 in three copies),一式四份(in quadruplicate 或 in four copies),一式五份(in quintuplicate 或 in five copies),一式六份(in sextuplicate 或 in six copies)等。

例如,原文:"本信用证凭受益人开具以我行为付款人按发票金额100%计算无追索权的即期汇票用款,该汇票一式两份,并须附有下列装运单据:发票一式五份,注明合同号码。重量单/装箱单一式两份,载明每箱毛重和净重。制造商出具的品质、数量/重量证明书一式三份。"译文:This credit is available by beneficiary's draft(s), drawn on us, in duplicate, without recourse, at sight, for 100% of the invoice value, and accompanied by the following shipping documents: Invoice in quintuplicate copies, indicating Contract No. Weight Memo/Packing List in duplicate, indicating gross and net weights of each package. Certificate of Quality, Quantity/Weight in 3 Copies issued by the manufacturers.

此外,在正式的企业介绍、项目介绍、合同协议等英文商务类文本中,经常运用结构复杂的长句(包括各种从句、修饰语)来使表述内容更为严谨、精确。被动态、非谓语结构也经常出现,使文本风格更为正式、客观。合同协议的内容较多涉及双方或各方的利益,情态动词 shall 出现频率较高,以明确双方或各方权利、义务。英译汉时往往需要采取分译,而汉译英时根据具体情况及其对应的英文平行文本,有时候可以有意识地采用其英文平行文本中经常出现的句型结构。例如,原文:Insurance shall, to the extent it is available on premium and terms comparable to those abroad and as required by applicable Chinese law, be obtained in China and such policies will be denominated in Renminbi or foreign currency or both, as appropriate. 译文:"如果中国具备与国外保险费和条款相类似的保险,且中国适用法律要求进行保险,则可以在中国投保。保险单根据具体情况应以人民币、外币或两种货币计价。"上例英文表述中,被动态出现了不止一处 Insurance shall be obtained in China, as required by ... 和 such policies will be denominated ... ,行文风格非常正式。英文中还出现了插入语 to the extent ... 来修饰限定主句中在中国投保的前提条件,而译成中文时,则需采取分译,将插入语译成两个条件从句。另一处分译则在于原文是用 and 连接的并列句,译文则用句号隔开这两个并列句。

9.3 商务类文本的翻译策略

商务类文本总的翻译原则是要做到准确性、专业性和规范性。在商务类文本翻译中,要做到这三点,首先必须要熟悉商务方面的相关术语和专业表述,掌握商务方面的专业知识;其次应该多阅读英文和中文商务类文本的平行文本,注意观察各自的行文风格、格式、用词及句型等细节。具体操作时,除了要注意商务术语的翻译、商务类文本(如信用证)的格式外,还应该注意商务类文本中否定句、定语从句、数量词、四字格等的翻译。

1. 术语的翻译策略

最常见的是关于"公司"的术语表述,除了 company(公司,商号),business(企业,商行等),corporate(公司的,法人的)之外,还有 concern(公司,商行,企业),exchange(交易所,公司),subsidiary(子公司),trust(托拉斯,指为减少竞争等联合的企业组织),以及一些缩略词,如 Inc.(或 inc.,完整形式为 incorporated,置于公司名称之后)。

例1:原文:Broadway Autos is a subsidiary of Broadway International Inc. of Portland, Oregon.

译文:百老汇汽车公司是设在俄勒冈州波特兰市的百老汇国际公司的子公司。

例2:原文:A "person" includes any individual, company, corporation, firm, partnership, joint venture, association, organization, trust, state or agency of a state.

译文:"人",包括任何个人、公司、社团、商行、合伙企业、合资企业、协会、组织、托拉斯、国家或国家机构。

国际贸易中还有许多关于询价方面的术语,例如:询盘/询价(inquiry),发盘/报价(offer),实盘/确盘(firm offer),虚盘(indefinite offer),还盘/还价(counter-offer),承诺/接受(accept 或 acceptance)等。

2. 否定句的翻译策略

英文文本中一般用 no, not, never, none, nothing, nowhere, nobody, neither, nor, neither... nor... 之类加上被修饰的成分表示全部否定。例如:The price I give you is lower rate and we have never quoted such low price to other of our clients. 译为"给你的价格是最低的,我们还从未报给其他客户如此低的价格"。

若句子已有上述否定标志,而后面又有 without... 就构成双重否定句。一般双重否定句可以译为双重否定句或肯定句。例 1:Expansion or reorganization should not be planned without the proper analysis of the accounting information. 双重否定译法译为"没有对会计资料进行恰当的分析,就无法计划公司的发展和重组"。肯定译法译为"只有在对会计资料进行恰当的分析后,才可以计划公司的发展和重组"。例 2:Unusual occurrences in exporting are not uncommon. 双重否定译法译为"不寻常的事件在出口的情况并不少见"。肯定译法译为"在出口贸易中不寻常的事情也是常见的"。

英文中有些句子在形式上是肯定句,但包含一些含有否定意义的词,此时在译文中需要注意译出原文的否定含义,并且根据不同情况可以选择保留原句被否定部分或转译被否定的部分。例如:In some cases shipments may be delivered directly to the retail store, bypassing the distribution center. 译为"有时货物可以直接运给零售商,不经过配送中心"。

3. 定语从句的翻译策略

英文中的定语从句可以译为定语,也可以根据不同情况选择译为谓语、状语等,或者译为另外一个单句。例 1:LVMH, the French luxury goods group, (which owns a string of prestige, brand names ranging from Louis Vuitton luggage to Hennessy cognac,) saw net profits rise by 7% to FFr. 1.29bn ($239 million) from FFr. 1.21 billion in the first half of the year in spite of the downturn in the luxury products industry. 译为"路易威登是一家法国奢侈品集团公司,(它)拥有从路易威登箱包到轩尼诗干邑的一系列

名牌产品。尽管奢侈品行业有下降趋势,今年上半年该集团净利增长7%,从12.1亿法郎升至12.9亿法郎(相当于2.39亿美元)"。原文较长,译文采用了分译,将which引导的定语从句分译为一个单独的补充说明的句子,并将原文谓语动词saw net profits rise ... in spite of ...译成具有自身完整主谓宾的句子。

例2:Wines and spirits, which have borne the brunt of the economic slowdown, suffered a fall in sales to FFr. 4.44bn from FFr. 4.76 billion, while operating profits slipped to FFr. 1.26bn from 1.51bn. 译为"葡萄酒和烈酒受到经济衰退的直接冲击,销售额从47.6亿法郎下降到44.4法郎,营业利润也从15.1亿法郎下滑到12.6亿法郎"。原文中which引导的定语从句变成了译文中第一个短句中主语后面的谓语陈述部分。

4. 数量词的翻译策略

商务类文本中,数词、量词常常与其源语货币、度量衡单位联系在一起,无论是英译汉还是汉译英都必须准确翻译,不出差错。即使原文只在第一处数字旁写明货币符号,而后面的数字并未每个都标上货币符号时,译者翻译成译入语时,也得与原作者求证后或依据上下文给每个数字都加上货币符号。例如:Luggage and leather products were also affected by Japan's instability, but managed to increase operating profits to FFr. 890 million from 827m on sales up to FFr. 2.33bn from 2.15bn. 译为"日本经济的不稳定也影响到行李箱包和皮革制品的销售,但这些产品的营业利润还是从8.27亿法郎上升到8.9亿法郎,销售额从21.5亿法郎上升到23.3亿法郎。"原文中,用画线标示的两个数字只有表示百万的million的缩写字母m和表示十亿的billion的缩写字母bn,但没有货币单位,但从上下文可以判断出是法郎(FFr.)。但译文并不会直译为"从8.27亿法郎上升到8.9亿"和"从21.5亿法郎上升到23.3亿",而是给每个数字都明确地加上货币单位,译为"从8.27亿法郎上升到8.9亿法郎"和"从21.5亿法郎上升到23.3亿法郎"。

当涉及度量衡单位时,汉译英的译文中可以将其适当转换为译入语的通用度量衡单位及换算后的数字来表达,但未必需要过度转换。例如,将中文的"2斤"表达为英文的"1 kilogram"即可,但未必需要换算成"... ounce"或"... pound";将中文的"10里"表达为"5 kilometers"即可,但未必需要换算成"... miles"。英译汉时,有时可以直译保留原文度量衡单位,例如"5 ounces"可以就译为"5盎司",此时未必需要译者过度换算译为"141.75克",既简洁明了,也避免出错。

当原文只是一种约数表达或习惯说法时,此时原文表达中的数量词未必直译或一一译出。例如,a half-baked idea 是"不成熟的想法",又如:——Can you come down a little? —Sorry, its one price for all. 译为"——你能便宜一点卖吗? ——对不起,不二价。"one price 或 one price only 在商业、贸易用语中一般译为"不二价",指固定价格政策或单一价格政策。

5. 四字格的翻译策略

四字格通常指汉语中由四个字构成的成语(有些不止四个字)、词组或短语,四字格的表述形式在各种商务文本如企业介绍、产品描述、行情报告、商业信函、合同协议中比较常见。例如:prompt shipment 迅速装船,a flow of orders 大量订单,an initial order 首次订货;又如 Citibank National Association 花旗银行,Bank of China 中国银行,HSBC 汇丰银行(英文全称是 The Hongkong and Shanghai Banking Corporation,直译为香港上海汇丰银行,简称汇丰),China Merchants Bank 招商银行等。

当一些汉语成语与英文表达已经有约定俗成的译法时,译者可以遵循约定俗成的译法,如汉语的"谋事在人,成事在天"译成英文一般是"Man proposes, God disposes";反之亦然。诸如此类的成语及俗语的翻译,译者可以遵循已有的表达。

另外还有一些四字格不能算成语,但已经成为比较固定的四字词组,例如本章开头提到的"如蒙早日复信,不胜感激。"译文可以译成"We will be very grateful to your early reply." 或 "Your early reply will be very much appreciated."常见的四字格词组的逻辑关系有并列(如:平等互利 equality and mutual benefit)、重复(如:招商引资 attract investment)、目的(如:退耕还林 return cultivated land to forest or pastures)、途径(如:按劳分配 distribution according to performance)、动宾(如:优势互补 complement each other's advantages)等。在这类词组中,把握原文的逻辑关系、信息内涵并译出原文的真正信息是关键所在。

需要说明的是,四字格是汉语行文的一大特色,英译汉时,可以在译文中适当采用四字格的润色处理方法。汉译英时则不能一概而论,需根据实际情况,直译意译相结合,以译出原文信息、不过分拘泥于原文格式的翻译处理为主。如在一些景区告示的翻译中,考虑到译入语景区文化及译入语读者的期待视野,一些汉语原文中的四字词组并不一定需要原原本本地直译成英语。例如:某景区告示中承诺:"① 牢固树立'以人为本'的服务理念,信守'游客至上'的服务宗旨,尽一切所能落实游客提出的合理化建议。② 工作人员服务规范,持证上岗,坚持微笑服务,文明待客,尽一切所能让游客感受到宾至如归的温馨。"如果直译的话,可能译文会采取类似以下的处理方法:1. With the "human-centered" philosophy as our service concept and the belief that "customer satisfaction is the top priority" as our principle, we will make every effort to implement tourists' proper suggestions. 2. The trained staff with certificates will welcome you with smiles, standard services and hospitality, hoping it will make you feel warm and at home. 而该译文的译者(上海外国语大学高级翻译学院的姚锦清教授)建议分别译为:We promise to provide you with the best possible services and appreciate your comments and suggestions for improvement. 和 We promise that our staff will act according to professional codes of conduct and ensure you are served with hospitality. 其原因是,"以人为本"原本用于政务宣传文本,一般在国家领导人讲话中出现,但在国内各种语境中被过度使用,景区告示尚不需如此"泛政治化"。因此译者并未直译第 1 句的"以人为本"、"游客至上",而是意译出汉语原文的深层内涵"provide you with the best possible services"(为游客提供尽可能好的服务);在第 2 句中,因为译者也并未直译"服务规范"、"持证上岗"、"微笑服务"等,而是采取意译的方法。话说回来,如果这些四字短语直译成英语(如 serve with smiles)也会让人感觉很怪。

9.4 翻译实例及点评

英译汉

【原文】

London: Industrial production in Britain fell a seasonally adjusted 0.3 percent in October (1) the Central Statistics Office reported Wednesday in a preliminary report. Output (2) was pulled down by a loss of North Sea oil production after the Piper Alpha platform disaster in July in which 167 people died, the office said. Although October production (3) showed a 2.2 percent increase from a year earlier, the decline from September (4) surprised analysts, who had expected an increase of about 0.8 percent (5). Production had risen 0.4 percent in September (6), revised upward from an earlier estimate of a 0.5 percent drop (7).

（戚云方，1996：256-257，311）

【译文一】

　　伦敦：周三，中央统计办公室在初步报告中表示，十月份英国工业生产指数周期性下降0.3个百分点（Ⅰ）。统计办还表示，七月发生的阿尔法平台事故造成167人死亡，此次事故使北海石油公司蒙受巨大损失，拉低了英国工业产量（Ⅱ）。尽管十月份工业产量（Ⅲ）同比增长2.2个百分点，但自9月份以来的下滑（Ⅳ）还是令分析家们大惊失色，因为他们原以为自九月以来会产生0.8个百分点的增长（Ⅴ）。九月份产量上涨0.4个百分点（Ⅵ），与预计的0.5个百分点相比有所下滑（Ⅶ）。

（学生课堂练习）

【译文二】

　　伦敦：中央统计局在周三发布的一份初步调查报告中称，由于季节差异，英国的工业产值十月份下降了0.3个百分点（Ⅰ'）。办公室发言人称，7月份派珀·阿尔法平台发生的事故导致167人丧生，北海石油产量下降，因而石油输出量（Ⅱ'）下跌。虽然十月份产量（Ⅲ'）较去年同期上升了2.2个百分点，分析师们仍然对九月份以来产量的下跌幅度（Ⅳ'）感到吃惊。此前，他们预期会上升0.8个百分点（Ⅴ'）。九月份产量上升了0.4个百分点（Ⅵ'），扭转了之前下降0.4个百分点的预期（Ⅶ'）。

（学生课堂练习）

【译文三】

　　伦敦：中央统计署星期三公布的一份初步报告表明，英国10月份工业产值经季节性调整后下滑0.3%[0.3个百分比]。据该署报告，工业产值因7月份派珀尔·阿尔法（Piper Alpha）（钻井）平台爆炸北海石油产量受损而下降，在那次事故中有167人丧生。尽管10月份的工业产值较去年同期/同比增长了2.2%，但与9月份相比的增速下降使分析家感到惊讶，他们原来预计10月份的工业产值比9月份增长约0.8%。9月份的工业产值上升了0.4%，由原先0.5%的跌幅估计转为上升/与此前预计的0.5%的跌幅相比，不降反增。

　　[备注：今年10月份与去年10月份相比是同比；今年10月份产值与今年9月份产值相比是环比。]

（戚云方，1996：256-257，311，有所改动）

【点评】

　　这组英译汉比较简短，但若要译得好，除了应具备一定的双语运用能力，还要对经济方面的知识有所了解。翻译过程中有两点要特别予以关注，一是对于关键词的把握，二是对于一些数字的理解和翻译。

　　在对关键词的把握上，原文的四个句子以四个类似的单词或词组 Industrial production，Output，October production 和 Production 开头。这四个词贯穿原文始终，究竟该怎么译，对译者的能力是一个考验。译文一分别译为："工业生产指数"、"工业产量"、"工业产量"和"产量"；而译文二处理成："工业产值"、"石油输出量"、"产量"和"产量"。也就是说，对于这两篇译文而言，这四个词的所指是不尽相同的。可是，对照译文三，这四个词却均被译为"工业产值"。于是，差异就出来了，译文的优劣情况自然也就一目了然了。

　　对于原文中一些数字的理解和翻译，译文一和译文二一开始的"下降0.3个百分点"当然没什么好讨论的，此后的"同比增长2.2个百分点"和"较去年同期上升了2.2个百分点"的翻译也与原文相符。但随后对于0.8、0.4和0.5个百分点的处理就出现偏差了。在这一点上，译文一尤其显得混乱、不清晰和不准确。

　　此外，译文一、二对于原文中 fell a seasonally adjusted 0.3 percent in October 中的 seasonally 和 the decline from September surprised analysts 中的 the decline from September 的理解和翻译也有误差。

汉译英

【原文1】

　　商品检验：双方同意以制造产出具之品质及数量或重量检验证明书作为

卖方向付款银行议付货款单据之一(1)。但货物的品质及数量或重量的检验应按下列规定办理。

(A) 一般货物：货到目的口岸 60 天内经中国商品检验局复验(2)，如发现品质或数量或重量与本合同规定不符时(3)，除属于保险公司或船行负责者外(4)，买方凭中国商品检验局出具的检验证明书向卖方提出退货或索赔(5)。

（戚云方，1996：132 - 133）

【译文一】

Inspection：Both parties involved agree to take the inspection certificate of the quality, quantity or weight of the products as one of the payment documents to the bank for the seller (Ⅰ). However, the inspection of the quality, quantity or weight of goods must follow the regulations below.

(A) General cargo：cargo will be reinspected by the China Commodity Inspection Bureau within 60 days after arriving the port of destination (Ⅱ). If it is found that its quality, quantity or weight is inconsistent with the provisions of this contract (Ⅲ), the buyer can demand for returning goods or claim for compensation with the inspection certificate issued by China Commodity Inspection Bureau (Ⅴ), apart from which are under the responsibility of insurance companies or shipping head (Ⅳ). All the costs and losses caused by returning goods or refunds (including inspection charges) should be paid by the seller.

（学生课堂练习）

【译文二】

Goods Inspection：The two sides agree to use inspection certificate (including quality, quantity and weight statistics) as one of receipts that the seller give to the paying bank in times of negotiating or paying back loans (Ⅰ'). However, the inspection of the quality and quantity of goods or weight should be according to the following regulations.

(A) General cargo：Cargo, arrived to the port of destination, would be reinspected by the China Commodity Inspection Bureau (Ⅱ') within 60 days. If the quality, quantity or weight is not consistent with the provisions, the insurance company and shipping lines should take responsibility (Ⅳ'), besides, the buyer can claim return and compensation from the seller with the inspection certificate issued by China Commodity Inspection Bureau. All the costs (including inspection fees) and losses due to return or compensation would be paid by the seller.

（学生课堂练习）

【译文三】

Inspection: It is mutually agreed that the certificates of quality and quantity or weight issued by the Manufacturer shall be part of the documents to be presented to the paying bank for negotiation of payment. However, the inspection of quality and quantity or weight shall be made in accordance with/(或者 according to, in conformity with, in line with) the following.

(A) For General Cargo: In case the quality, quantity or weight of the goods be found not in conformity with/(或者 found inconsistent with) *those stipulated in this Contract*/(或者 the provisions of this contract) after reinspection by the China Commodity Inspection Bureau within 60 days after arrival of the goods at the port of destination, the Buyers shall return the goods to or lodge claims against the Sellers for compensation of losses upon the strength of Inspection Certificate issued by the said Bureau, with the exception of those claims for which insurance companies or shipping lines（船行）are liable/responsible.

（戚云方，1996：132-133，有所改动）

【点评】

这组汉译英的原文属于典型的商务文本类型，言简意赅、措辞严谨，其内容也体现出较强的专业特点。与此相对应，在翻译过程中如果要想取得好的效果，就应当遵循此类文本翻译的一些基本要求，即尽量照顾到译文的准确性、专业性和规范性。

从译文一和译文二的表现来看,还存在着一些问题。问题主要存在于专业性和规范性不足上面,由于两篇译文对这两方面的处理不甚理想,结果就对译文的准确性造成了损害。

第一段:对于原文的第一句,针对"双方同意……"的翻译,若采用被动态 It is mutually agreed,会比采用主动态 The two sides agree 感觉更为正式,更符合合同条文正式、严谨、严肃的风格。可惜,两位译者采用的都是主动语态。此外,译文一、二均未能准确译出"作为卖方向付款银行议付货款单据之一"这一部分。无论是译文一中的 as one of the payment documents to the bank for the seller,还是译文二中的 as one of receipts that the seller give to the paying bank in times of negotiating or paying back loans,都有不足。

第二段:对于原文中"货到目的口岸60天内经中国商品检验局复验"部分,译文一的翻译比译文二要好。接下来,对"除属于保险公司或船行负责者外"部分的翻译,两个译文都出了点差错,意思表达不确切。

此外,译文一的 If it is found that its quality, quantity or weight is inconsistent with the provisions of this contract, the buyer can demand for returning goods or claim for compensation … 看起来更像是日常英语,似乎缺少了商务合同文本应有的专业性和严谨性。类似的问题还有不少,如 weight statistics, the two sides, one of receipts 等,要么语言表达不准确,要么不符合文本的语言特征。对照译文三的选词用词和句式的使用,读者可以做出判断。

【原文2】

(B) 医药商品:进口的医药商品应受中华人民共和国法律及规章的约束,凡不合格的医药商品不准进口(1)。双方同意本合同所订此类商品之品质应以货物到达目的口岸后60天内经中国商品检验局检验并以该局所签发之检验证为最后依据,双方均须遵守之(2)。不合格货物卖方应予收回,并赔偿买方货款及因退货而遭受的运输、储藏、保险、利息、检验等费用损失。

(戚云方,1996:132-133)

【译文一】

(B) Pharmaceutical products: pharmaceuticals imported into China are subject to laws and regulations of the People's Republic of China, all unqualified medical products are not allowed to be imported (Ⅰ). The parties agree that the quality of the order for such goods of this contract shall be in Canon of 60 days after the goods arrive at the destination port of China commodity inspection bureau inspection and the inspection certificate issued by the bureau for the basis, the two sides are to be complied with (Ⅱ). Unqualified goods the seller shall take back, and damages suffered by the buyer's payment and return the transportation, storage, insurance, interest, and inspection costs.

(学生课堂练习)

【译文二】

(B) For pharmaceutical: The imported pharmaceutical goods shall be bound by the laws and regulations of the People's Republic of China, such disqualified goods shall be prohibited to be imported (Ⅰ'). Both sides agree that the quality of such designated goods herein shall take the inspection certificates issued by the China Commodity Inspection Bureau after inspection the goods within 60 days since the arrival at the port of destination as final (Ⅱ'), and binding upon both sides. The sellers shall take back all the disqualified goods and compensate the buyers for the expenses of the goods as well as the losses as a result of the return of the goods, such as freight, storage, premium, interest and inspection charges etc.

(学生课堂练习)

【译文三】

(B) For Pharmaceuticals/Pharmaceutical products: Pharmaceuticals imported into China are subject to laws and regulations of the People's Republic of China. Disqualified pharmaceuticals are prohibited to be imported. It is mutually agreed/(或者 Both sides agree) that for the quality of the contracted goods in this category, the Inspection Certificate issued by the China Commodity Inspection Bureau after inspecting the goods within 60 days from the date of arrival at the port of destination shall be taken as final and binding upon both Parties. The Sellers shall take back all the disqualified goods and compensate the Buyers for the value of the goods plus all losses sustained due to return of the cargo, such as freight, storage charges, insurance premium, interest, inspection charges, etc.

(戚云方,1996:132-133,有所改动)

【点评】

和本章的前一组汉译英一样,这里所选的原文内容也属于商务合同文本的范畴。

译文一:除了首句还算可以接受以外,余下的部分在行文上、遣词造句上漏洞还是比较多,有些地方的问题甚至十分严重。比如,在以下这个相对冗长的句子中,就有几个可疑之处。The parties agree that the quality of the order for such goods of this contract shall be in Canon of 60 days after the goods arrive at the destination port of China commodity inspection bureau inspection and the inspection certificate issued by the bureau for the basis, the two sides are to be complied with. 一是 Canon 一词究竟指什么,无从说起。二是 the two sides are to be complied with 也不妥,这里的 comply with 一般都用在主动句中,不会出现在被动句中,这是基本的用法问题。第三,从语法的角度来看,这个句子也不符合语法规范,可以说从 destination port 之后就陷入了混乱。译者把多个不同层次的信息挤进了一个句子里面,但与此同时没有相应地增加有关的动词或从句以理清关系(如能在 China commodity inspection bureau 之后加上 has inspected the goods,再在 inspection certificate 以及 issued 之间加上 has been 就会好一些,但也只是略有所改善)。若要从根本上完善这个句子,还要作综合的考虑。另外,译文中 China commodity inspection bureau 中的后三个单词的首字母也应大写。

译文二:总体情况略好一些,但也不乏低级的失误和令人产生疑惑的地方。比如,一开头的 The imported pharmaceutical goods shall be bound by the laws and regulations of the People's Republic of China 中 be bound by 的使用就是一个比较严重的问题。be bound by 的确有"受到约束"的意思，只不过它都被用来指某人受到何种约束。请看例句：We don't want to be bound by any excessive rules. /We also agree to be bound by the Terms and Conditions on the reverse hereof. /Subscriber of the Site will be bound by the terms and conditions of this Agreement. 因此，像译文二把 The imported pharmaceutical goods 置于句首作为主语，再以 shall be bound by the laws and regulations ... 如此处理有所不妥。对照译文三的处理，Pharmaceuticals imported into China are subject to laws and regulations of the People's Republic of China. Disqualified pharmaceuticals are prohibited to be imported. 这里的 are subject to laws and regulations ... 就是标准、准确的译法。此外，该句的后半部分，即 such disqualified goods shall be prohibited to be imported，与前半句不协调、不匹配，特别是 such 一词放在这里很突兀。对照译文三，这个部分完全可以独立出来，成为第二个句子。即便要把它放在第一句里，至少也需要在逗号后面加上一个 and。

第十章

政务宣传翻译

10.1 政务宣传类文本的概念

政务宣传类文本种类较多,包括政府机构颁布的行政法规、命令、通知、公告,政府机构网站的介绍、信息发布等材料,也包括事业单位如国家公立高校及其网站上的介绍内容、信息发布等材料。

政务宣传类文本不同于科技类文本、商务类文本(如合资企业的商务合同),后两者在一些术语表达、行文、格式、风格上都有比较一致的中英文表达与行文规范。因国别、地域、政治文化背景与思维方式不同,不同政务宣传类文本的行文风格会有所差别。中文的政务宣传类文本中多用四字格(例如中共十八大报告以及李克强总理政府工作报告中出现的"简政放权"一词,其官方对应英译是"streamline administration and delegate more power to lower levels"),喜用对仗、排比等,行文有时较庄严,间或引用俚语、俗语、古今中外名言警句和诗句等来托物寄情、抒发情怀或表示强调等(例如国家主席习近平讲话中的"打铁还须自身硬")。英文的政务宣传类文本讲究语言形式的逻辑性与严谨性,提倡语言的自然流畅,有时也引用名言、诗句、警句等来加强文本表达效果。

在进行政务宣传类文本英中互译时,译者既要注意源语国家与译入语国家不同的政治制度、表达习惯与行文规范,还要有政策意识和政治意识,做到既传递原文信息又不出现政治性的错误。

10.2　政务宣传类文本的基本特征

　　政务宣传类文本的首要特征是政策性和信息性。政策性是指因为政府机构颁布的行政法规、命令、通知、公告等政策性和信息性都极强，译者需要保持对国家大政方针、相关政策的高度关注与政治敏感，仔细衡量待用词汇的政治含义，才能做好政务宣传文本的英中互译工作。在一些敏感问题的表述上，译者还需要遵循特定的译法，不出差错。而对一些新事物、新政策、新提法、新表述的原文与官方译文表述，译者要注意搜集、整理与积累，不断扩充、更新自己的知识储备。

　　信息性要求译者准确传递原文本的信息内涵，面对信息量较大的原文文本，译者需要仔细分析其逻辑层次与深层内涵，不遗漏、不啰嗦，清晰地用译入语语言表达出来。面对一些原文文本不够精练、不够清晰的政务宣传类文本时，译者还需在脑海中先对原文进行处理，再译成译文。还需要注意的一点是，有时候政务宣传文本会引用译入语国家的名言、警句、诗句，译者将原文译成译入语时，需要搜索到这些名言、警句、诗句的原有的译入语表达，而非自己另行翻译。

　　政务宣传类文本的第二个特征是规范性。政务宣传类文本的发出者往往是各级政府机构，代表着各级政府形象，其行文必须具有规范性。政务宣传类文本中的一个重要部分即政府公文更是如此。具体而言，政府公文，如通报、公告、通告、通知等的标题命名方法、正文组成内容、标题与正文字体颜色及大小、公文中标点符号用法、数字用法等均有严格规定。而对于政府网站上的一些介绍性文字，虽然不如公布的政府公文的格式严谨，但相关表述还是要遵循政府公文中一贯的规范表述。

　　政务宣传类文本的第三个特征是其显著的宣传性特征。无须讳言，无论是美国的白宫网页，还是我国各级政府机构的政务宣传类文本，都有此特征。例如，当今美国总统奥巴马每周一次的 radio speech，不仅是宣传其执政理念、执政方针的宣传工具，还被他用来团结民众、号召民众支持他"减税"和医改法案的政策并呼吁民众反对反对派的斗争工具，还经常被用来向世界宣扬美国精神、美国理念。然而，政务宣传类文本的宣传性特征并不意味着译者可以将一些宣传色彩过浓的字眼原原本本地转换成译入语，相反，此时译者有时候需要淡化翻译文本文字表面的宣传色彩,这样才更容易被译入语读者所接受。在这一点上,好的政务宣传类文本(包括原文本与翻译文本)如同好的广告,不会引起其目标受众的反感,不会轻易让人察觉这是广告,但又起到了优秀广告的广而告之的宣传效果,让受众在不经意间自然地接受它。

10.3 政务宣传类文本的翻译策略

政务宣传类文本总的翻译原则是准确性、专业性和规范性。译者既需要准确把握原文的意思,也需要用符合译入语表达习惯的语言来表述,尤其要注意文化差异导致的一些中英文词汇在内涵和外延上的差异,避免译文表述在译入语读者中引起误解、歧义或负面效应。在具体操作时,要注意以下四点:

1. 吃透原文精神、加强政策意识

政务宣传类文本包含许多政策性信息,不同国家的政务宣传类文本还往往带有其本国的政治立场与主张,具有较强的政治性和政策性。因此,译者在翻译政务宣传类文本时,一定要吃透原文意思、保持政治敏感、加强政策意识。英译汉时,当遇到一些原文在敏感问题的表述、情感色彩与政治立场上与译入语社会文化中的文本表述、情感色彩与政治立场截然相反的情况时,译者即使不进行"归化"式翻译,也至少要进行"中性化"处理与翻译。而汉译英时,当涉及一些敏感问题或领土主权时,译者应译出原文内涵。如汉译英时,"台湾"一般译为"Chinese Taipei"或"Taiwan, China"。例如:"大陆和台湾虽然尚未统一,但两岸同属一个中国的事实从未改变。"译文:Although the mainland and Taiwan are yet to be reunified, the fact that they belong to one and the same China has never changed. 此处,"尚未统一"译成"are yet to be reunified"比否定感更强的"are not yet reunified"更符合原文意思与内涵。又如:"支持工业反哺农业。"译文:Encourage industry to support agriculture in return for agriculture's earlier contribution to its development. 译文清晰地传递了"反哺"的内涵,让人更明白这么做的理由。

2. 优化原文文字及译文处理

优化原文文字及译文处理可以细分为以下5点:

(1) 纠错——纠正原文表述的错误

面对一些原文表述不够准确、缺乏专业性和规范性的地方,译者需要灵敏

地判断、识别出原文的错误,自行纠正或请原文作者修改后再翻译。例如:"中华人民共和国合同法由中华人民共和国第十届全国人民代表大会常务委员会第二十八次会议于2007年6月29日通过。"此句主语应该增加书名号,改为《中华人民共和国合同法》。译文可为:The Labor Contract Law of the People's Republic of China was adopted at the 28th Meeting of the Standing Committee of the Tenth National People's Congress of the People's Republic of China on June 29, 2007.

(2) 地道——用地道、清晰的译文表述原文信息

一些外宣文本、机构介绍等的译文可以向国外同类文章的语言表述靠拢,用清晰、地道的译文传达原文信息,这样更容易使译文取得好的交际效果。这也是我们一贯强调的"平行文本"在职业翻译中的作用。例如,国内公立大学网站推出英文版时,"学校概况"可以翻译为英文的 About Us(也可将其中的 Us 替换成具体的大学的英文名字),而不一定要逐字译为 General Situation。国外大学网站中一般有 About 一项,内容是 About Us 之类的介绍(如哈佛大学网站就有 About Harvard College 网页)。

一些政策性更强的政务宣传类文本也是如此。近年来,政务宣传类文本的翻译方式发生了一些变化:在语言上更注重细节,不再套用或搬用过去一些常用的甚至看起来还不错的翻译。例如,"信息化"不再译为 informationization,因为 informationization 属于中国人造的英语单词,并未被英语国家人民接受。可译为 IT application。"科学发展(观)"不再是最初译成的 scientific development,而是 The Scientific Outlook on Development,有时也译为 develop the economy in a scientific way,因为 scientific development 回译为中文实际是"科学(领域)的发展"。"稳增长"不再译为 to stabilize economic growth,因为 stabilize 有 make sth stable or become firm 之意,to stabilize economic growth 反而有了"使 economic growth 僵化在一个固定的水平上"的歧义。目前"稳增长"可以译为 to ensure stable growth。还有非常重要的一点,从党的十八大报告英文版中可以看出:"政治体制改革"不再译为 political restructuring,因为 restructuring 有"推倒重来"的意思;目前"政治体制改革"更常译为 political reform 或者 reform of the political structure。此外,"基层民主"并不译为 primary-level democracy 或 grass roots level(草根阶层)democracy,而译为 community-level democracy,所以"基层民主不断发

展"可译为 Community-level democracy has steadily developed。"文明"不能机械地译为 civilization，在中国政治语汇中，"文明"的使用在语义上要比英文中的 civilization 广得多，不能机械地对译；"文明"根据上下文有时可以译为 progress。如"精神文明"不宜译为 spiritual civilization，可译为 cultural and ethnical progress，因为 cultural 指"文化的"，ethnical 指"人种的、种族的"。"生态文明"不宜译为 ecological civilization，可译为 ecological progress。

（3）不如不译——冗余信息可以简化或不译

需要注意的是，中文与英文有时行文风格极为不同。例如，有时候中文会用许多华丽的形容词来形容某个事物、某处开发区或某个项目，而英文读者则对一些更实实在在的信息感兴趣。又例如，一些地方政府及其机构在一些报告、总结中常用一些口号（此口号一般不具有全国影响力与认知度），此时如果逐字翻译为英文，效果不一定好，也不一定为读者所欣赏。因此，当面对以下两种情况时，我们主张冗余信息可以简化或者不译。一种是翻译描形状物的文字时，各种空洞华丽的词藻不可硬译，一般"虚"译为"实"，有些过虚的形容性文字可以简化或不译。另一种是对于一些地方政府部门出于工作需要临时编撰的一些口号、标语可以不译，译出原文真正的信息点即可。

此外，还有一种情况，原文信息即使不"冗余"，但未必为译入语读者感兴趣，或者并不是译入语读者重视的信息，在这种情况下，译者可以根据自己的理解酌情简化原文或省译部分信息。例如，中国某公立大学网站汉语介绍中写道："XX 大学，……<u>是教育部直属并与上海市共建、进入国家'211 工程'建设的全国重点大学</u>，……<u>筚路蓝缕，奋发有为</u>，现已发展成一所培养高端国际型外语人才的多科性、国际化、高水平特色大学，<u>蜚声海内外</u>"，其对应的英文介绍有明显的简化与省译："XX University ... is an internationally recognized, prestigious academic institution distinctive for its multidisciplinary, globalized nature, committed to preparing innovative professionals and future torchbearers for a wide range of international expertise to address the critical challenges of our times."可以看出，中文介绍中画线部分在英文译文中都被省译了。但这种情况需要译者在译文定稿上拥有比较高的"话语权"或权威程度才可行，至少这种处理能被原文作者或翻译任务委派者认可才可以进行。否则，译者即使秉着职业翻译的精神、以专业的翻译态度进行简化处理或部分省译,却有可能被原文作者或翻译任务委派者认为译者翻译水平有限或不能胜任该翻译工作并被炒鱿鱼,所以碰到这种情况时,译者在可能的情况下,可以与原文作者或翻译任务委派者沟通说明。

(4) 淡化宣传色彩——改掉宣传色彩过浓的字眼

在翻译政务宣传类文本时,译者有时候需要换掉原文宣传色彩过浓的字眼,并对某些提法做淡化或中性化处理,使译文呈现出一种不卑不亢、语气平和的风格。例如,"公有制在经济中占有<u>主导地位</u>。"过去曾经译为 The public sector is dominant in the economy.,而如今可以译为 The public sector is the leading sector/mainstay of the economy. 分析可知,sector 是"部分、部门、领域"的意思,mainstay 是"支柱、中流砥柱"的意思。"主导地位"译为 dominant 有点不妥,因为 dominant 指占统治地位,和 monopoly(垄断)相似。又如,有时中文文本出现类似这种字句"项目建设中,各参建单位冒严寒、战酷暑,积极克服时间紧、任务重等不利因素影响,按照时间节点,抢时争速,全力加快建设。"这类字句在翻译成英文时一些短语可省译或改译。如译为:During the project construction, participating units overcame the heavy tasks under tight schedules and managed to complete the project on time.

(5) 分析原文逻辑关系,调整句型结构

在原文句子较长、所表达信息内容较多时,译者应对原文信息及逻辑层次关系进行深入分析,必要时可以调整原文的句型结构后再翻译成译文。例如,原文与译文分别如下。

原文:我们将继续<u>同发达国家加强战略对话</u>,增进互信,深化合作,<u>妥善处理分歧</u>,推动相互关系长期稳定发展。我们将继续贯彻与邻为善、以邻为伴的周边外交方针,加强<u>同周边国家</u>的<u>睦邻友好</u>和务实合作,积极开展<u>区域合作</u>,共同营造和平稳定、平等互信、合作共赢的地区环境。我们将继续<u>加强同广大发展中国家的团结合作</u>,深化传统友谊,扩大务实合作,提供力所能及的援助,维护发展中国家的正当要求和共同利益。

译文:<u>For developed countries</u>, we will continue to <u>strengthen strategic dialogue</u>, enhance mutual trust, deepen cooperation and <u>properly manage differences</u> to promote long-term, stable and sound development of bilateral relations. <u>For our neighboring countries</u>, we will continue to follow the foreign policy of friendship and partnership, <u>strengthen good-</u>

neighborly relations and practical cooperation with them, and energetically engage in regional cooperation in order to jointly create a peaceful, stable regional environment featuring equality, mutual trust and win-win cooperation. For other developing countries, we will continue to increase unity and cooperation with them, cement traditional friendship, expand practical cooperation, provide assistance to them within our ability, and uphold the legitimate demands and common interests of developing countries.

原文谈的是中国与三种不同类型的国家的关系。译文把 For developed countries, For our neighboring countries 和 For other developing countries 放在三个句子的句首，使得译文读起来层次清晰、条理通顺、逻辑关系也更清楚。

3. 不使用绝对化的字眼及表述

翻译政务宣传类文本时，用词要留有余地，不说过头话，也不使用一些绝对化的字眼或表述。"完善"不再译为 perfect（使达到完美状态）、optimize（使最优化）等词，因为这些词都太绝对化，并且"完美状态"实际上是达不到的，不如不用这种表述。事实上，许多政务宣传类文本中的"完善"的实质是"改善"（improve），所以"完善开放性经济"可以译为 to improve the open economy，"完善机制"可以译为 to improve the mechanism of ... "规范化"以前的旧译法是 standardize（标准化），十八大报告中的新译法是 adopt due standards to govern ... 或 do something according to due standards/procedures。"严格规范执法"的旧译法是 to ensure law enforcement is standardized，新译法是 to ensure law enforcement is conducted in a strict way according to due procedures 或 to ensure procedure based law enforcement。"保障"的旧译法是 guarantee（一种比较绝对，不留余地的说法），新译法是 ensure，如"为党和国家事业发展提供了强有力的保障"现在译为 ensuring progress in advancing the cause of the Party and the country，而不是 providing a powerful guarantee。"矛盾"不译为 contradiction，可译为 problems, conflicts，因为 contradiction 指"抽象意义上事物处于对立的状态，带有不可调和"的意思，而在中文语境下的"矛盾"实际上常是指一些亟须解决的问题。

4. 吸收新鲜语汇，淘汰过时词汇

淘汰过时词汇主要指淘汰一些早期苏联式英语，并且在现代英语中具有贬义色彩的词汇。"干部"不再译为 cadres，这是早期苏联式英语用法，在现代英语中有贬义。"干部"可译为 officials。"群众"不译为 masses，译成 people 即可。masses 是早期苏联式英语用法，在现代英语中也有贬义。因为《牛津高阶英汉双解词典》(第7版)对 the masses 的英文释义是 the ordinary people in society who are not leaders or who are considered to be not very well educated。因此"广大人民群众"不必译成 the broad masses of the people，译成 all the people 即可。"指导思想"不译为 guiding ideology，可译为 guiding theory/philosophy。因为 ideology 或 ideological 在现代英语中贬义较强，多用于贬义语境。如：He is ideological in his views. "他意识形态偏见很强。" xx's foreign policy is ideologically motivated. "xx 国的外交政策受意识形态影响很严重。"此外，"精神追求"的旧译法是 spiritual pursuit，而新译法是 intellectual/cultural pursuit，因为 spiritual 有较强的宗教含义，在翻译政治文件中应慎用。而"国民经济"旧译法是 national economy，此译法受早期苏联式英语的影响，national 属冗余信息，应删去。"国民经济"译成 the economy 即可。"团结"过去译法是 solidarity（含 A 和 B 共同对付 C 的意思），现在译法是 unity。"新局面/新形势"旧译法是 new situation，这是典型中式英语，新译法是 in a new environment, facing new developments 或 under new conditions。

此外，政务宣传翻译需要注意吸收国外"平行文本"中经常出现的新鲜词汇，如 motivate, leverage (类似于 affect largely), holistic, systemic 等。"发挥某某的积极性"可以译为 keep sb. motivated 或 motivate sb. to do sth.；"充分发挥某人的力量"可译为 to fully leverage sb.'s strength。

10.4 翻译实例及点评

英译汉

【原文】

APEC

APEC operates by consensus (1). Members conduct their activities and work programs on the basis of open dialogue with equal respect for the views of all participants. In terms of the global economic and trade climate, two major scenarios distinguish the APEC meetings of this year (2). One is that some of the major members have suffered economic slowdown such as the United States and Japan; and the other is whether to launch a new round of WTO talks this year remains uncertain. Given that, this year's APEC meetings are focused on the following two issues: a. Strengthening the cooperation between and among the APEC members in the face of potential economic slowdown for confidence rebuilding. b. Furthering the liberalization and facilitation process of trade and investment and supporting the development of the multilateral trading system by pushing forward a new round of WTO talks at an earlier date. <u>By analyzing the objective environment and practical needs that APEC is facing</u> (3), and <u>condensing the ideas from various parties</u> (4), <u>we have agreed upon the theme of APEC 2001 as "Meeting New Challenges in the New Century: Achieving Common Prosperity through Participation and Cooperation."</u> (5). This theme was mainly aimed at guiding the APEC members towards the 21st century and against the backdrop of the economic globalization and New Economy, seeking favorable positions, exploring new opportunities and enhancing cooperation for the common prosperity. Following this way of thinking and considering the present APEC cooperative framework, we worked out three sub-themes, which are: a. Making all APEC members benefit from the globalization and New Economy <u>by promoting capacity building and exploring future opportunities</u> (6). b. Advancing Trade and Investment for the establishment of a more reasonable multilateral trading system. c. Creating a favorable macro-environment for the sustainable economic development in Asia and Pacific.

(邹力,2005: 105 – 106)

【译文一】

亚太经合组织

亚太经合组织(APEC)根据一致同意的方式来运转(Ⅰ),其成员国所有的活动和工作安排都基于所有参与者意见得到同样的尊重并且互相公开对话的前提。由于全球经济和贸易的氛围,今年的 APEC 会议有两个不同的情景(Ⅱ)。一是一些主要成员国,比如,美国和日本,它们的经济增长速度放缓;二是

WTO是否要在今年启动新一轮谈判还不确定。考虑到这些因素,今年的APEC会议将主要强调两个问题:① 加强 APEC 成员之间的合作,以便应对潜在的经济衰退,也为了重新树立信心;② 继续推进贸易和投资自由化和便利化进程,支持多边贸易体系的发展,以及争取尽早启动 WTO 新一轮谈判。通过分析客观环境与 APEC 实际的需要(Ⅲ),通过浓缩个不同党派的意见(Ⅳ),我们同意把"迎接新世纪的新挑战:参与、合作、实现共同繁荣"作为 2001 年 APEC 会议的主题(Ⅴ)。这一主题的目的在于指导 APEC 成员面向 21 世纪,在经济全球化和新经济的形势下,抓住有利时机,开拓机遇,加强合作,以便实现共同繁荣。按照这样的思路,并考虑到 APEC 目前的合作框架,我们拟定了三个分主题:① 通过促进能力,开拓更多机会(Ⅵ),使各成员从全球化和新经济中获益。② 促进贸易与投资,推动建立更加合理的多边贸易体制。③ 为亚太地区经济的可持续发展创造有利的宏观环境。

(学生课堂练习)

【译文二】

亚太经合组织

亚太经合组织(APEC)内部按照一致同意的原则来操作(Ⅰ'),其成员所开展的活动和工作安排均建立在意见均等和公平、公开对话的基础之上。鉴于全球经济和贸易的大环境,今年的 APEC 会议呈现出不同以往的两大特点(Ⅱ'):一是一些主要成员国,如美国和日本,其经济增长速度放缓;二是 WTO 能否在今年启动新一轮谈判尚无定论。基于此,今年的 APEC 会议将着重关注两个方面的问题:① 加强 APEC 成员之间的合作,以应对可能出现的经济衰退,重树信心;② 推动新一轮的世贸会谈尽早展开,以期在贸易和投资领域,进一步开放市场,简化流程,同时推动多边贸易机制的发展。在综合考虑 APEC 面临的客观环境与现实需要(Ⅲ'),并且在征求各方意见的基础上(Ⅳ'),我们一致同意把"面对新世纪的新挑战:通过参与和合作来实现共同繁荣"作为 2001 年 APEC 会议的主题(Ⅴ')。这一会议主题旨在引导 APEC 成员如何面向 21 世纪,在经济全球化和新经济的形势下,如何发掘积极因素、抓住新机会,深化合作,以求共同繁荣。遵循这种指导思想,并考虑到 APEC 现有合作框架,我们拟定了三个分主题:① 促进产业发展、紧握未来机遇(Ⅵ'),以求所有 APEC 成员共享经济全球化和新兴经济发展所带来的红利。② 促进贸易与投资,推动建立更加合理的多边贸易体系。③ 为亚太地区经济可持续发展创造有利的宏观环境。

(学生课堂练习)

【译文三】
亚太经合组织

亚太经合组织(APEC)实行的是协商一致的原则。成员的活动和工作计划建立在公开对话、平等尊重的基础上,征集所有参与者的意见。今年举办 APEC 会议,就全球经济贸易环境来说,主要面临两个大背景:一是一些主要成员经济增长速度减缓,如美国和日本;另一个是 WTO 能否在今年启动新一轮谈判问题。因此,今年的 APEC 会议将主要侧重于以下两个方面:① 加强 APEC 成员之间的合作,共同应对可能出现的经济衰退,重树信心;② 继续推进 APEC 贸易投资自由化和便利化进程,支持多边贸易体制发展,推动 WTO 尽早启动新一轮谈判。根据 APEC 面临的客观环境与现实需要,在征求各方意见的基础上,我们已确立了"新世纪、新挑战:参与、合作、促进共同繁荣"作为 2001 年 APEC 会议的主题。这一思路主要立意于引导 APEC 成员面向 21 世纪,在经济全球化和新经济的形势下,趋利避害,开拓机遇,加强合作,实现共同繁荣。按此思路,并考虑到 APEC 现有合作框架,我们拟定了三个分主题:① 加强能力建设,开拓未来,发展机遇,使各成员从全球化和新经济中受益。② 促进贸易与投资,推动建立更加合理的多边贸易体制。③ 为亚太地区经济可持续发展创造有利的宏观环境。

(邹力,2005:105-106,有所改动)

【点评】

本组英译汉的原文的内容涉及亚太经济合作组织于 2001 年 10 月在上海召开的首脑会议和部长级会议。从具体的行文来看,比较规范和正式,没有拖泥带水的成分,这也符合此类文本政策性、宣传性和规范性的特点。

译文一和译文二的总体质量都还不错,并且译文二更胜一筹。译文一的不足主要反映在两点:一是出现了两处误译,即译文意思违背了原文作者的意图;二是在选词和用词方面有时把握不够准确和规范,与此类文本的翻译要求有些距离。前者的例子是把 condensing the ideas from various parties 和 by promoting capacity building 分别翻译成"通过浓缩不同党派的意见"和"通过促进能力",这样的处理显然与原文的意思有出入。至于后者的例子也有一些,比如,把 two major scenarios distinguish the APEC meetings of this year 中的 scenarios 机械地译为"情景",把 By analyzing the objective environment 直接译为"通过分析客观环境"也有生硬之嫌。相对而言,译文二并未出现明显的误译。不过,它也存在一些不够专业和规范化的处理。比如,一开始的"按照一致同意的原则来操作"中的"操作"一词就和全文的基调不甚匹配。还有,在"我们一致同意把'面对新世纪的新挑战:通过参与和合作来实现共同繁荣'作为2001年APEC会议的主题"这个句子中,引号里面的部分显得冗长。既然是一个大会的主题,恐怕不宜把它处理成一个拖沓的句子,而应该要尽量浓缩和精炼。

汉译英

【原文1】

一、历史沿革(1):

1922年10月,由国民党人和共产党人联合创办了上海大学(2)。时任校长于右任,总务长邓中夏,社会学系主任瞿秋白(3)。学校秉承"养成建国人才,促进文化事业"的宗旨,培养了大批进步青年和社会精英(4)。1927年"四一二"事变后(5),上海大学即被国民党当局强行关闭。

(上海大学校史)

【译文一】

1. Historical Evolution(Ⅰ)

In October, 1922, the national party and communist party established Shanghai University together(Ⅱ). At that time, the principal was Yu Youren, the procurator was Deng Zhongxia, and the dean of sociology department was Qu qiubai(Ⅲ). Adhering to develop founding talents and promote cultural undertakings, Shanghai University has cultivated a large capacity of progressive youth and society elite(Ⅳ). Since the 412 incident of 1927(Ⅴ), Shanghai University was forced to close by the national party.

(学生课堂练习)

【译文二】

1. Historical Development（Ⅰ'）

In October 1922, some party members of Kuomintang and Chinese Communist Party co-founded Shanghai University（Ⅱ'）. At the time of its establishment, Yu Youren was appointed president of the university, Deng Zhongxia, dean of general matters, and Qu Qiubai, dean of sociology department（Ⅲ'）. The university, taking "cultivating great talents and endeavouring to promote cultural development" as its motto, was successful in turning out a large group of progressive youth and social elites（Ⅳ'）. In the wake of April 12 Incident（Ⅴ'）, Shanghai University was forced to close by the Kuomintang administration.

（学生课堂练习）

【译文三】

1. Our History

Our history began in October 1922 when members of Chinese Nationalist Party (or Kuomintang) and Chinese Communist Party co-founded Shanghai University. At the time of its establishment, Yu Youren was appointed president of the university, Deng Zhongxia, dean of general affairs, and Qu Qiubai, chair of the sociology department. Adhering to the mission of "developing founding talents and promoting cultural undertakings", Shanghai University cultivated a large number of progressive youth and social elites. However, after the "April 12th Incident" in 1927 which was an anti-Communist purge, Shanghai University was forcibly closed by the Kuomintang administration.

（本书作者译）

【点评】

这组汉译英的原文比较简短，只有四句话，但是要翻译得好也不容易。因为它既涉及如何把握翻译原则的问题，同时也和译者的知识面、语言能力，及其对翻译技巧的运用等有关。

和此前的英译汉一样,译文一和译文二中,译文二的表现要更好。现在来看一下译文一的具体情况。对于原文首句的"由国民党人和共产党人联合创办了上海大学",译文一把"国民党人"译成 the national party。这里有几个问题:一是表述不准确,二是没有把这个专有名词的首字母大写,三是即使可以这样翻译"国民党",可还是漏掉了"人"字。译文一将原文第二句中的"校长"、"总务长"和"系主任"分别译为 principal,procurator 和 dean 也不恰当。而且整个句子的句式运用也有不足之处。译文一的第三句中,Adhering to 后接的两个动词 develop 和 promote 应该加上 ing,并且应该和原文一样使用引号。此后的 has cultivated 属于时态使用不当,而 a large capacity of 和 society elite 则又是用法问题。最后一句中的 412 Incident 显得突兀,应附上相应的说明文字或补充说明信息才比较合适。

从译文二来看,第二句开头的 At the time of establishment 比译文一的 At that time 表义更加具体和清晰。第二句中句式的选用也较为合理。当然,general matters 应为 general affairs,而且 dean 应为 chair。最后一句中有关"'四一二'事变"的处理虽好于前者,但是建议应像译文三那样作另外的说明。至于对小标题"历史沿革"的翻译,译文一、二的处理均不理想。

【原文 2】
中国经济体制改革

中国正在由计划经济向市场经济转轨,<u>因此我们的经济体制改革必然会涉及到外国投资政策的调整,而调整的目的是为了加速与国际接轨的过程</u>(1)。

<u>为了逐步使我国的关税(tariff)总水平达到发展中国家的平均水平</u>(2),我们将在近年来几次降低关税率的基础上继续大幅度降低关税率。这样做不仅是为了达到世界贸易组织对关税的要求,<u>而且也是我国建立社会主义市场经济的自身需要</u>(3)。

我们将根据市场经济的国际惯例和要求<u>废除各种有关进口减免税的条例</u>(4),逐步统一本国企业与外资企业的税收政策。这样做的目的旨在使税收制度标准化,创造企业与企业之间、地区与地区之间公平竞争的条件,进一步改善投资环境。

(邹力,2005:107-108)

第十章　政务宣传翻译

【译文一】

China's Economic System Reform

China is now experiencing the transformation from planned economy to market economy, <u>therefore the adjustment of foreign investment policies would be inevitably involved in the economic restructuring, so as to rapidly internationalize the economy of China</u>(Ⅰ).

<u>In order to gradually lower our custom tax level to the average level of developing countries</u> (Ⅱ), in the past few years, china has lowered her custom tax rate several times, and we will continue to substantially lower the rate. In this way we can not only meet the requirements of WTO on custom tax, <u>but also meet our own needs of build socialist market economy</u>(Ⅲ).

We will, according to the generally accepted international practices and the requirements of the market economy, <u>put an end to various regulations governing import tax exemptions and reduction</u> (Ⅳ), and gradually unify taxation policies concerning Chinese and foreign-funded enterprises. The purpose of doing this is to standardize the tax system, create equal competition between enterprises as well as between regions, and further improve the investment environment.

(学生课堂练习)

【译文二】

China's Reform of Economic System

China is transforming itself from planned economy to market economy, <u>and so our economic system reform will naturally mean to have foreign investment policy adjustment, which is to be carried out because we wish to quicken our steps in globalization</u>(Ⅰ').

<u>In order to let our general tariff level come down to the average level of developing countries</u>(Ⅱ'), we will continue to reduce our tariff rates considerably after all these tariff rate reductions over the past several years. This will not only enable us to meet the tariff requirements of the

World Trade Organization, but also to meet China's requirements for building a socialist market economy.

We will, according to the generally accepted international practices and the requirements of the market economy, get rid of various rules about import tax exemptions and reduction(Ⅲ'), and gradually unify taxation policies about Chinese and foreign-funded enterprises. Our purpose is to standardize the tax system, create an equal competition environment for enterprises as well as different regions, and better improve our investment environment.

（学生课堂练习）

【译文三】

China's Reform of Economic System

China is undergoing the process of transition from a planned to a market economy. Therefore, our reform of the economic system is bound to involve readjustments in some foreign investment policies, the goal of which is to accelerate links with the usual international practices.

In order to gradually bring our general tariff level in line with the average level of developing countries, we will, based on tariff rates which have been lowered several times in recent years, continue to introduce significant reductions in tariff rates. This effort will not only fulfill the tariff requirements of the World Trade Organization, but also meet China's requirements for establishing a socialist market economy.

We will act, in accordance with generally accepted international practices and the requirements of the market economy, to abolish various regulations governing import tax exemptions and reduction, and gradually unify taxation policies governing Chinese and foreign-funded enterprises. The aim of doing so is to standardize the tax system, create conditions for equal competition between enterprises as well as regions, and further improve the investment environment.

（邹力,2005:107-108）

【点评】

　　这组汉译英的原文的内容涉及中国经济体制改革以及相关政策调整等问题，文字规范、内容比较正式，且具有一定的政策性。

　　总体上来看，译文一和译文二的表现尚好，基本能反映出原文的本来面貌。当然也存在一些不足之处。译文一的问题在于：一是某些表达不符合英文习惯，有比较明显的中式英语的痕迹。开首一句中的 therefore the adjustment of foreign investment policies would be inevitably involved in the economic restructuring, so as to rapidly internationalize the economy of China 就是一个例子。二是某些词语的选择与文体特征不相匹配，比如，put an end to various regulations governing import tax exemptions and reduction 中的 put an end to 就显得口语化，不够正式和严谨。三是译文中出现了几处基本的语法和语言运用问题。比如，but also meet our own needs of build socialist market economy，实际应为 but also meet our needs of building a socialist market economy。译文二的情况也差不多，在此仅指出其中几个有缺陷的地方：其开首一句不但表达不够准确和严谨，而且所谓 quicken our steps in globalization 和原文的意思也有出入。至于 let our general tariff level come down to the average level of developing countries 和 get rid of various rules about import tax exemptions and reduction，在性质上和译文一中出现的问题大致相同。

参考文献

1. Nord, C. Translating as a Purposeful Activity—Functionalist Approaches Explained [M]. Shanghai: Shanghai Foreign Language Education Press, 2001.

2. Nida, E. A. Language, Culture, and Translation[M]. Shanghai: Shanghai Foreign Language Education Press, 1993.

3. Gibson, S. The Problem of Abortion: Essentially Contested Concepts and Moral Autonomy[J]. Bioethics, 2004, 18 (3): 221-233.

4. Zhu W. The Tort Law of P. R. China and the Implementation of Informed Consent[J]. Asian Bioethics Review, 2014, 6 (2): 125-142.

5. Roberts, W. H. & Turgeon, G. About Language: A Reader for Writers [M]. Beijing: Foreign Language Teaching and Research Press, 2000.

6. International Society for Stem Cell Research (ISSCR). Guidelines for the Clinical Translation of Stem Cells[M/OL]. 2008. http://www.isscr.org/docs/default-source/clin-trans-guidelines/isscrglclinicaltrans.pdf

7. Sager, J. C. Terms[C]//Mona Baker (ed.) Routledge Encyclopedia of Translation Studies. Shanghai: Shanghai Foreign Language Education Press, 2009.

8. Reiss, K. Type, Kind and Individuality of Text—Decision-making in Translation [C]//The Translation Studies Reader, Lawrence Venuti (ed.), Susan Kitron (tr.). London and New York: Routledge, 2000.

9. Newmark, P. Approaches to Translation[M]. Shanghai: Shanghai Foreign Language Education Press, 2001.

10. 陈宏薇. 汉英翻译基础[M]. 上海：上海外语教学出版社，1998.

11. 李长栓. 非文学翻译理论与实践[M]. 北京：中国对外翻译出版公司，2004.

12. 李龙. 文学性问题研究——以语言学转向为参照[M]. 北京：人民出版社，2011.

13. 林语堂. 论翻译[C]//罗新璋主编. 翻译论集. 北京：商务印书馆，1984.

14. 陆乃圣. 英汉差异及翻译[M]. 上海：华东化工学院出版社，1993.

15. 罗新璋. 我国自成体系的翻译理论[C]// 罗新璋主编. 翻译论集. 北京：商务印书馆，1984.

16. 茅盾. "直译"与"死译"[C]//罗新璋主编. 翻译论集. 北京：商务印书馆，1984.

17. 戚云方. 外贸英语(第二版)[M]. 杭州：浙江大学出版社，1996.

18. 任志强. 任你评说：任志强评说地产中国[M]. 北京：中信出版社，2010.

19. 萨拉·B. 波默罗伊, 斯坦利·M. 伯斯坦, 沃尔特·唐兰, 等. 古希腊政治、社会和文化史[M]. 傅洁莹，龚萍，周平，译. 上海：上海三联书店，2010.

20. 石忠义. 关于"文学性"的定义[J]. 文艺理论研究，2000(6)：文讯.

21. 孙万彪. 英汉法律翻译教程[M]. 上海：上海外语教育出版社，2002.

22. 王东风. 小说翻译的语义连贯重构[J]. 中国翻译，2005(3)：37-43.

23. 王东风. 异化与归化——矛与盾的交锋？[J]. 中国翻译，2002(5)：24-26.

24. 王佐良，丁往道. 英语文体学引论[M]. 北京：外语教学与研究出版社，1987.

25. 魏清光，魏家海. 我国学术翻译译德失范的原因及解决之道[J]. 东北师大学报(哲学社会科学版)，2012 (6)：128-131.

26. 许根顺. 第一夫人在上海[M]. 上海：上海锦绣文章出版社，2010.

27. 严俊仁. 新英汉科技翻译[M]. 北京：国防工业出版社，2010.

28. 张培基等. 英汉翻译教程[M]. 上海：上海外语教育出版社，1980.
29. 张亚权. 论学术翻译的文献回译——以梅尔清《清初扬州文化》中译本为例[J]. 南京大学学报（哲学·人文科学·社会科学版），2005(3)：128-136.
30. 张宗美. 科技汉英翻译技巧[M]. 北京：宇航出版社，1992.
31. 邹力. 商务英语翻译教程（笔译）[M]. 北京：中国水利水电出版社，2005.
32. 朱敏彦. 上海历史上的今天[M]. 上海：上海锦绣文章出版社，2009.
33. 左旭初. 民国商标图典[M]. 上海：上海锦绣文章出版社，2013.

附录一

非文学翻译的实施步骤

基于非文学翻译的性质，为了确保翻译任务高效完成，我们可以把整个翻译过程细化为几个操作环节，具体步骤如下：

1. 接受任务

这是整个非文学翻译过程的开始，它包括雇主和译者或译员双方的接洽、商谈以及最后签订合同等。在这个阶段中，双方需要确认翻译的内容、质量要求、交稿日期、报酬和支付的方式以及可能的违约处理。在某些情况下（如因涉及专利或商业秘密等），雇主还会在合同中作出一些特殊的约定，规定译者需要遵守保密条款、不得向第三方透露译文内容等。

2. 吃透原文

这是正式实施非文学翻译的第一个环节。在这个阶段，译者开始真正密切接触翻译素材。他/她需要反复通读原文，力求把握其主旨，明确其重点和难点以及总体的行文风格等。同时，还需梳理原文中明显或隐性的内容疏漏、逻辑失当或表达不甚明确的地方，以便在翻译时做出适当的补充和调整。在此基础上，他/她应考虑并基本明确采取何种主要的翻译方法。

3. 查找资料

这是非文学翻译过程中的重要一环，一般需要在动笔之前落实完成。在翻译过程中若发现缺乏相关资料，也可边查找、补充边实施翻译。非文学翻译的特点之一是内容覆盖面广、专业性强，因此，对于文本内容之外的延伸材料（如背景知识、专业术语等）的查找和储备是必不可少的。

4. 阅读平行文本

这也是非文学翻译过程中不容忽视的重要环节。所谓平行文本（parallel

text),一般指与原文内容相关或相近(即"平行")的译入语参考文本。它的形式不拘,可以是一部专著里面的某个章节,也可以是一篇或几篇严肃的学术论文,或者是报章杂志刊载的一般性文章,甚至还可以是百科全书里的条目和网络搜索引擎提供的网上资源等。阅读平行文本可以弥补译者在专门知识和特定语言构造方面的不足和欠缺,比如,可以帮助其获得专业知识、熟悉专业术语、借鉴表达方法和模仿行文风格等。换言之,在着手翻译之前或翻译进行的过程中,尽量多参阅性质相似、内容接近的平行文本,有助于译者实现由"外行"角色向"内行"角色的转变,从而也有利于其更好地完成翻译任务。

5. 着手翻译

有了前面几个环节的准备和铺垫,现在应该是正式落笔的时候了,也就是到了通常所说的"把一种语言转换成另一种语言"的时候了。这个阶段中所要做的基本上是一个串联和整合,当然,其间必然也还需要进行思考和调整。至于持续的时间,则可长可短,要依据原文的具体容量而定。有时候一天即可完成,还有可能需要数天、数周,甚至几个月或更长的时间才能完成。

6. 修改和完善

这是非文学翻译(实际上,文学翻译也莫不如此)过程中不可缺少,但往往容易受到忽视的一个环节。翻译,毕竟涉及两种或多种不同的语言。即便译者的外语能力再强、其对译入语的历史文化以及其他背景知识再熟悉,也仍然难免出现疏漏和差错。再者,如前所述,非文学翻译多属于实用文体的范畴,其涵盖的内容跨度极大,有时候专业性非常强,这就意味着译者在翻译时有可能面临专业知识不足等先天缺陷,因此,在翻译完成之后更加需要仔细校读,以便及时发现问题并予以修改和完善。还有,在不少情况下,非文学翻译往往体现出时间紧、任务重的特点。为了按时交稿,译者有时候需要加班加点。基于此,也十分有必要在完成之后再进行细致的审阅和修改。不但如此,视具体的翻译情况或根据雇主的要求,译者还有可能须对其完成的译文进行二校或三校。可以说,这个环节既是整个翻译过程中一个有机组成部分,同时也可反映出译者的责任心和对待翻译任务的态度。

7. 交稿

这是非文学翻译实施流程中的最后一环。随着前面几个步骤的顺利结束,至此整个翻译活动才可谓大功告成。

附录二

非文学翻译的质量控制

对于翻译质量的评判不外乎译文是否准确、译笔是否地道、风格是否忠实于原作等。如此标准，从广义上来说，应该适用于所有翻译活动，当然也包括非文学翻译。不过，对于非文学翻译，因其体现出的有别于文学翻译的诸多特点（如科学性、专业性、商业性和实用性等），所以，在评价译文优劣的时候应首先考察其是否能够全面、忠实和有效地反映出原文本的信息，而其他诸如语言是否优美、风格是否鲜明等则处于从属地位。此外，鉴于相当一部分非文学翻译活动实际上可被视为某个商业活动的一个组成部分，在讨论译文质量时还应当充分考虑译者的职业操守和合同意识。具体来说，非文学翻译的质量控制流程可大致归结为如下几点：

1. 确保译文内容忠实、准确、可靠

一般认为，非文学文本的目的多强调信息传递，而非侧重于审美意趣或社会教化。因此，在翻译过程中，信息传递的准确性和清晰有效性应该是一个主要的考量。要做到译文内容忠实、准确和可靠，译者必须首先对原文有一个全面和准确的把握，否则这一切就无从谈起。

2. 确保译文表述流畅、合理，逻辑性强

非文学文本多讲究从事实出发，行文简明流畅、逻辑严密，且往往会包含一系列的实验参数和统计数字等。与此相对应，译文在具体的遣词造句和篇章组织方面也应该力求言简意赅、严丝合缝。只有这样，才能有助于准确和有效地传递原文的信息。

3. 确保译文的专业性

非文学翻译多涉及专门领域，其表达体系中时常包含专业的词汇和语汇。

在翻译过程中,译者应充分考虑到此类表达与日常用语之间的区别,确保体现出文本原有的专业性。

4. 确保不出现随意改译和漏译的情况

这一点主要针对非文学翻译内容覆盖面广、专业性强的特点,而译者由于自身条件的限制,不可能对每一个知识门类都了如指掌,这就使得其在翻译过程中难免会遇到各种困难。不过,这不应成为其做出随意改译和漏译的理由。非文学翻译所要实现的一大目标即是全面、准确和迅速有效地传递信息,任意删减内容、避重就轻只会使译文的质量打折扣。当然,一些文本的原文也可能存在表达比较随意和逻辑相对混乱的情况,译者对此作出相应的调整则是另一回事。

5. 确保译文格式规范

如前所述,就非文学翻译而言,译文的风格以及文本总体的审美效果应被认为居于次要的地位,唯有内容,也就是信息本身才是检验翻译质量的主要依据。不过,考虑到非文学文本的特殊性,其内容往往含有大量的示例、插图、列表等;而且,不少合同、公证书等一般都有自己固定的格式。对此,译者应尽力确保译文的体例和格式与原文相符,以体现其科学性和严肃性。

6. 确保译者在整个过程中体现出应有的职业操守和合同意识

非文学翻译如今发展势头迅猛,其职业化前景已是大势所趋。在这样的情形之下,对于非文学翻译质量的控制,除了要衡量译文本身各方面的表现是否合格以外,还需要考虑译者在这个过程中是否体现出其应有的职业操守和合同意识。比如,要考察他是否遵守合同规定按时交稿,是否按照合同的其他约定遵守保密义务、不向无关的第三方泄露信息等。

附录三

英汉互译练习

英译汉

I

India's Family Welfare Programme is the oldest government sponsored fertility reduction programme in the world. Since its inception in 1952 the programme has undergone quantitative and qualitative changes. An overview of the contraceptives promoted by Government of India over the years clearly indicate a continuous shift from simple methods to highly medicalised harmful devices which impose excessive health risks on women. Realisation of reproductive rights warrants presence of enabling conditions or social rights. In the absence of such enabling conditions to say that reproductive technologies have enabled women to have control over their bodies is a myth.

The second issue pertains to misuse of pre-natal diagnostic techniques for sex selection and female foeticide. Pre-natal diagnostic tests are medically meant for the detection of foetal abnormalities and prevention of the birth of defective children. But unfortunately in a country like India where sons are preferred over daughters these tests are (mis)used for the detection of the sex of the foetus so that female foetuses could be aborted. Such sex-selective abortions have become a significant social phenomenon in several parts of India. Law alone cannot mitigate the problem is clear from the recent estimates which says that two million abortions are performed after sex determination tests in a year. The impact of these illegal abortions on women's health could well be appreciated if we consider the fact that abortions account for one quarter of the estimated 100,000 maternal deaths which still occur in India. Another recent shocking development is the use of techniques such as sedimentation or centrifugation, Ericson's method, electrophoresis, ion exchange through flotation etc for sex pre-selection and clinics with the name board "baby of your choice" are openly found in major cities in India. At this rate women will become an "endangered species" in the near future.

(Dr. K. Shanthi 向"国际女性生殖健康研讨会"提交的论文)

II

Stem cell research holds tremendous promise for the development of novel therapies for many serious diseases and injuries. While stem cell-based treatments have been established as a clinical standard of care for some conditions, such as hematopoietic stem cell transplants for leukemia and epithelial stem cell-based treatments for burns and corneal disorders, the scope of potential stem cell-based therapies has expanded in recent years due to advances in stem cell research.

At the same time, the scale of media coverage for early-stage stem cell research has raised the hopes of many patients afflicted with currently incurable diseases and disabling conditions. Those involved with testing novel stem cell-based interventions should be keenly aware that patients may bring unrealistic expectations to clinical trials of experimental therapies.

The public, too, should recognize that in all areas of medicine, the maturation of an early-phase, experimental intervention into an accepted standard of medical practice is a long and complex process usually involving many years of rigorous preclinical and clinical testing and many setbacks and failures. Only with time and experience do most new clinical treatments come to be accepted by medical professionals.

Attempts to develop a stem cell-based intervention into an accepted standard of medical practice are particularly difficult processes for the following reasons.

♯ Stem cells and their direct derivatives represent, in most cases, an entirely novel product, requiring that investigators assist in the design and development of both the manufacturing process and the assays that assure the safety, purity, stability, and potency of the final product.

♯ Stem cell self-renewal and differentiation are difficult to control, leading to long experiments with unavoidable heterogeneity in results.

♯ Animal models of many diseases do not accurately reflect the human disease and toxicological studies in animals are sometimes poor at predicting toxicity in humans.

♯ Transplantation studies where human cells are implanted in animals cannot provide full prediction of immune or other biologic responses to human cells in patients.

♯ Stem cells and their derivatives may act on several targets and exert both beneficial and detrimental effects, most notably, the risk of ectopic tissue and tumor formation. Thus, preclinical evidence of safety is of utmost importance.

♯ Cellular transplants may persist for many years in patients, or their actions may be irreversible, thus necessitating careful patient monitoring and extended follow-up.

♯ Stem cells may be harvested from donors of different ages, sexes, and ethnicities, bearing different molecular signatures. The standardization of donation procedures and the establishment of rigorous quality control for harvested somatic (adult) stem cells have only just commenced.

Such considerations underscore the need for independent expert peer review prior to clinical investigation to ensure the integrity of the research and informed consent processes.

(ISSCR, 2008)

III

For many centuries, as we have seen, the growing City State gained slowly in prosperity, bringing the distant lands under cultivation or pasture and consolidating its authority over men's minds and lives. Outside her were the landless adventurers, infesting the narrow seas and barring the mountain passes; but within her well-marked borders the farmer and the shepherd, and the craftsman and small trader beside them, were serving the State and preparing themselves for self-government. We have now reached the point in our rapid sketch of the economics of the growing City, where, after centuries of isolation, the old seclusion is interrupted and the states of Greece began to be brought into relation with their neighbors.

The change was due to very simple and natural causes. Greece is by nature, as we have seen, a poverty-stricken country. Her bare hills and plains provide in themselves food for but a small population. Under the rude methods of cultivation then in use, a time was bound to come, in every City State area, when the land could yield no more increase. It became peopled up to its natural limits. If the slightest mischance occurred, if the rains came late or a sudden storm spoilt the harvest, the State would be face to face with famine. This point seems to have been reached in the development of the leading City States in the eighth or seventh century before Christ. On an earlier page we watched some of the consequences to which this led in the sphere of politics or citizenship. Here we are concerned only with its economic results.

When population presses upon subsistence, and there is not enough food to go round, there are only two immediate remedies — less people or more food, to send away emigrants or to bring in supplies from outside. Leaving the question of emigration aside till our next chapter, let us turn to the question of fresh supplies.

How is the food to be procured? It cannot be bought, for there is nothing to buy it with. There are as yet no surplus products or manufactures. It must be hunted or stolen, "led off or carried off," as the

Greek phrase ran. In other words, the city must make her peace with the hunting instinct and learn to use it in her service. She must learn how to conduct war.

(萨拉·B. 波默罗伊等,2010)

IV

As it has been found possible to tabulate, to the satisfaction of some people at least, the world's Hundred Best Books, so, twenty years ago, it might have been possible to enumerate and and set down the hundred least worthy that had then appeared under the imprint of reputable publishers. The enormous output since that time, however, has made such a task impossible in a literal sense. Even the most patient and plodding student, tabulating for his doctorate degree, would sink appalled before the herculean task of selecting the hundred worst from the thousands sufficiently poor.

The causese for this unprecedented eruption of inferior literature have been several, and the invention of the American typewriting machine is surely not the least of them. When one of the first of these machines was shown to George Eliot by an Oxford professor, she exclaimed with prophetic fervor: "Ah, I can see that it will be responsible for many a bad book, and we have poor ones enough as it is." There can be no doubt, that the mere facilitating of the mechanical labor of authorship has induced many young people who were otherwise unemployed to try their hands at literature, and only too often they have produced what other idle youngsters like themselves found readable enough. A class of ephemeral fiction has resulted which might well be called that of the stenographers' school, consisting of novels made by the almost unassisted efforts of the machine.

The great increase of publishing firms, many of which are frankly and solely interested in satisfying the lowest element of the reading public, has had, no doubt, much to do with this plague of books which, rated at nothing, would be overestimated. But it seems probable that the public library, despite many a good turn it has done for culture, is even more guilty in this general debauching of public taste. People will read a great many more novels borrowed from a public library than they would ever buy, and the great majority of people, reading many, will happen upon more poor ones than good ...

(http://www.en84.com/article-9283-1.html)

V

A day of celebration generally is in the first place dedicated to retrospect, especially to the memory of personages who have gained special distinction for the development of the cultural life. This friendly service for our predecessors must indeed not be neglected, particularly as such a memory of the best of the past is proper to stimulate the well-disposed of today to a courageous effort. But this should be done by someone who, from his youth, has been connected with this State and is familiar with its past, not by one who like a gypsy has wandered about and gathered his experiences in all kinds of countries.

Thus, there is nothing else left for me but to speak about such questions as, independently of space and time, always have been and will be connected with educational matters. In this attempt I cannot lay any claim to being an authority, especially as intelligent and well-meaning men of all times have dealt with educational problems and have certainly repeatedly expressed their views clearly about these matters. From what source shall I, as a partial layman in the realm of pedagogy, derive courage to expound opinions with no foundations except personal experience and personal conviction? If it were really a scientific matter, one would probably be tempered to silence by such considerations.

However, with the affairs of active human beings it is different. Here knowledge of truth alone does not suffice; on the contrary this knowledge must continually be renewed by ceaseless effort, if it is not to be lost. It resembles a statue of marble which stands in the desert and is continuously threatened with burial by the shifting sand. The hands of service must ever be at work, in order that the marble continue lastingly to shine in the sun. To these serving hands mine also shall belong.

The school has always been the most important means of transferring the wealth of tradition from one generation to the next. This applies today in an even higher degree than in former times for, through modern development of the economic life, the family as bearer of tradition and education has been weakened. The continuance and health of human society is therefore in a still higher degree dependent on the school than formerly.

Sometimes one sees in the school simply the instrument for transferring a certain maximum quantity of knowledge to the growing generation. But that is not right. Knowledge is dead; the school, however, serves the living. It should develop in the young individuals those qualities and capabilities which are of value for the welfare of the commonwealth. But that does not mean that individuality should be destroyed and the individual become a mere tool of the community, like a bee or an ant. For a community of standardized individuals without personal originality and personal aims would be a poor community without possibilities for development. On the contrary, the aim must be the training of independently acting and thinking individuals, who, however, see in the service of the community their highest life problem. As far as I can judge, the English school system comes nearest to the realization of this ideal.

But how shall one try to attain this ideal? Should one perhaps try to realize this aim by moralizing? Not at all. Words are and remain an empty sound, and the road to perdition has ever been accompanied by lip service to an ideal. But personalities are not formed by what is heard and said, but by labor and activity.

The most important method of education accordingly always has consisted of that in which the pupil was urged to actual performance. This applies as well to the first attempts at writing of the primary boys as to the doctor's thesis on graduation from the university, or as to the mere memorizing of a poem, the writing of a composition, the interpretation and translation of a text, the solving of a mathematical problem or the practice of physical sport.

（阿尔伯特·爱因斯坦于 1936 年 10 月 15 日在纽约州立大学举行的"美国高等教育 300 周年纪念会"上的演说词《论教育》）

Ⅵ

Never was there a more outrageous or more unscrupulous or more ill-informed advertising campaign than that by which the promoters for the American colonies brought settlers here. Brochures published in England in the seventeenth century, some even earlier, were full of hopeful overstatements, half-truths, and downright lies, along with some facts which nowadays surely would be the basis for a restraining order from the Federal Trade Commission. Gold and Silver, fountains of youth, plenty of fish, venison without limit, all these were promised, and of course some of them were found. It would be interesting to speculate on how long it might have taken to settle this continent if there had not been such promotion by enterprising advertisers. How has American civilization been shaped by the fact that there was a kind of natural selection here of those people who were willing to believe advertising?

Advertising has taken the lead in promising and exploiting the new. This was a new world, and one of the advertisements for it appears on the dollar bill on the Great Seal of the United States, which reads *novus ordo seclorum*, one of the most effective advertising slogans to come out of this country. "A new order of the centuries" — belief in novelty and in the desirability of opening novelty to everybody has been important in our lives throughout our history and especially in this century. Again and again advertising has been an agency for inducing Americans to try anything and everything — from the continent itself to a new brand of soap. As one of the more literate and poetic of the advertising copywriters, James Kenneth Frazier, a Cornell graduate, wrote in 1900 in *"The Doctor's Lament"*:

> This lean M.D. is Dr. Brown
> Who fares but ill in Spotless Town.
> The town is so confounded clean,
> It is no wonder he is lean,
> He's lost all patients now, you know,
> Because they use *Sapolio*.

The same literary talent that once was used to retail Sapolio was later used to induce people to try the Edsel or the Mustang, to experiment with Lifebuoy or Body-All, to drink Pepsi-Cola or Royal Crown Cola, or to shave with a Trac II razor.

(Roberts & Turgeon, 2000)

Ⅶ

When one thinks about the ethics of abortion, one inevitably thinks about rights, since it is in terms of the concept of rights that much of the debate has been conducted. This is true of overtly feminist as well as non-feminist accounts. Indeed, some early feminist writers — Judith Jarvis Thomson and Mary Ann Warren, for example — employ a model of rights that is indistinguishable from that of their non-feminist counterparts. However, more recent feminist writers have developed a different understanding of "a woman's right to choose".

In this paper, I will begin by outlining the non-feminist debate over the moral permissibility of abortion. Referring to W. B. Gallie, I will suggest that this debate is irresolvable, since at its heart is an "essentially contested concept", that of personhood. I will then consider the way in which feminists have attempted to reconceive the terms of the abortion debate and suggest an expanded account of women's right to abortion, drawing on the work of Susan Sherwin. Finally, I will argue that there is a further element to a "woman's right to choose" that expands on and links together the feminist and non-feminist understanding of abortion.

When one thinks about the ethics of abortion, one inevitably thinks about rights, since it is in terms of the concept of rights that much of the debate has been conducted. This is true of overtly feminist as well as non-feminist accounts. Indeed, some early feminist writers — Judith Jarvis Thomson and Mary Ann Warren, for example — employ a model of rights that is indistinguishable from that of their non-feminist counterparts. However, more recent feminist writers have developed a different understanding of "a woman's right to choose".

From the perspective of mainstream, non-feminist philosophy, the abortion debate can be characterised as follows: the rights of the woman are pitted against those of the foetus. Women have rights to privacy, self-determination, bodily integrity or rights over property in the person that might or might not outweigh the competing rights of the foetus. An examination of the literature shows that there is at least some agreement over what rights a woman possesses, but disagreement over what these rights amount to; this disagreement arises out of conflicting accounts of the moral status and consequent moral rights of the foetus. Three basic positions can be delineated: (i) the foetus has a right to life from the moment of conception; (ii) the foetus comes into possession of the right to life at some stage during pregnancy; (iii) the foetus does not at any stage of gestation have a right to life. These are referred to as the "conservative", "moderate" and "liberal" positions respectively. Where the foetus has a right to life from the moment of conception, abortion becomes impermissible except in perhaps a small minority of cases, since whatever rights a woman does have regarding what happens in and to her own body do not outweigh the right to life. Similarly, where the foetus comes into possession of the right to life at some point during pregnancy, abortion becomes impermissible after that point. Finally, where the foetus does not have a right to life, the woman has a right to abortion at any stage during pregnancy since her rights are stronger than any lesser rights that the foetus might possess, if indeed the foetus can be said to possess any rights at all.

The abortion debate, then, becomes a debate not so much over women's rights but over foetal moral status, and for this reason it is interminable. Just as foetal rights are grounded in foetal moral status this status in turn rests on the concept of "personhood", and this, I will show, is an example of what W. B. Gallie terms an "essentially contested concept".

(Gibson, 2004)

汉译英

I

本演讲将从自主性作为自主决定和自由选择的概念着手,阐明对遗传咨询中的自主个人和自主行动的分析,不应局限于行动主体和行动本身,如受咨询者是否有能力作决定,咨询者是否提供足够的信息,提供的信息是否是非指导性等,以及最后的选择是否是独立和自主的行动。本演讲认为,考察遗传咨询中的自主性更应着眼于社会、经济和文化的环境。演讲将从中国在遗传检测方面存在的现实问题,以及特有的社会经济文化因素,来说明遗传咨询中尊重和实现被咨询者自主性模式的困难。演讲者认为,基因歧视的存在与对个人隐私的保护不力,实际的社会不公平的存在,传统养老观念,以及男女不平等的现状,都在一定程度上妨碍了被咨询者自我决定和自由选择的可能。为此本演讲认为,解决遗传咨询的困难,既需要假以时日,进行制度的变革,也需要从伦理和法律方面作相应的努力。

(朱伟,德国柏林"遗传咨询中的社会伦理问题国际研讨会"发言)

II

宋朝是中国古代植物学发展的一个高峰时期,其显著标志是植物谱录的大量出现和园艺业的高度发达。佛教的内在教义和宋朝寺院经济的发展,促进宋朝佛教界人士积极参与了植物学的研究与实践工作,并取得了一定的成就。通慧大师赞宁及其《笋谱》就是其中杰出的代表。

(某大学教务处课程简介)

Ⅲ

"知情同意"一词在20世纪50年代被正式命名以来,成为生命伦理学的一条重要原则,并在医学临床和研究中,被视为保护病人的有效武器。不过,对于知情同意原则内涵的理解,及其如何在实践中得到有效的运用,历来存在着不同的看法和争议。这可以从知情同意在相关立法和伦理准则中不断被修改体现出来。中国有关知情同意的立法,也已经历了这样的过程。2010年7月1日正式生效的《侵权责任法》,就是对知情同意原则在法律上的又一次重大的改进和完善。它的颁布,再一次引起了医学、法学和伦理学界对知情同意原则如何在中国有效运用的关注。

本文试图对《侵权责任法》中有关知情同意的内容和条文进行阐释,分析其与以往相关法规存在的不同之处,并指出新条文的现实意义,同时,论文试图从知情同意的内涵、目的和意义的角度,进一步分析和论证《侵权责任法》存在的不足,及在理论和实践中可能遇到的困难,并在此基础上提出相关的建议。

(Zhu Wei,2014)

Ⅳ

商标是社会商品经济发展到一定的高度而必然出现的产物。早在汉代(公元前202—公元220年),我国工业生产已有较大发展,特别是在金属冶炼加工、陶器制作等诸多方面,已出现使用产品商标的现象。如1964年、1973年分别在陕西咸阳和河南长葛县出土的西汉铁器(如铁铲、铁锤)上,就发现都铸有一个"川"字,在北京市郊大葆台的西汉古墓出土的文物中,考古人员发现了铁斧上都铸有一个"渔"字。这是西汉时期用商品产地名称作为商品的标记,用现代商标理论专业知识来表述,这实际上就是一种地理名称的商标。它是我国古代使用商标的雏形。

到了唐朝(618—907年),我国各地传统手工业生产已相当发达。那时,既有官方的手工作坊,也有民间手工作坊。为了提高和保证产品质量,唐朝的一些分管手工业的官府曾规定某些产品必须注明工匠名字、店铺或作坊的名称,即"物勒工名",然后才可销售自己的产品。其目的很明显,就是要让买主查看产品质量和生产单位后,能认牌购物。如果制造商违背了有关产品质量和产品标识的有关规定,就要被官府治罪。

(左旭初,2013)

V

《民国商标图典》为一本全面介绍民国时期(1911—1949年)我国厂商(包含部分在华外商)注册使用产品商标图样的资料性工具书。

辛亥革命已经100周年了,海内外专家学者对民国时期的政治、军事、经济、社会和文化诸领域的研究已站在一个新的历史高度来思考,并已获得不少新的研究成果。通过对民国时期商标图样的研究,能从一个重要的方面形象地反映出民国时期社会经济发展历史的一个缩影。因此,本书对于研究民国经济史乃至整个民国历史均具有珍贵而形象的史料价值。

1911年,伟大的民主革命先行者孙中山先生领导的辛亥革命推翻了清王朝,建立了中华民国。但中国社会并没有进入资本主义阶段,近代中国半封建半殖民地社会之性质也没有改变。综观民国38年的历史,国内外战乱不断,社会动荡不安,中国民族工商业发展之路举步维艰,因此民国商标的发展历程也是充满坎坷。

本书内容具有较强的学术性和丰厚的人文价值。书中不仅叙述了许多中国近代著名的爱国民主人士、民族工商实业家,如张謇、张弼士、陈嘉庚等人艰苦创业的传奇故事;而且还涉略到不少中国近代著名的历史人物,如民主革命先行者孙中山,民国元老蔡元培、于右任,孙中山夫人宋庆龄,抗日爱国将领李宗仁、张学良、冯玉祥,文化艺术界名流康有为、柳亚子、齐白石、刘海粟、徐悲鸿等人关注民族工商业和中华名牌商标发展的珍贵史实。

根据编辑策划设计,本书分为文字与图片两部分。"第一篇:话说民国商标"为文字部分;"第二篇:民国商标单色图样"和"第三篇:民国商标彩色图样"为图片部分。文字部分共分八章,简要回顾了世界和中国商标发展史;介绍了民国时期政府对厂商注册使用商标之行政管理和民国商标书刊之出版发行的概况;叙述了民国商标之最和民国时期政要名流对国货商标的关注;阐述了民国商标之特色,并对如何辨析民国商标图样表述了独到的见解。

(左旭初,2013)

Ⅵ

中国工业品生产(包括手工业生产)历史悠久,最早可追溯到 2 000 多年前的夏、商、周时代。当时,在手工业生产行业中出现过许多能人,生产过很多知名产品。如东周时期的酒仙杜康就是一位知名度很高的酿酒大师,由他酿造的酒远近闻名。还有如春秋时期的范蠡,不仅是一位杰出的政治家、思想家和谋略家,而且对当时工商业的繁荣发展也作出一定的成就,他是我国古代著名的经营者、实业家和品牌创立者。

我国古代众多的能工巧匠生产过很多富于中国民族特色的传统工艺产品,如丝绸、瓷器和青铜器等,其品质精良,闻名于世。这些生产技术在经过不断改进后,均达到炉火纯青之地步。此外,我国古代造纸、火药、指南针、印刷术等四大发明,更是在当时世界工业史上处于领先地位。

在当今全国各地出土的一些古代生产的丝绸、瓷器和青铜器上,并未发现留下制作者、生产组织者或产品商标等名字和名称。虽然偶尔也留有一些生产产地名称或生产者名字,但以现代社会所要求的产品生产企业和产品商标的概念来衡量还是有很大距离。当时,人们在产品上留有的一些简单标记,最多也只能说是我国古人使用产品商标的一种雏形。

(左旭初,2013)

Ⅶ

清朝时期(1616—1911 年),各地企业经营者在创建知名产品商标方面,也同样取得有不错的成就。当时不仅出现了大量企业家所创立的知名企业和产品商标,还有一些企业家在自己使用的产品商标被同行非法假冒后,一度要求政府有关部门查处非法假冒行为,以保护自己企业和产品商标良好的社会声誉。

在清朝纺织行业中有很多创业能人高手,如清乾隆年间(1736—1795 年),江苏松江府(今上海市松江区)东门外双庙桥,有一位擅长织布的巧妇——丁娘子创办的织布社名声很响,人们将她所织出的棉布称之为"丁娘子"布,而"丁娘子"实质上就是她所使用的棉布商标。

我国古代和近代在化妆品生产方面,可谓历史悠久,特别是江浙一带,有很多能工巧匠曾生产出深受宫廷仕女和广大城乡妇女喜欢的知名化妆产品,如当时市场上的"谢馥春"、"戴春林"和"老庙香室"等香粉、胭脂等。

(左旭初,2013)

VIII
现代科技与社会发展

现代科技不仅极大地改变了自然的面貌,也深刻地影响着人的精神面貌,现代社会的特征很大程度上是由现代科技所造就的。本课程在较宽阔的背景下,以多维视角探索现代科技与社会发展的关系。在叙述现代科技基本特征的基础上,着重论述现代科技对社会经济系统、社会政治运作、科学教育、管理现代化、生活方式、社会变革、马克思主义哲学、伦理道德等影响。本课程具有鲜明的文理交叉、通识教育的性质,不仅有助于学生掌握科学、技术、社会有关的知识,更是引发当代大学生对科学技术与社会关系问题的关注,认识到科技对社会的正反面的影响,以唯物辩证法的基本观点考察现代科学技术,提高科学素养和人文素养。

(某大学教务处课程简介)

IX
周庄之行

周庄是典型的中国水乡古镇,位于上海与苏州之间。周庄虽历经900多年沧桑,至今仍保存着完整的水乡古镇风貌。10月21日,嘉宾们在周庄古镇游览了古桥楼、双桥、沈厅等景点,领略了古镇的民俗风情。嘉宾们分别乘坐在一艘艘由当地船姑们划动的小船,穿河道、过小桥。古镇的桥、古镇的人、古镇的水、古镇的每一处景观都深深地吸引着每一位前来观光的嘉宾。她们尤其对民宅另一边的几位农妇发生了兴趣,原来农妇们正在手工缝制一双双花布婴儿鞋,这一双双民风淳朴、造型别致、乡土味十足的民俗花布婴儿鞋,着实让嘉宾们大感了一番兴趣。

……

APEC峰会虽然已经圆满地落下了帷幕,但与会期间部分经济体领导人配偶们的精彩之旅为中外友好交往史,留下了一个个生动的镜头和美好的记录。与此同时,上海又一次向全世界展示了自己的新形象。

(APEC峰会简讯)

附录四

本书附录三参考译文

英译汉

I

印度的家庭福利计划是世界上最早由政府资助的人口出生减少计划。自1952年实行以来,该计划经历了量变和质变。就过去几年印度政府对避孕药物和用具的推广而言,我们可以清楚地看到,它走过了一段从使用简单方法到使用对妇女健康有极大危害的高端医疗器械的持续变化历程。生殖权的实现需要有可实现的条件或社会权力的保证。在不具备此等可实现条件的情况下,谈论所谓生殖技术使妇女得以控制自己的身体只是痴人说梦。

第二个问题涉及把产前诊断技术错误地用于性别选择和人为致死女婴胎儿。从医学意义上来讲,产前诊断是检查胎儿畸形、防止生育有缺陷婴儿的一种手段。但不幸的是,像印度这样重男轻女的国家,这种检查却被(错误地)用于检测胎儿的性别,使女婴胎儿被流产掉。这种因性别选择而导致的堕胎,在印度不少地方已成为严重的社会问题。根据最近的统计数字,印度每年经性别检查后实施的堕胎有两百万例。显然,这不是仅靠法律就能解决的问题。如果我们清楚这样的事实,即在印度全年约十万名因生产而死亡的妇女中,由于流产导致的死亡人数占了四分之一,那么,我们就会深切地感受到非法堕胎对妇女健康造成的危害是多么巨大。最近,另一个可怕的发展趋势是采用像沉积、离子、埃里克森方法、电泳现象等技术,或通过漂浮离子交换来进行性别预选择。在印度的一些大城市,有些诊所公然打着"你自己选择的婴儿"这样的招牌招徕生意。长此以往,在不久的将来妇女将成为"濒危物种"。

(本书作者译)

II

  干细胞研究为许多严重疾病和损伤的创新治疗提供了广阔的前景。在某些情形下,基于干细胞的治疗已成为临床治疗标准,如白血病中的造血干细胞移植,用上皮干细胞对烧伤和角膜患者进行治疗等。近年来,由于干细胞研究的发展,基于干细胞的治疗范围得到了拓展。

  与此同时,媒体对早期干细胞研究的报道也唤起了不少正遭受目前还无法治愈的疾病折磨的病人以及残疾患者的希望。不过,正在对干细胞干预进行试验的研究人员应该清醒地认识到,患者可能因此而对实验性治疗的临床试验产生不切实际的期望。

  公众也应该明白,在医学的所有领域,一个早期的、实验性的干预,从其成熟到被临床实践接受应用是一个漫长、复杂的过程,往往需要经过多年严格的临床前及临床试验,并会经历诸多挫折和失败。对于大多数全新的临床治疗方法,只有经过长时间的实验和实践,才会被医学专业人员所接受。

  将干细胞的干预转化为临床可接受的标准是一个非常艰难的过程,其原因如下:

  大多数情况下,干细胞及其直接衍生物是一种全新的产物,要求研究人员在其操作和分析环节参与进行设计和改进,以确保最终产品的安全性、纯度、稳定性和有效性。

  干细胞的自我更新和分化较难控制,这就导致试验过程冗长,且不可避免地在最终结果上出现不均一性。

  许多疾病的动物模型并不能准确反映人类的疾病,并且动物的毒理学实验有时对预测人体的毒性反应较差。

  人类细胞植入动物机体的移植研究,并不能完全预测当人类细胞用于病人时,病人对此产生的免疫和其他生物反应。

  干细胞及其衍生物会作用于多个靶点,并同时产生有益或者有害的作用,更重要的是,还会产生异位组织和肿瘤。因此,临床前的安全性证据显得尤为重要。

  细胞移植会在病人身上持续数年,其作用也可能是不可逆的,这就使得对病人的仔细监测及长期随访变得十分必要。

干细胞组织可能从不同年龄、性别、种族的捐赠者采集而来，它们含有不同的分子标记。而对捐赠程序的标准化，以及对采集成体干细胞的严格质量控制的工作才刚刚起步。

基于上述情形，十分有必要在开展临床研究以前，先由独立的同行专家进行评审，以确保研究与知情同意过程的完整性。

（朱伟等译）

Ⅲ

正如我们所看到的，几百年间，崛起的城邦渐见繁荣，连偏僻之地也变得田舍俨然，其治下的百姓则安分守己、恭顺温良。城邦辖区之外是没有土地的冒险者的天地，这些人出没在地形狭隘的海边和山口。但城邦之内，农夫、牧羊人、手工艺者和小本经营者却各司其职、有条不紊地维持着城邦的运行。至此，循着新兴城邦经济发展的轨迹，我们来到了希腊历史上的一个重要阶段。经过几百年的封闭之后，现在旧有的格局已被打破，希腊各邦开始不得不要和周围的邻国产生联系。

这样一个变化的出现是自然而然的事情。我们已经注意到，希腊在本质上是一个非常贫穷的国家。她那贫瘠的山地和平原所产出的粮食只够一小部分人口之用。再加上当时的耕作技术十分落后，因此，对于每一个城邦来说，迟早必然面临粮食产量不足的问题。到了那个时候，它的人口就趋于饱和。一旦稍有不测，比如持续干旱，或收割的季节突遭暴雨袭击，那么，国家就会陷入饥荒。在公元前8世纪或7世纪，那些先进的城邦在其发展过程中似乎就曾到达过这一临界点。在前几页，我们关注了由这一临界点所带来的政治、公民的权利和义务等方面的负面影响。在这一章，我们将只关注其在经济方面造成的不利影响。

当人口问题对生存构成威胁，造成缺乏足够的粮食周转的时候，只有两个行之有效的对策：要么减少人口，要么增加粮食供应。也就是说，或者把人口转移出去，或者从外界补充粮食供给。我们暂且把人口迁移问题搁置一边（留待下一章再来讨论），这里先来讨论增加供给的话题。

那么，如何来获取粮食呢？这粮食不可能用钱去买，因为根本就没有钱。此外，也没有其他多余的物产或制成品可用于交换粮食。因此，这所谓的粮食只能靠猎取或偷盗,用他们自己的话来说,是"拿来或要来"。换句话说,对于老百姓的这种盗抢习性,城邦当局还必须表现出足够的宽容,并尝试以此来服务于它的统治。它需要学会战争之道。

(傅洁莹等译)

IV

既然如今我们认为足以开列全球"百本最佳图书"(至少这是某些人乐意看到的),那么,早在20年之前,我们也可能检点并列出由知名出版商推出的一百本最没有价值的书籍。不过,20年后的今天,鉴于出版数量之巨,要想完成这样一项任务却已变得根本不可能。即便是最耐得住寂寞、为了博士头衔而一心埋头苦读的研究者,面对数以千万计质量低下的图书也会望而生畏,也会觉得从中去挑选一百本最拙劣的书实在是一项无比艰巨的任务。

造成这种伪劣图书大肆泛滥的原因有好几个,打字机在美国的发明即是其中最重要的因素。想当年,当一位牛津教授把最早一批打字机中的一台在乔治·艾略特面前展示的时候,艾略特氏曾以富于预见性的语气惊呼:"哎呀,我可以想象这玩意儿将会催生出不少蹩脚的书来!事实上,我们现在的劣等书已经够多的了!"毫无疑问,打字机有助于减轻写作的负担,正是这一点促使不少原本无所事事的年轻人敢于在文字领域一试身手。而在绝大多数情况下,他们写出来的东西竟然能得到另外一批像他们一样没有多少正经事可做的年轻人的青睐。于是乎,一类或可被称为速记派的短命小说诞生了,它们几乎完全拜打字机所赐,堪称速记时代的产物。

与此同时,出版机构数量激增,其中公开打出旗号、纯粹致力于满足最低层次读者需要的也绝不在少数。这一现状无疑也和时下劣等书(这类书再怎么受到贬低和鄙视也不为过)大行其道密切相关。不过,公众的审美趣味之所以一落千丈,公共图书馆或许更应该受到指责,尽管它也曾对文化多有贡献。这是因为比起读者自己购书来读,他们从图书馆去借来阅读的书要多得多,而绝大部分的读者,读的书越多,碰到的劣等书总比好书多。……

(本书作者译)

V

美好的一天通常首先应该以回忆和追溯开始,尤其是追忆那些为人类文明发展建立特殊功勋的人们。我们决不能忘却这些先贤的丰功伟绩，因为唯有将他们铭记在心才能激励心地淳厚的后来者继续努力。不过，这样的缅怀不该由像吉普赛人那样四海为家的人来完成，而应该由从小生长在这个国家、熟悉这个国家历史的人来完成。

　　基于此，我实际上并不适合在此高谈阔论，或许，只有和教育相关的一些话题（因其不受时空的制约），我还可以说上几句。但在教育方面，我也不敢妄称权威。古往今来，不知有多少智慧和善良的人们已经就教育问题进行了大量的阐述，提出了许多精辟的见解。作为一个不太懂教育的门外汉，我深知需要鼓起极大的勇气才敢于站在这里。因为，除了自身的经验和信仰，我并无其他可资借鉴的东西。假如我们今天的讨论纯粹属于科学的范畴，也许，仅凭这些倒已足够令人信服。

　　但是，教育事关人类的心智活动，它没那么简单。在这儿，仅仅拥有真知灼见还不够；相反，必须不断努力去丰富和更新学识，这样它才不至于湮灭。人类的知识仿佛一座竖立在沙漠中的大理石雕像，随时都有被流沙掩埋的威胁。必须有勤劳的双手细心呵护，它才能始终在阳光下发出耀眼的光芒。我愿自己也加入这呵护的行列。

　　多少年来，学校始终是传承和推动浑厚的传统文化的最重要途径。今天，伴随着社会经济生活的飞速发展，家庭作为传统认知和教育担当者的作用已日渐衰微，因此，学校的重要性就比以往显得更加突出。可以说，当今的人类社会，其薪火相传和繁荣昌盛，无不更加需要大力仰仗学校之功。

　　有时候，人们仅仅把学校看作是向年轻一代灌输大量知识的工具。但这种观点是错误的。知识是死的，而学校服务的对象却是活的。学校应该培养年轻人的集体意识和能力，使之更好地为社会的福祉贡献力量。当然，这并不意味着允许扼杀个性，允许个人沦为集体的附庸，就像一只无足轻重的蜜蜂或蚂蚁那样。这是因为，当一个社会处处雷同，其中的成员缺乏个性、失去生活的目标，那么，这将是一个不幸的社会，它不可能得到发展。恰恰相反，学校教育的目标必须强调学生独立思考和行为的能力。当学生以自己所长服务于社会时，他们也同时看清了自己的最高人生目标。据我所知，英国的学校教育体系最接近于实现这样的理想。

　　那么，人们应该如何来实现这样一个理想呢？是否可以通过加强道德教化来实现呢？大可不必。口头的说教向来空洞无物，在通往地狱的路上从来都不缺少高谈阔论。但人的个性是通过行动和实践造就的,而不是凭着口舌之功。

有鉴于此,最有益的教育方法始终在于强调学生的实际动手能力。这种能力既可以指学童发蒙的试笔,也可以指大学里博士生的论文撰写,抑或仅仅是背诵一首诗歌,写出一篇文章,翻译一个文本,解决一个数学难题,或者还可以是参加某个体育活动。

(本书作者译)

VI

纵观历史,若要论广告之大胆、出格,广告之信口雌黄、天花乱坠,以及广告之无所不用其极,当首推北美殖民当局策划的意在吸引欧洲移民的宣传招数。17世纪(甚至更早)时,在英国印刷发行的不少宣传小册子通篇充斥着诱惑性的夸大其词,还有半真半假的玩意儿和彻头彻尾的谎言。即便是间或夹杂其中的一些货真价实的内容,以今天的标准来衡量,也足以使联邦贸易委员开出一道禁止令。所谓遍地的金银财宝、青春不老泉水、欢跳的鱼儿、享用不尽的野味……总之,在他们的笔下,可以说是一切应有尽有。当然,其中确有真实的成分,不能说全部都是空穴来风。想来不免令人称奇,若不是当初那些野心勃勃的创意大师发起了这一轮广告宣传攻势,不知要历经多少年北美大陆才能变得如此人丁兴旺。另一个有趣的问题是,美国文明的孕育和发展显然得益于大批笃信报章杂志宣传、甘愿来此落地生根的外来移民,可这一切又是怎样发生的呢?

广告的作用首当其冲体现在描摹和实现全新的未来之上。北美大陆是一个崭新的世界,它为自己所做的广告之一出现在一美元纸币背面的美国国玺上,上面用拉丁文写着"时代的新秩序"。这可以说是美国有史以来最成功的一句广告语。所谓"时代的新秩序",意思就是要相信新生事物,要让每一个人都敞开胸怀拥抱新生事物。这一点,无论过去或现在,特别是在当今美国人的日常生活中,已经深入人心。多少次,每当美国人走出标新立异的第一步——大到当年远涉重洋、千里迢迢赶赴北美大陆,小到转而使用一款新的肥皂——都可以看到广告神奇的影子。前康奈尔大学高才生詹姆斯·肯尼斯·弗雷泽是广告文案策划的圣手,他在1900年曾写过一篇著名的"哀医者":

这位消瘦的医学博士人称布朗医生,

> 他在一尘不染小镇过得好不郁闷。
> 小镇莫名其妙天天光鲜整洁，
> 难怪布朗医生面容憔悴荷包瘪，
> 你知道的，他的病人现在全都跑掉，
> 只因为大家都用上了萨博留牌肥皂。

像这种文质高雅的叫卖之术后来又不断地被其他广告商复制，以此来诱导消费者掏钱购买爱泽尔或野马汽车、卫宝牌肥皂或通体牌护肤用品、百事可乐或皇冠可乐，还有双刀片刮胡刀等。

（本书作者译）

Ⅶ

当人们思考流产所涉及的伦理问题时，不可避免地会想到权利，因为此类争论大多围绕权利的概念而展开。就这一点而言，无论是女性主义者还是非女性主义者的论述莫不如此。诚然，一些早期的女性主义学者，如朱迪丝·贾维斯·汤姆逊和玛丽·安·沃伦等，在探讨这一问题时所采用的权利模式与非女性主义学者并无明显的区别。不过，后来的女性主义学者对于"妇女选择权"一词却形成了不同的理解。

在本文中，我将首先略述非女性主义者关于流产的道德可行性的论证。参照 W.B.加利的理论，我将指出她们的论证是无法导出结论的，因为在她们理论的核心部分，即对于"人"的解释方面，"本质上充满了争议"。接下来，我将探讨女性主义者如何试图就有关流产的讨论进行重构，并且，在参考苏珊·舍温研究的基础上，提出一个对妇女流产权利的扩充论述。最后，我将指出，围绕妇女流产的问题，并不仅仅只是"妇女的选择权"那么简单，还有更深层次的考量，而这关乎女性主义者和非女性主义者对这一问题的不同理解。

按照主流的、亦即非女性主义哲学的观点，有关流产的争论，归结到一点无非是妇女的权利与胎儿的权利之间相互对立。妇女拥有隐私权、自我决定权，保持身体完整性的权利或财产的处置权，这些权利也许超过胎儿的权利，也许并没有超过。对相关文献的考察表明，在妇女拥有哪些权利的问题上，至少存在着某些比较一致的看法。但是，对于这些权利的权限有多大，却存在着分歧。之所以出现这样的情形，是因为人们对胎儿的道德地位和相应的道德权利的看法不相一致。在这方面，有三种基本的观点：(i) 从怀孕时起胎儿就具有生命权;(ii)在怀孕期间的某个阶段胎儿开始具有生命权;(iii)胎儿在妊娠的任何阶段都不具有生命权。与此相对应,上述观点分别被称为"保守派"、"温和派"和"自由派"的观点。按照从怀孕时起胎儿即具有生命权的观点,除了在极少数情况下,流产是不被允许的,因为无论妇女对在她身体内和身体的其他部分所发生的一切拥有怎样的权利,这些权利都无法超过生命权。相应地,按照在怀孕期间的某个阶段胎儿拥有生命权的观点,那么,在这一阶段后流产即是不被允许的。最后,按照胎儿不具有生命权的观点,则女性有权在妊娠的任何阶段流产,因为即便胎儿真的拥有什么权利的话,妊娠妇女的权利也要超过胎儿可能拥有的任何权利。

至此,关于流产的争论与其说是关于妇女权利的争论,倒不如说成了关于胎儿道德地位的争论。由此,这场争论还会继续下去。这是因为,胎儿的权利建立在胎儿的道德地位基础之上,而对于道德地位的界定又取决于我们对"人"的概念的理解。所谓"人",在 W. B. 加利看来,恰恰是"本质上充满争议的一个概念"。

(本书作者译)

汉译英

I

Beginning with an analysis of the concept of autonomy, which is interpreted as self-determination and free choice, the speaker in this presentation argues that in addressing the issues concerning genetic counseling, we should not let our discussion focus only on aspects of autonomous agent and autonomous action, such as the counselee's ability or inability for autonomous decision-making, and the amount of information provided by the counselor and its effectiveness or ineffectiveness. Instead, we should weigh more of the socio-cultural and economic factors when treating the topic of autonomy in genetic counseling. The speaker here, before bringing up the issue of general failure to honor the autonomy model in genetic counseling in China, outlines briefly the problems with genetic testing in the country and its unique social and economic environment. She holds that among other negative contributors, genetic discrimination, violations of privacy, social inequality, gender discrimination and conventional attitude towards aging are especially to be held responsible for affecting autonomous decision-making by the counselee. She concludes by pointing out three solutions for this dilemma in genetic counseling in China, and they are institutional reform, ethical and legal breakthrough, and patience.

（本书作者译）

II

The Song Dynasty, when gardening was highly developed and encyclopediacal reference books on botanical studies came out in large numbers, witnessed the flourish of botanical studies in China. This phenomenon is not unrelated to the spread of Buddhist teachings and the rise of monastery economy at the time, which resulted in more involvement by the religious figures in the study and practice of botany. Among the important works in the field of botanical studies, *The Book on Bamboo Shoots* by Master Tong Hui (Zanning) is a prominent example.

（本书作者译）

III

Informed consent, a norm denominated formally in the 1950s, has become accepted as a very important principle in bioethics, and it is now looked upon as an effective tool for the protection of patients in medical practice and research. However, for a long time, opinions differ as regarding the nature of informed consent and how it may be applied effectively in real practice. This is reflected in the way informed consent has been defined and redefined in laws of the past times. This, too, is the situation in China. Now, with the new *Tort Law of P. R. China*, which came into force on July 1, 2010, the issue of informed consent, its significance, its implementation and its feasibility again triggers a new wave of heated discussion among scholars in the medical, legal as well as ethical fields.

This paper, revolving around how informed consent is described in the *Tort Law*, will first seek to point out the new characteristics in the treatment of informed consent in this law as compared with those in other laws before and try to grasp the realistic meaning of such change. In the meantime, the author, taking the perspective of the connotation, purpose and significance of informed consent, will further discuss the limitation such adoption of informed consent in the *Tort Law* may contain, and the possible difficulties that may arise in both theory and practice in the implementation of the law. Finally, the author will point out that much still remains to be done in China to push forward the work involving the implementation of informed consent and the protection of patient/subject benefit and right.

（本书作者译）

IV

The adoption of trademark is something that happened naturally when commodity economy of the society developed to a certain degree. In as early as the Han Dynasty (202 BC—220 AD), industrial production in China was already highly developed, and product labeling began to be seen in metal smelting and processing, and pottery making. For example, on the ironware of the West Han Dynasty discovered respectively in Xianyang, Shanxi Province in 1964, and in Changge, Henan Province in 1973, the Chinese character "Chuan", was identified. And on the iron axes unearthed in the tombs of the West Han Dynasty near Beijing, the character "Yu" was noticed. These seem to indicate that it was the normal practice for people of the West Han Dynasty to mark on the articles the place of make, which, by modern standard, is something similar to country of origin. These obviously represent the earliest attempts at product labeling in ancient China.

By the Tang Dynasty (618 AD—907 AD), traditional handicraft industry in China was further developed. At that time, both government-sponsored and private handicraft workshops were engaged in various kinds of production activities. To ensure good quality, the local authorities in charge of the handicraft industry sector made it a rule that certain finished products had to bear the name of the maker/producer or that of the workshop/store before being marketed. This was known as "Carving the Names on the Products". And whoever violated such requirement would be punished. The purpose for doing this was obvious: to encourage the buyers to cultivate the consciousness of brand names and to enable them to check quality first before making the decision to pay for anything.

(本书作者译)

V

An Illustrated Book of Trademarks in Modern China, a panoramic book about trademarks in China, offers a comprehensive look at the trademarks applied by home enterprises (as well as some foreign businesses operating in China) during the Republic of China period (1911—1949).

On the occasion of the 100th anniversary of Xinhai Revolution (or the Revolution of 1911), we are pleasantly surprised to notice that research about the Republic of China has been carried to a new height in almost all areas. This book, devoted exclusively to the study of trademarks, is yet another modest attempt to record faithfully the gigantic social, cultural and political shifts the Chinese society underwent during that period of time. Detailed and informative, this book is of special help for the study of the economic development, if not the overall societal development, of the Republic of China.

Xinhai Revolution, initiated by Dr. Sun Yat-sen, is responsible for the end of the reign of the Qing Dynasty and the founding of the Republic of China. With the change of the political system, China, however, did not enter into the period of a capitalist society; instead it remained a country with typical semi-feudal and semi-colonial characteristics. Taking its brief history of 38 years as a whole, the Republic of China has always been troubled by ceaseless fights and turbulent social upheavals, and as a result, the growth of China's national industry and commerce, not to mention the growth of its home trademarks, has also been largely hampered.

This book, a serious academic endeavor, is rich in its historical and cultural implications as well. On the one hand, it contains vivid accounts of the pioneering work of such patriotic industrialists as Zhang Qian, Zhang Bishi and Tan Kah Kee. On the other hand, it chronicles, with a treasure trove of materials, the care for and support to the development of China's home industry and commerce and the cultivation of famous home brands from such historical figures as Sun Yat-sen, Tsai Yuanpei, Yu Youren, Soong Ching-ling, Li Zongren, Zhang Xueliang, Feng Yuxiang, Kang Youwei, Liu Yazi, Qi Baishi, Liu Haisu and Xu Beihong.

In terms of structure, this book is composed of two parts. Part I, with "An Overview of Trademarks before and during the Republic of China Period" as its general topic, is text-based. In the eight chapters in this part, the focal points include the history of trademark building both at home and abroad, trademark administration and publications on trademark building before and during the Republic of China period, the most renowned trademarks during the Republic of China period, support for home trademarks from the influential figures, the characteristic features of the trademarks and trademark designs of the period, and etc. Part II and Part III, "Single-color Patterns of Trademarks of the Republic of China" and "Color Pattern of Trademarks of the Republic of China", are picture-based.

（本书作者译）

Ⅵ

China has a long history in industrial production (including the production of handicraft goods) and its earliest production activity may be traced back to the Xia, Shang, and Zhou Dynasty, which was more than 2,000 years from now. At that time, there emerged a large number of competent craftsmen who were expert at making things well liked by the people then. Du Kang in the Eastern Zhou Dynasty, for example, who was praised as "Celestial Being of Wine", was a master brewer. Wine made by him was famous far and near. Also famous was Fan Li in the Spring and Autumn Period, who was not only an outstanding thinker, strategist and statesman, but also a successful businessman and promoter of trademark building. He made noticeable contributions to the growth of industry and commerce at his time.

Historically, the skillful craftsmen in ancient China were responsible for the making of many high quality products (fine silk, chinaware, bronze ware, and etc.) with rich Chinese national color. These fine handicraft articles, made with ever-improving technical expertise and skills, soon became famous around the world. And China's "Four Great Inventions", i.e. paper making, gunpowder, printing and the compass, all represented the top industrial achievement of the world at the time.

Surprisingly enough, however, on the ancient silk, chinaware and bronze ware unearthed in many places in China, no any written word about the maker or organizer of the production activity or anything resembling the brand name of today has been identified. Although some unearthed articles do bear the place of make or the name of the maker, these, however, can hardly be termed as trademarks by modern standard. The simple marks left on some of the ancient articles are, at most, the primitive form of branding.

（本书作者译）

Ⅶ

In the Qing Dynasty (1616—1911), more achievement was made in trademark building and protection. During that period, a large number of powerful enterprises in many places in the country, together with the well-trusted brand names they created, rose to fame. Some of these enterprises had strong trademark protection consciousness, and when cases of illegal use of the brand names by other producers were discovered, these trademark owners would even urge the government to help investigate and punish such counterfeit labeling.

In the textile industry, in particular, there emerged quite many competent people. For example, during the reign of Emperor Qianlong (1736—1795), in a place called "Shuang Miaoqiao" (Bridge of Twin Temples) in Songjiang, Jiangsu Province (now a place in Songjiang, Shanghai), there was a skillful housewife named "Lady Ding", whose workshop of weaving was quite well known. The cloth made by her was called "Cloth of Lady Ding". Actually, "Lady Ding" became something quite like her trademark.

Historically (both in ancient times and modern times) China is strong in producing cosmetics. For a long time, in the areas of Jiangsu and Zhejiang provinces, lots of capable people produced well known cosmetics that were favored by ladies of different social status. Popular brand names marketed over the years include "Xie Fu Chun" (a trademark in Yangzhou), "Dai Chun Lin" (another trademark in Yangzhou) and "Lao Miao Xiang Shi" (Old Temple with Incense Rooms), and these were brand names for face powder, rouge and so on.

（本书作者译）

VIII

Science and Technology and Its Impact on Social Life

The development of modern science and technology brings about gigantic change not only to the natural world, but to the human society as well. This course, interdisciplinary in nature and appropriate for general education, is designed to explore the close connection between modern scientific and technological advancement and the evolution of human society. Highlighting the characteristic features of modern science and technology first, the course lays more emphasis on how scientific and technological breakthroughs have affected the social-cultural-political-economic aspects of human existence. It is expected that the students, after taking the course, will not only have a better knowledge of the latest scientific and technological achievements, but grow more conscious of both the positive and possible negative effect science and technology may produce on human life.

（本书作者译）

IX
The Visit to Zhouzhuang

Zhouzhuang, a water village with a history of more than 900 years, stands between Shanghai and Suzhou. It is well known for its complicated waterways, stone bridges of the past times, and well-preserved local-style dwelling houses. On Oct. 21, 2001, the first ladies went to Zhouzhuang for a visit. They first went to the ancient bridge tower, the twin bridges, the Shens Hall and other scenic spots. After that, they went on a boating tour around the village, during which time they were especially attracted by several local housewives hand-making cute baby shoes by the riverside. They were so amazed by everything around them that they felt they themselves became part of this enchanting water village.

...

While the APEC Summit Meeting has had to draw its curtain, the friendship developed among the first ladies during the meeting and the sweet memory of their time together will remain long with them. In the meantime, Shanghai, the host city of the Summit Meeting, has come under the spotlight of the world stage through this conference and other related activities.

（本书作者译）